Echoes of Soviet Urbanism
Exploring Modernist Housing Narratives

Perspectives on Heritage, Transformation, and Community
Dynamics in East European and Eurasian Microrayons

Echoes of Soviet Urbanism
Exploring Modernist Housing Narratives

Perspectives on Heritage, Transformation, and Community
Dynamics in East European and Eurasian Microrayons
–
Edited by Barbara Engel

Contents

Introduction.
Soviet housing heritage 6
Barbara Engel

01 **Ajapnyak in Yerevan, Armenia.**
The case of the earliest microrayons:
transforming (in)formalities 12
Heghine Pilosyan

02 **Chilanzar district in Tashkent, Uzbekistan.**
Analysing legislative transformations,
economic reforms, and migration dynamics 34
Dona Kulmatova

03 **Dubki micro-district in Taganrog, Russia.**
The missing social dimension in urban
development and heritage-making 46
Elena Batunova and Elena Chernysheva

04 **Microrayon No. 41 in Kamensk-Uralsky, Russia.**
Sparkles of heritage-making in the realm of inertia,
ignorance, and dismay in the Brezhnev legacy 60
Albina Davletshina and Ivan Bushlanov

05 **Khimmash neighbourhood in
Sverdlovsk-Yekaterinburg, Russia.**
The Soviet palace: from social hub to remnant of
the past and back again 74
Polina Gundarina

06 **Lazdynai in Vilnius, Lithuania.**
Creative touches in Soviet mass housing 92
Barbara Engel

07 Olaine, Latvia.
Tacitly embracing the heritage of the Soviet monotown:
social and infrastructural dynamics 108
Guido Sechi, Kārlis Lakševics, and Māris Bērziņš

08 Purvciems microrayon in Riga, Latvia.
Unravelling the inherited residential patchwork 124
Marina Sapunova and Ekaterina Gladkova

09 North Saltivka in Kharkiv, Ukraine.
Spatial neighbourhood development:
from socialist city plans to post-war reconstruction 140
Hlib Antypenko

10 Solnechny in Samara, Russia.
A microrayon's urban renewal prospects through
the eyes of planners and residents 156
Vitaly Stadnikov

11 Universitetsky in Irkutsk, Russia.
Identifying the value of functional balance 172
Anastasia Malko and Lyudmila Kozlova

12 Vazha-Pshavela block VI in Tbilisi, Georgia.
Community-driven spatial transformations 190
Barbara Engel

13 Vyhurivschyna-Troieshchyna in Kyiv, Ukraine.
A housing estate with supergraphics and
colour composition 208
Semen Shyrochyn

Index 234
Authors 236

Introduction.
Soviet housing heritage

Barbara Engel

The large housing estates that were built throughout the USSR from the 1960s to the 1980s continue to shape the urban landscape in many post-Soviet cities. Since the dissolution of the Soviet state, these residential areas have undergone phases of intense transformation. The transition in the ex-Soviet countries from planned to market economies, the redistribution of land ownership, and the establishment of new rules have had a major impact on the urban environment, including built fabric and open spaces. As these neighbourhoods represent a major resource of housing and a testament to post-war modernist planning principles, the question arises as to how they can be further developed in a sustainable manner. How can these former socialist urban ensembles be transformed to meet the needs of today's citizens and functional requirements while preserving the traces of their history and providing opportunities for identification?

The book at hand presents 13 'district stories' from seven post-Soviet countries, written by experts from a variety of disciplines, including architecture, urban and regional planning, public policy and social sciences, and human geography. The authors take a critical look at various aspects and discuss the housing heritage from different perspectives. They present observations of spatial, social, and functional transformations as well as of the formal and informal frameworks, planning strategies, and concepts that lie behind the physical development. They discuss spatial patterns and their modifications with a view to future heritage-sensitive development of the neighbourhoods. Some authors include discussions of values and perceptions by professionals, residents, and politicians. In addition to exploring how the different stakeholders influence urban development, the texts identify risks and opportunities in the revealed civic and institutional practices. By doing so, they formulate new narratives for large housing estates and identify potential challenges for responsible planning and action required.

Depending on their location – in a prospering or a declining area – large housing estates can perform very differently. We find renovation, densification with additional elements or new buildings (sometimes with total replacement of historical buildings), but also deterioration. One key feature of transformation and change in these neighbourhoods since the end of state socialism has been the privatisation of buildings and, in some countries, also land. On the one hand, the new economic opportunities have brought more and different functions to former monofunctional areas. Newly created shops, restaurants, and services have demonstrated the demand for better amenities in the neighbourhoods. On the other hand, the implementation of new functions and

buildings has mostly taken place not in accordance with a holistic plan or strategy but rather in a chaotic manner that severely disrupts the clearly organised urban layout of a modernist configuration with its fluidity of open spaces.

The end of state regulation of urban development and the change in economic conditions have brought new freedoms and new actors onto the scene: homeowners, private developers, and local authorities. Their different interests must be taken into account, but these must also be weighed against the public interest. So far, the enforcement of private interests has usually prevailed; implementation of city-controlled and regulated strategies has been subordinated to monetary forces. The new private actors could be used to empower neighbourhoods – whether through civil society engagement or private investment in development. They could support development that is more diverse, more mixed, and importantly, more socially balanced. However, this would require new, clear regulations and their acceptance and implementation, as well as control of private activities and governance and planning strategies and policies.

Built to promote a new socialist way of life, the large housing estates were put forward as remarkable achievements of Soviet industrial policy-making. However, although recognised as part of national heritage, in many cities Soviet urban structures and architecture remain controversial, provoking emotions that range from admiration and nostalgia to criticism and rejection. In this regard evaluation of these districts has to take into account other aspects besides discussions of aesthetic and functional values.

The era of mass housing construction under the leadership of Khrushchev and Brezhnev was characterised by speed and quantity of housing construction as well as by industrialisation and streamlining of construction methods. The result was a unification of the entire production process – from the development of standardised housing types to the awarding of contracts. However, the microrayons and panel blocks of that time varied considerably.[1] Despite the fact that all the districts examined here were planned during the Soviet era, governed by rigid planning rules and within the framework of the technological possibilities of the time, the variations between them are manifold and substantial – from adaptation to a specific geographical context through use of local materials to the freedom and creativity claimed and established by urban planners at the time when the large housing estates were being built and the individual approach taken to transforming a particular neighbourhood. The various approaches to

Introduction

large settlements since the end of the Soviet Union reflect local specificities – in terms of depth of intervention in the conversion and how it is carried out, as well as with regard to land policy, planning regulations, and planning culture in the respective cities and countries.

The observations and reflections on the 13 case studies in this book – Ajapnyak (Armenia); Chilanzar (Uzbekistan); Dubki, Kamensk-Uralsky, Khimmash, Solnechny, and Universitetsky (Russia); Lazdynai (Lithuania); Olaine and Purvciems (Latvia); Saltivka and Vyhurivschyna-Troieshchyna (Ukraine); and Vazha-Pshavela (Georgia) – bring out both similarities and differences in these districts' histories and current situations. To what extent are the developments specific to individual context, and what is comparable? The stories point to the need for an exchange of experiences, in the sense of 'lessons learned', that could be fruitfully applied beyond post-Soviet neighbourhoods – to eastern European large housing estates and western European large housing estates as well. It is hoped that this publication will act as a stimulus for such an exchange as the value of postwar modernist urbanism and architecture in the post-Soviet states has not yet been widely recognised and most initiatives for its study and popularisation refer to iconic, exceptional buildings. Expanded international exchange between practitioners and academics on the further development of large housing estates in both East and West could provide valuable insights and impulses. This publication aims to contribute a more holistic understanding to the discussion of post-war modernist housing estates with their urban and functional – but also cultural and social – values and meanings.

This publication has been produced within the framework of 'cities.building.culture – Built Heritage in Post-Soviet Urban Development', a collaborative research project in the field of area studies funded by the German Federal Ministry of Education and Research (BMBF) and involving the Karlsruhe Institute of Technology (KIT), RWTH Aachen University, and the Leibniz Institute for the History and Culture of Eastern Europe (GWZO). Carried out from 2021 to 2024, the project dealt with the housing heritage of post-Soviet cities and developed new approaches to the sustainable management of cultural heritage in the post-Soviet space. It involved an international and interdisciplinary dialogue at the intersection of cultural, historical, social, planning, and environmental sciences. By looking at selected residential neighbourhoods from the pre-socialist and socialist eras of the late nineteenth and twentieth centuries, the project examined values, rooted in both the past and the present, that are attributed to the variously

1 Microrayon: (micro-district): in Soviet urban planning a primary unit of urban development comprising a complex of houses and services infrastructure connected with and bounded by main transport arteries. Roughly equivalent to the concept of the 'neighbourhood unit' devised by the American urban planner Clarence Perry in the early twentieth century.

endangered housing heritage. Approaches to monument preservation, urban planning, and civic engagement were analysed with regard to their effectiveness for the sustainable development of our housing heritage. Launched in 2021, the project initially focused on Russian cities; the expansion of its geographical scope was intended from the outset for a second funding period.

Russia's attack on Ukraine in February 2022, with the ongoing war in Ukraine and its consequences, is fundamentally changing the landscape of post-Soviet urban research. This requires essential theoretical discussions on issues such as the concepts of the post-Soviet city and post-socialism. Existing networks and collaborations have been called into question, and methodological opportunities for primary empirical research in Russian cities are now severely restricted or even non-existent. The organisational and structural foundations for cooperation have been torn apart. The war requires reorientations at multiple levels and updates in the collegial, international, and interdisciplinary dialogue. However, there is a crucial need for differentiated research on spaces in the territory of the former USSR and for critical investigation and contextualisation of the transformation of the built heritage in its different political and socio-economic conditions. It is important to prevent Russia from becoming a *terra incognita*. There is a serious risk that research will be carried out either from afar, by exiles or non-Russians, or in a reduced manner by the Russian government.

Each author in this publication condemns the war, but scientific pursuits should be grounded in professional, value-based exchange, and collaboration should certainly not be dictated by politics. The authors share the understanding that the only way to a prosperous future is through cooperation and dialogue. Solutions to the common problems that should be the focus of our efforts can be found through active partnership.

By sharing knowledge of different 'stories' of districts of mass housing, we hope to foster the exchange of knowledge and thereby increase understanding of the genesis and transformation of and challenges facing districts of mass housing. The contributions presented here are excerpts from observations. They focus on specific issues, reveal very different facets, and demonstrate the complexity of the challenge we face and must address as leaders – whether in planning practice or academia. Our texts point to endangered spatial qualities, to values in building culture, and to the need for long-term, simultaneous planning strategies. They point out the uniqueness of details and the fact that *genius loci* makes a difference. The synopsis of contributions from different countries is an invitation to take a closer look and learn from each other.

01

Ajapnyak in Yerevan, Armenia. The case of the earliest microrayons: transforming (in)formalities

Heghine Pilosyan

Figure 1:
Map showing the location of Ajapnyak district in Yerevan, relative to the central Kentron district.
Source: Heghine Pilosyan

1   Cheryomushki: a district of Moscow built up with early types of panel building in the 1950s and 1960s.

The story of the urban district of Ajapnyak began over six decades ago, across four hundred fifty hectares of land along the right side of Hrazdan Gorge – thus earning its name from the words *aj* ('right') and *ap* ('riverbank'). The accelerated construction of mass housing in the subsequent decades saw the district spread across the wider peri-urban territory, neighbourhood after neighbourhood, such that today it measures more than five times its original area. Shaped through several stages of sociopolitical and technological transformation, the first neighbourhoods in Ajapnyak are now adding another chapter to a history encompassing several generations of residents and their individual stories woven into the district's urban fabric. Narrated by the residents themselves, excerpts from these stories are retold below, adding valuable perspectives from within. Much of this combined narrative is accordingly built on unstructured observations and accompanying conversational interviews with residents (conducted over the course of several days in July 2023), some of whom were among the first to relocate to Ajapnyak. Geographically, this research was predominantly limited to the first two neighbourhoods of this large district and their residents.

An Armenian Cheryomushki: laying the foundations [1]

Progress in industrialised housing construction – spearheaded by the pivotal All-Union Congress of Soviet Builders and Architects in 1954 – coincided with and underpinned the fastest era of urbanisation in Armenia. The urban population was steadily growing through repatriation and rural–urban migration. In Yerevan, where demographic growth was most dramatic and has repeatedly exceeded projections set out in the city's master plans (of which there have been five: in 1924, 1935, 1951, 1970, and 2005), the shortage of housing units was particularly pressing. In an act of planned urban expansion to accommodate the growing urban population, several districts were designed with new types of apartment building. Due to technological advances and productive capacity, standardised housing construction in Armenia can effectively be split into two chapters: the early stage of industrialisation between 1956 and 1970 and the period of full prefabrication from 1970 to 1990 – marked by growth in both efficiency and building height. The pre-independence period of construction was in effect cut short by the earthquake of 1988, whose physical and psychological consequences are still evident to this day.

Located in the northwest of Yerevan, Ajapnyak is the first local example of a residential district composed of microrayons – in line with the urban-planning ideology propagated by the 1957 Housing Decree. Following in the footsteps of its precursors in other Soviet cities, the new residential district colloquially became known as 'Cheremushka' (an Armenianised version of the Russian 'Cheryomushki'). Constituted by standardised residential blocks clustered into separate neighbourhoods and built in several stages, Ajapnyak illustrates the transformations in approaches to the urban configurations of microrayons and the evolution of the standardised buildings in them. As opposed to the central Kentron district with its densely built-up historical urban fabric (which limited both the scale and pace of new development), the undeveloped land in Ajapnyak was a *tabula rasa* which allowed for the construction of larger, self-contained micro-districts with schools, kindergartens, and local trade and consumer services.

As in European countries, the rapid post-war progress in the provision of housing across all Soviet states was a continuation of the early modernism that had emerged between the 1920s and 1930s – the Soviet Constructivist movement later banned as formalism in disguise. The genetic relationship between Ajapnyak's first micro-districts and earlier modernist mass-housing projects is further attested in work by Mikael Mazmanyan. Recognised as one of the pioneers of Constructivist architecture in Armenia but then exiled when Constructivism fell out of favour with the Soviet authorities, Mazmanyan was dispatched to Norilsk, the northernmost city in the USSR, to co-lead the construction of the Neoclassical industrial city. His involvement in the design and construction of Ajapnyak between 1955 and 1965 was his grand return, marking the beginning of the era of de-Stalinisation.

The standardised buildings constructed in the first neighbourhoods in Ajapnyak – Series 1-451P – underwent a decades-long evolution of their own, both in terms of engineering and informal *ad hoc* modifications. A combination of several local circumstances – an unsettled prefabrication process, coupled with centuries-long masonry traditions owing to the wide availability of stone – resulted in the use of traditional masonry techniques (the Armenian *midis* wall) for the envelope of the earlier design series, thus making these buildings more resilient to the local climatic and seismic conditions (based on the longest surviving architectural heritage). At this stage the only prefabricated element was precast hollow-core panels as a

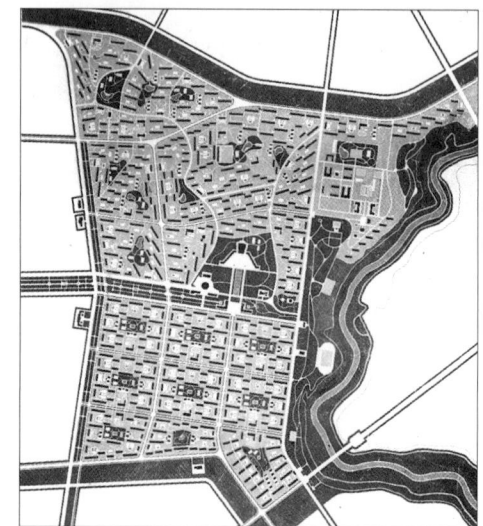

Figure 2:
The first master plan for Ajapnyak, by Mikayel Mazmanyan and Sargis Nazaryan, 1956.
Source: personal collection of Mikayel Mazmanyan

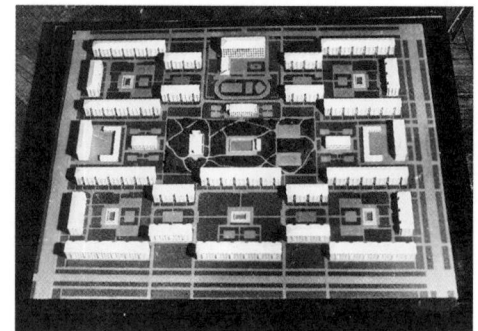

Figure 3:
An early model of Microrayon 2 in Ajapnyak.
Source: personal collection of Mikayel Mazmanyan

replacement for the traditional timber floors. As a result, the district was essentially formed by a single linear typology of four-storey buildings varying solely in length according to the number of contiguous blocks. So-called 'improved' versions of this series would later be slotted into already-built neighbourhoods and would be used to form complete new microrayons.

Early on, the project was criticised for complete disregard of the natural features of the Hrazdan Gorge and its surroundings.[2] To this day, the vast Tumanyan Park on the sloping riverbank is physically cut off from the residential districts by the six lanes of Halabyan Street.

Shifting traditions: from stone to panel, from multi-generational to nuclear family

The issues that arose within the context of the first microrayons ran deeper than urban planning. It is unquestionable that in terms of living conditions, the new apartments in Ajapnyak were an improvement for most tenants who were rehoused. Before long, however, the urban lifestyle in these new dwellings came into conflict with the long-standing mores of the relocated families – rooted in generations of place-making in both older Yerevan neighbourhoods and outlying rural settlements. Henceforth, particularly at this stage of urbanisation, there was an obvious discrepancy between what was conceived as the Soviet urban family – a nuclear family unit living in 'a separate, comfortable flat' – and the established model of the multi-generational extended family in Armenia.[3] Despite smaller family units becoming the trend, by the mid-1960s around a quarter of all Armenian families were still multi-generational; mostly, they comprised three generations.[4]

Similar to in other early mass housing series constructed throughout the Soviet Union and christened *khrushchevkas*, the apartments in Ajapnyak were cramped, prompting the newcomers to adapt the standard layouts to their personal needs. Open balconies, which had always been ubiquitous in Yerevan's urban dwellings, lost their prominent role when they were enclosed and turned into 'useful' space, often to provide an extra bedroom for elders or a newly wed couple. Some of the drawbacks voiced by the new tenants – low ceilings causing poor ventilation, bathrooms and toilets combined to form a single space, walk-through rooms, and small kitchens – were to a certain extent addressed in the later, 'improved' Series 1A-450, which, like its precursor, had stone walls and precast hollow-core panel floors.

2 Grigoryan, Artsvin, and Tovmasyan, Martin, *Architecture of the Soviet Armenia* (Moscow: Stroyizdat, 1986), p. 128.

3 See: Vardanyan, Lilia, and Ter-Sarkisiants, Alla (eds), *Armyane, Seriya 'Narody i Kul'tury'* [Armenians, 'nations and cultures' series] (Moscow: Nauka, 2012), pp. 320–321.

4 Ter-Sarkisiants, Alla, *Sovremennaya sem'ya u Armyan* [The modern Armenian family] (Moscow: Nauka, 1972), p. 41.

Figure 4:
The earliest standardised housing series, Series 1-451P, in Ajapnyak.
Photo: Arsen, 2023

Once the infrastructure or prefabrication was fully established in the 1970s, the layouts were reproduced in precast panel structures (namely, Series A1-451KP) allowing for taller multi-apartment buildings of nine to 17 storeys. This was seen as a much-needed step towards introducing diversity into the skyline of these new 'dormitory' districts. The fully prefabricated tower blocks became an element from which entire districts could be built and also served as infill housing in the earlier microrayons and older central neighbourhoods in an attempt to promote urban diversification and densification.

As the engineering and technological aspects of industrialised housing evolved, Armenian architects became increasingly vocal about the need to revise standardised housing layouts in order to take better account of the diversity of local climate zones and demographics, as well as to deliver improved aesthetics. Indeed, it was inevitable that a standardised housing construction campaign of the magnitude that propelled Soviet urbanisation would have to contend with the 'aesthetic of numbers'.

In an article published in 1972 Levon Babayan – one of the leading local architects working on housing types with flexible dwelling layouts – urged his colleagues to sort experimental housing structures (built using three main techniques: precast concrete large panels, precast concrete frame, and concrete lift-slabs with concrete frames) into a handful of flexible types.[5] In view of the country's relatively small output of industrialised housing (compared to the

5 Babayan, Levon, 'Voprosy Arkhitektury Jilishcha' [Housing architecture], *Arkhitektura SSSR* [Architecture of the USSR], No. 2, 1972, pp. 15–18.

6   Ibid., p. 17.

7   Ibid., pp. 16–17.

8   See: Azatyan, Karen, 'Bnakeli Bjji Zargats'man Himnakan P'ulery Yerevani Verjin Haryuramyaki Chartarapetut'yan Mej' [The main stages of evolution of the dwelling unit across the architecture of the recent century], *Scientific Papers of National University of Architecture and Construction of Armenia*, vol. 59, No. 4, 2015, pp. 3–12.

Figure 5:
The evolution of the first standardised typology of mass housing (from left to right): Series 1-451P – the first standardised series, composed of stone masonry walls and hollow-core concrete floors, five storeys high; Series 1A-450 – an improved version of the previous series, with more diversity but still built of the same materials, with most of the balconies incorporated into the main body of the building; Series A1-451KP – reproduction of the same layouts using prefabricated concrete panels, typically nine to 17 storeys high.
Source: Heghine Pilosyan

rest of the USSR), 'overcoming the "childhood illnesses" of industrial construction' was the only avenue available for ensuring diversity in available types of housing.[6]

In the same article Babayan discussed the advantages of making summer spaces transformable, allowing for year-round use, which would curtail the chaotic modifications to the façades – a practice that started in Ajapnyak within the first few years of tenants being rehoused. At the same time, Babayan questioned the trend of shrinking Armenian families and the growing tendency of young couples to separate from their extended families, arguing that 'living in a household of three generations enriches one's inner culture … and in a way mitigates the problem of personal alienation. Such an arrangement of living together is also congruent with Armenian tradition.'[7]

The spatial concentration of significant routine social interactions went beyond intra-familial ties – spilling over into kinship with neighbours, thus turning shared areas and courtyards into relevant structural elements. The crucial role of courtyards as spaces of neighbourly kinship (and their spatial link with balconies) was a long-established trait stretching back centuries – with its roots in traditional Armenian houses.[8]

Over the course of the twentieth century the processes shaping Yerevan's modern urban fabric repeatedly reinstated courtyards as a basic element uniting residential complexes, although on different

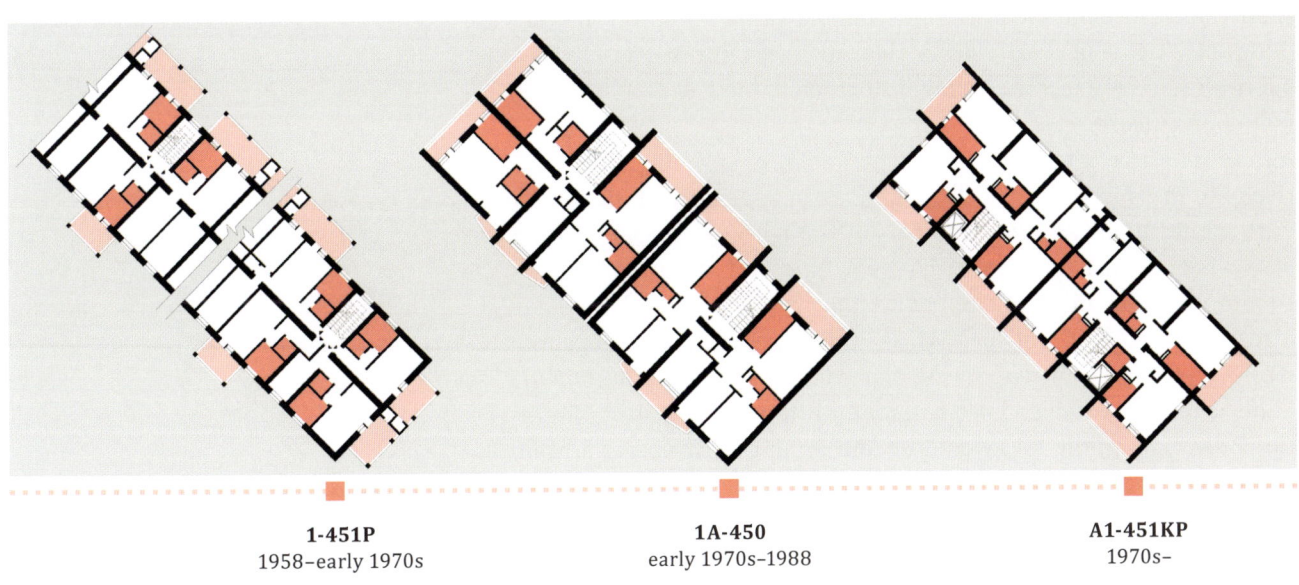

1-451P
1958–early 1970s

1A-450
early 1970s–1988

A1-451KP
1970s–

Figure 6:
Ajapnyak in 1964: some of the loggias are already glazed, but the landscaping is not yet complete.
Source: HinYerevan.am

scales: first in enclosed multi-section apartment blocks ion the master plan by Alexander Tamanyan (drawn up in 1924); then in Constructivist experiments based on communal living, including a residential complex for workers by Mikael Mazmanyan himself; and then in the perimetrally positioned standardised houses in Ajapnyak's first micro-districts. Today the same courtyards remain a prominent feature in Yerevan's daily life, shaping the city's urban landscape and architectural and cultural heritage. The extent to which courtyards continue to influence residents' self-identity – their role as a social meeting place and play area for children's outdoor activities – is vividly made clear in Taline Ter-Minassian's account of her research in archival documents and examples taken from pop culture.[9]

As the average housing area per person kept growing, the practice of living in separate nuclear families increasingly found favour with modernising Armenian society. Although a matter for another ethno-sociological inquiry of its own, this shift raises the question of whether the first families to move to Ajapnyak would have already abandoned the persisting multi-generational household model had they been given the option – leading to faster human urbanisation and a reduced propensity for often unauthorised alterations. Or, one might ask, would encouraging the three-generation arrangement through an increased number of enlarged dwelling units with inbuilt flexibility have been a better way to address long-term social goals?

[9] Ter-Minassian, Taline, Erevan, *Konstruirovanie Stolitsy v Sovetskuyu Epokhu* [Yerevan, the construction of a Soviet-era capital] (Yerevan: Antares, 2019), pp. 194–201.

Two big quakes: 1988 and independence

The accelerated housing construction of the 1970s could not but affect the socio-demographic setting in Ajapnyak as well: along with new neighbourhoods being absorbed into the district, older neighbourhoods were undergoing densification with infill tower blocks. The latter were mostly built in courtyards; this may have contributed in some way to residents' perceptions – signalling that these spaces were subject to greater transformability.

The efficiency with which housing construction trusts were churning out new housing units led to controversial results in the long run. On one hand, the 60–70 per cent increase in production capacity made it possible to (re)house a vast number of urban dwellers faster than ever before – for the first time earning the construction organisations positive recognition from municipal and central authorities as well as from city dwellers.[10,11] On the other hand, the quickly assembled multi-apartment buildings contributed to a larger number of casualties per building in the Spitak earthquake of 1988: the highest mortality rate per building was in the precast-concrete frame

[10] Ibid., p. 217.
[11] Ibid., pp. 206–210.

Figure 7:
A full-length view of the earliest standardised housing series, Series 1-451P, in Ajapnyak.
Photo: Arsen, 2023

01 Ajapnyak in Yerevan, Armenia

type.¹² Analysis of damage patterns indicated poor performance for the masonry multi-apartment building series (1-451P and 1A-450): the joints between the stone walls and precast hollow-core floor slabs were inadequate in terms of both design and construction quality.¹³ Additionally, all buildings showed signs of poor on-site workmanship, which was a major contributing factor in the extensive collapse of buildings.

Predominantly developed on the basis of the stone-masonry Series 1-451P, residential buildings in the first neighbourhoods built in Ajapnyak sustained considerable damage, which has been further exacerbated over the years by unstable soil conditions and a lack of maintenance. Three decades on, the devastating effects of the earthquake are still experienced by residents of the remaining unsafe and dangerous buildings in Ajapnyak.

In the ensuing years the building codes and construction practices were reviewed several times: higher magnitudes were assigned to all seismic zones nationwide, and many residential buildings were accordingly left unfinished. Paradoxically, unauthorised alterations did not cease but instead intensified in the hands of current owners, further compromising the structural integrity of the buildings. Relatively minor modifications deemed acceptable prior to 1991 – i.e. alterations sufficiently non-invasive to be tolerated by municipal authorities upon receipt of a bribe – spread in an unrestrained manner in the wake of the privatisation launched in 1993, governed by the principle that 'whatever is not prohibited is allowed.'¹⁴

In an environment of weakened oversight, communal spaces and courtyards have undergone significant modifications as well – fragmenting the undefined in-between spaces and mirroring the level of informality in each neighbourhood. Yet the modifications that have affected the façades and communal spaces in Ajapnyak's first neighbourhoods differ in character from those that have occurred in most other neighbourhoods in Yerevan, yet the motif that is common to both kinds of neighbourhood is ubiquitous free-standing garages. In Ajapnyak most of the green areas adjoining first-floor windows have been fenced in by residents: *'It had to be done: the windows are too close to the ground, it was too easy for every passer-by to peek in'*, they explain today. To extend their apartments, residents of Ajapnyak glazed in and walled up balconies and loggias and appropriated recessed spaces in front of stairwells, compromising their natural light and ventilation. When asked, the residents involved in such alterations draw a picture of amicable mutual agreement:

12 Noji, Eric K., et al., 'The 1988 Earthquake in Soviet Armenia: A Case Study', *Annals of Emergency Medicine*, vol. 19, No. 8, 1990, pp. 891–897.

13 Rescue Service, Ministry of Emergency Situations (RS), 'The Project for Seismic Risk Assessment and Risk Management Planning in the Republic of Armenia. Final Report: Volume II; Main Report 1', Yerevan City risk assessment, 2012, pp. 5-21–5-22.

14 Vermishyan, Harutyun, et al., *Lokal Ink'nut'yunnery Yerevanum: K'aghak'ayin Taratsut'yan Karruts'vatsk'nery* [Local Identities in Yerevan: the structures of urban space] (Yerevan: Publishing House of Yerevan State University, 2015), p. 94.

Figure 8:
An unfinished lift-slab building in the last, sixteenth, micro-district of Ajapnyak, begun in the early 1980s. Called 'Norashen' (*nor*: 'new'; *shen*: 'structure'), this district is better known as the 'sixteenth neighbourhood'.
Photo: Arsen, 2023

Resident 1
'Well, we shared the staircase landing, my next-door neighbour and I ... No, none of the other neighbours in the building expressed any objections, we have extremely warm relationships.'

A man in his early 60s, whose family relocated to Ajapnyak in 1960. Since the early 2000s he has run a small shop in the courtyard of his building.

In contrast, elsewhere in Yerevan (particularly in the central Kentron district), the extensions are much larger; the enclosed courtyards present a patchwork of extensive volumes protruding from inner façades, with up to three storeys constructed on top of roofs, and multiple first-floor apartments turned into autonomous units through the creation of private street access and large verandas. Several factors may have contributed to such remarkable differences in spatial configurations.

The most consequential period of modifications to residential buildings nationwide was in the early 2000s, facilitated by the significant socio-economic advances of the time and by investments in electricity networks and other sectors. In 2000 several government decrees marked the beginning of structural reinforcement projects and relocation programmes for families residing in irreparably damaged

Figure 9:
The evolution of ad hoc modifications undertaken by residents in the first standardised series in Ajapnyak.
Source: Heghine Pilosyan

Figure 10:
One of the buildings in Microrayon 1, 2023: most of the loggias have been walled in; the recesses in front of the stairwells have been filled in as appropriated annexes to the apartments, leaving the stairwells themselves mostly without natural light and ventilation.
Photo: Heghine Pilosyan, 2023

buildings, most of which were located in Ajapnyak. To this day, numerous families are waiting for their apartments to be included in exchange programmes while judiciously refraining from investing in their crumbling dwellings; in a sense they find themselves once again in the position of the *osvoenets* in Soviet-era resettlement programmes.[15] Wherever modifications have occurred, the moderate investments may be attributed to the lower incomes in these neighbourhoods and to lower returns on investment due to the less desirable location in the city.

Akin to the way in which technological advances in the 1970s came to transform communal areas in Ajapnyak's neighbourhoods – by claiming intra-block spaces for new residential tower blocks and garages (to accommodate the ever-increasing number of vehicles) – the present resettlement initiatives are now reshaping physical and social constructs in these neighbourhoods, reversing long-accumulated informalities in the process. Through agreements with private developers, municipal authorities facilitate the construction of new multi-apartment buildings that meet the revised seismic standards on the sites of entire buildings, or portions thereof, that have been deemed dangerous, thus allowing resident families to be relocated within their original district of residence. These initiatives are particularly noteworthy when viewed in the context of ownership transition – from state-owned housing at the time of the earthquake to the current private property market (with an overall nationwide owner-occupancy rate of 96 per cent).

Was it gentrification back then?

The current in-situ redevelopment programmes, though not yet participatory, are in stark contrast to the previous Soviet scheme of housing allocation, which, in line with the programmed urbanisation of the era, frequently involved expropriation of centrally located makeshift dwellings through eminent domain to make room for new urban street networks.

Much has been written about the inbuilt spatial injustice of the occupation-based housing-allocation model in socialist cities, which ultimately 'produced [...] residential segregation of occupational groups'.[16] A comparable outcome emerged in Yerevan too, where the location of one's dwelling correlated with one's position in the Soviet socio-economic hierarchy. Furthermore, the mismatch between formal procedures of housing allocation and the true underlying

---

15 *Osvoenets*: a colloquial term derived from Russian and used in reference to people waiting to be resettled on the sites of their demolished dwellings.

16 Szelényi, Iván, 'Housing Inequalities and Occupational Segregation in State Socialist Cities: Commentary to the Special Issue of IJURR on East European Cities', *International Journal of Urban and Regional Research*, vol. 11, No. 1, 1987, pp. 1–8, here: p. 7.

Figure 11:
A new residential building in Microrayon 2, built on the site of a damaged standardised building. The formalisation process that accompanied the plot clearance has redefined the boundaries between urban elements, reinstating public and private spaces.
Photo: Heghine Pilosyan, 2023

informal mechanisms has perpetuated a cycle of grievances that are still expressed by older residents.[17] Overall, perceptions about new housing have been influenced by people's previous location of residence and its respective attractiveness. Identical sentiments are common among elderly residents who moved to Ajapnyak as children in the early 1960s.

Resident 2
'We didn't want to move from our home, but they were going to demolish it to build new streets. I loved my school there [one of the oldest schools in central Yerevan] and did not want to be transferred to this one. But my parents would not allow me to keep going to my old school. And it was difficult for them as well. We were the last family to be moved to this building, but the surroundings were still unfinished; it was like a desert.'
A woman in her 70s who moved to Ajapnyak in 1962 as a child. In 1996 she became the first president of one of the first condominiums in Ajapnyak.

Resident 3
'We moved here in 1961. Our home was on Khanjyan Street [a prime central location in modern-day Yerevan]. Many of the older residents did, of course, move elsewhere … but with the housing prices today, you know, you couldn't afford even a garage …'
A woman in her 70s whose family moved to Ajapnyak in 1961.

Notwithstanding the biases inherent in memory recall, people interviewed in present-day surveys whose families were averse to the prospect of relocation consistently express a shared sense of nostalgia for their 'old houses' and frustration at having to integrate in a new locality.[18] Some of the discontent might, in retrospect, stem from a sense of lost opportunity cost that is nurtured in the current framework of the market-based housing system. Ostensibly, these shifts in population composition are reminiscent of the post-2000 series of controversial redevelopment projects in high-value central urban areas – involving construction of housing for the elite – accompanied by unfair compensation for the long-term residents and, ultimately, gentrification.[19] Such parallels become less significant when viewed in the respective contexts of spatial planning and the objectives inherent in them. Housing allocation in accordance with geography of employment was conceived as one of the pillars of the

---

17 Vermishyan, Harutyun, 'Ideological and Cultural Practices in The Soviet Housing Space: The Case of Allocation and Obtaining of Apartments in Yerevan', *Studies of Transition States and Societies*, vol. 13, No. 2, 2021, pp. 23–38.

18 For more such examples, see: Vermishyan, Harutyun, et al., *Lokal Ink'nut'yunnery Yerevanum: K'aghak'ayin Taratsut'yan Karruts'vatsk'nery* [Local identities in Yerevan: the structures of urban space] (Yerevan: Publishing House of Yerevan State University, 2015), pp. 86–88.

19 See: Zenobi, Vincenzo, 'Le trasformazioni urbane nella Yerevan post-sovietica. Note su élite, economia e retorica della continuità' [Urban transformations in post-Soviet Yerevan: Notes on elites, economy and the rhetoric of continuity] in Comai, Giorgio, et al. (eds), *Armenia, Caucaso e Asia Centrale. Ricerche 2019* [Armenia, Caucasus and Central Asia: Research 2019] (Venice: Edizioni Ca' Foscari, 2019), p. 317.

industrialisation-driven planning of the twentieth century.[20] In today's market-oriented housing supply, individuals' choice of location is primarily defined by affordability – an issue that is rapidly afflicting Yerevan to an ever increasing extent.[21]

In search of adequate housing solutions, citizens of Yerevan are creating new commuting patterns characterised by longer distances and travel times, accompanied by other externalities such as worsening traffic congestion and environmental problems. Currently, there are several occupation-based affordable housing construction programmes subsidised by the government and labelled as 'social'. Catering to young professionals, academics, and civil servants, these initiatives are invariably located in urban areas far from the workplaces of the beneficiaries covered by the programme. In most cases the new houses are still reminiscent of the large panel buildings disliked by urban dwellers for their monotonous appearance and lack of diversity.

The latest chapter in Ajapnyak's story

As the first Armenian microrayons undergo another stage of spatial transformation, the residents are once again faced with shifting definitions of formal and informal and of private and public ownership. Ahead of their forthcoming relocation, inhabitants of Ajapnyak are individually taking measures to legalise the communal spaces they have taken over in order to ensure compensation from private developers for their properties' total area.

Walking through these neighbourhoods today, one sees a patchwork of façades and communal spaces divided up among neighbours – a tangible manifestation of a history marked by repeated transfers of supervision. It seems that the six decades of shared habitation, spanning several generations, have not forged reliable alliances for collective place-making, but rather that top-down initiatives continue to be relied upon for organising and maintaining spaces for social practices. In the same vein, the transfer of jurisdiction from the preceding *ZhEK* housing-maintenance offices,[22] operating on behalf of city councils, to tenant-controlled condominiums has not gained significant traction since the reform was put in place in 1996. The latter organisations remain largely misunderstood, perceived by residents as a structure within and supervised by local municipal offices, and are consequently incapacitated by non-payment of tenant fees. Cases in point are the handful of newly built playgrounds funded by the municipal

20 Grigoryan, Artsvin, and Tovmasyan, Martin, *Architecture of the Soviet Armenia* (Moscow: Stroyizdat, 1986), p. 190.

21 Pilosyan, Heghine, 'Is Housing in Armenia Affordable?', *Urbanista*, 4 May 2022, <https://urbanista.am/affordable-housing-eng>, accessed 23 October 2023.

Figure 12:
Part of a damaged building slated for demolition, whose residents are in the process of negotiating for compensation equivalent to the value of their property, including adjacent land appropriated in the 1990s and 2000s.
Photo: Arsen, 2023

22 *ZhEK*: abbreviated from the Russian *zhilish'no-ekspluatatsionnye offisy*.

office and one particularly well-maintained building with adjoining publicly accessible green spaces where, according to the residents, the young head of the municipal office lives with his family.

Resident 2
'As the first condominium president, I had to fight for everything. See that playground over there? Had it not been for my devotion to the interests of this community, there would have been no space left for it to be built; they would have built garages everywhere. And now kids from other neighbourhoods come here to play ...'

To judge by what is admittedly a limited set of interviews, the younger generation raising their families in Ajapnyak overall demonstrates a heightened awareness of the right to the city. Compared to their elders, younger *Ajapnyaktsis* are more aware of and vocal about situations where neighbours' actions limit their and their children's access to shared communal spaces or interfere with their rights of way. [23] However, such concerns are often not acted upon, seen as futile given the imminent prospect of relocation – whether such a project is underway for a particular building or the residents assume it to be the case based on the stories of neighbouring buildings.

[23] Ajapnyaktsi: a colloquial term for inhabitant of Ajapnyak in Armenian.

Figure 13:
A playground built by the local municipal office in one of the few intra-block areas where garages have not occupied all the green space.
Photo: Heghine Pilosyan, 2023

Resident 5
'There is no room left for my kids to play in the vicinity of our home, I have to cross the highway [Halabyan Street] for them to play in a safe green space ...'

'Look, see that large green space? How can you explain a situation like this? It's been this way for as long as I can remember. Someone just randomly decided to build a fence with a locked door in it, and now my kids and the rest of the neighbours can't use it. If, say, I am hanging my laundry on the rope out of the window and a piece of clothing falls, I then have to go to him and ask him to unlock the door and let me pick it up.'

A woman aged 27. Both she and her husband grew up in the first neighbourhoods in Ajapnyak and now manage a small grocery shop near their house.

Resident 4
'No, I don't know who fenced in that space, they probably had a good reason ... Go ask the municipality, let them be the snitch ...'

A senior resident encountered nearby, about the same fenced green area.

Perceptions of general obsolescence in regard to all housing types in Ajapnyak are deeply intertwined with local ideas about stone. The *midis* stone walls used in the first housing series are still recognised by the general public as the most reliable construction technique suitable for the local climate and seismicity. Thinking back to the 'dark and cold years', the senior residents of this type of *khrushchevka* are still grateful for the thick stone walls which were much better at providing warmth, comparing them favourably with panel houses and, sometimes, the newly built '*vysotkas* with thin walls'.[24] Simultaneously, the widespread use of pink Artik tufa in the stone facing of virtually all the mass housing built between the late 1950s and the 1980s has aroused complex feelings on the part of Yerevan dwellers and the professional community alike.

At the height of construction, as new districts kept breaking ground on the slopes surrounding central Yerevan, the contemporaries started to express a feeling of 'pink boredom', alluding to visual monotony. In contrast, the fading chromatic uniformity of modern Yerevan – as a result of the expanding palette introduced by new-builds on the one hand and the demolition of pre-1990 buildings clad in Artik tufa on the other – has led several generations of city

Figure 14:
A building in Microrayon 2; its external perimetral and green spaces have been fenced in by one of the residents.
Photo: Heghine Pilosyan, 2023

[24] *Khrushchevka*: early prefabricated building of the type built all over the USSR during Nikita Khrushchev's campaign to house the general population in separate apartments (as opposed to in hostels, barracks, or communal apartments).

dwellers to nostalgically bemoan the loss of the 'pink city'. In retrospect, if we compare the pink volumes that constitute the urban fabric of Ajapnyak to the unadorned concrete surfaces that are common across all ex-Soviet states, the former undoubtedly make for a much livelier urban environment.

… and post-scriptum

With sufficient temporal distance from the onset of mass housing construction, the professional communities have now gained the vantage point needed to reconsider the placement of these districts and buildings on the timeline of Yerevan's urban development. The story of the first microrayons in Ajapnyak is a complex interplay of multiple plot lines: Mikayel Mazmanyan's modernist legacy mixed with decades of remodelling guided by residents' individual sense of agency over their own habitat. The Soviet microrayons were never intended to have inbuilt capacities for co-production and incrementality. Yet a confluence of circumstances has continually reshaped the appearance of these residential neighbourhoods, dispelling the notion of their rigidity at the scale of both individual dwelling and cluster of buildings.

Several development phases spanning six decades, accompanied by formal and informal processes and relationships, have shaped Ajapnyak's neighbourhoods as they are today. At the outset there were centrally driven programmes of urban cohabitation in the first microrayons. These were followed by formal densification and semi-formal alterations, the latter flourishing into unregulated land-capturing practices in the 1990s and early 2000s. The resulting problems are now being resolved in multilateral deals between homeowners, private developers, and municipal bodies. With these contemporary redevelopment initiatives underway, the imperative arises for a new set of regulations governing spatial transitions.

As has been made clear by previous spatial transmutations, a combination of poorly defined (as opposed to flexible) clusters of buildings with lenient planning regulations undermines the principles of a just community. Regulatory control over fair use of communal spaces – frequently perceived as intermediate between public and private – and over the building–street interface may ultimately cultivate a sense of collective control among residents that is necessary for the successful operation of condominiums since they constitute the body responsible for regular maintenance. As it is, in an

Figure 15: (left page):
Several generations of spatial transformation in one image: garages and fenced-in green areas flanked by a road with no clear separation of pedestrian and vehicle paths (foreground); a building from an early standardised series facing a prefabricated panel tower block (middle); nd a new building that has replaced a dangerous structure (background).
Photo: Arsen, 2023

increasingly unaffordable, gentrifying Yerevan, new generations of born and bred Ajapnyaktsis enjoy a comfortable location in the city – adjacent to a renovated park which houses an important educational centre for creative technologies (the TUMO innovation centre, built in 2011). The latest phase of transformations in and around these first microrayons presents a fresh opportunity for their inhabitants to find a deeper sense of identity and belonging, enabling the development of a bespoke framework for collective place-making.

References

Azatyan, Karen, 'Bnakeli Bjji Zargats'man Himnakan P'ulery Yerevani Verjin Haryuramyaki Chartarapetut'yan Mej' [The main stages of evolution of the dwelling unit across the architecture of the recent century], *Scientific Papers of National University of Architecture and Construction of Armenia*, vol. 59, no. 4, 2015, pp. 3–12.

Babayan, Levon, 'Voprosy Arkhitektury zhilishcha' [Housing architecture], *Arkhitektura SSSR* [Architecture of the USSR], No. 2, 1972, pp. 15–18.

Grigoryan, Artsvin, and Tovmasyan, Martin, *Architecture of the Soviet Armenia* (Moscow: Stroyizdat, 1986).

Noji, Eric K., et al., 'The 1988 Earthquake in Soviet Armenia: A Case Study', *Annals of Emergency Medicine*, vol. 19, No. 8, 1990, pp. 891–897.

Pilosyan, Heghine, 'Is Housing in Armenia Affordable?', *Urbanista*, 4 May 2022, <https://urbanista.am/affordable-housing-eng>, accessed 23 October 2023.

Rescue Service, Ministry of Emergency Situations (RS), 'The Project for Seismic Risk Assessment and Risk Management Planning in the Republic of Armenia. Final Report: Volume II; Main Report 1', Yerevan City Risk Assessment, 2012.

Szelényi, Iván, 'Housing Inequalities and Occupational Segregation in State Socialist Cities: Commentary to the Special Issue of IJURR on East European Cities', *International Journal of Urban and Regional Research*, vol. 11, No. 1, 1987, pp. 1–8.

Ter-Minassian, Taline, *Erevan, konstruirovanie stolitsy v sovetskuyu* epokhu [Yerevan, the construction of a Soviet-era capital] (Yerevan: Antares, 2019).

Ter-Sarkisiants, Alla, *Sovremennaya sem'ya u Armyan* [The modern Armenian family] (Moscow: Nauka, 1972), p. 41.

Vardanyan, Lilia, and Ter-Sarkisiants, Alla (eds.), *Armyane, seriya 'Narody i Kul'tury'* [Armenians, 'Nations and Cultures' series] (Moscow: Nauka, 2012), pp. 320–321.

Vermishyan, Harutyun, et al., *Lokal Ink'nut'yunnery Yerevanum: K'aghak'ayin Taratsut'yan Karruts'vatsk'nery* [Local identities in Yerevan: the structures of urban space] (Yerevan: Publishing House of Yerevan State University, 2015).

Vermishyan, Harutyun, 'Ideological and Cultural Practices in the Soviet Housing Space: the Case of Allocation and Obtaining of Apartments in Yerevan', *Studies of Transition States and Societies*, vol. 13, No. 2, 2021, pp. 23–38.

Zenobi, Vincenzo, 'Le trasformazioni urbane nella Yerevan post-sovietica. Note su élite, economia e retorica della continuità' [Urban transformations in post-Soviet Yerevan: Notes on elites, economy, and the rhetoric of continuity] in Comai, Giorgio, et al. (eds.), *Armenia, Caucaso e Asia Centrale. Ricerche 2019* [Armenia, Caucasus and Central Asia: Research 2019] (Venice: Edizioni Ca' Foscari, 2019).

Figure 16:
Bird's-eye view of Ajapnyak's first microrayons in 2023. Adjacent to the first series of standardised buildings, the taller new-builds can be discerned – replacing demolished dangerous parts of the former. *Photo: Davit Gevorgyan*

02

Chilanzar district in Tashkent, Uzbekistan. Analysing legislative transformations, economic reforms, and migration dynamics

Dona Kulmatova

The evolution of urban planning in Tashkent

Urban planning is a critical dimension of socio-economic development, embodying the cultural and historical peculiarities of a society. The urban planning history of Tashkent spans more than 150 years, forming a distinctive research domain that enables the elucidation of evolving dynamics and pivotal developmental stages in the city.

In its formative years Tashkent succumbed to the influences of various factors as it responded to economic and political vicissitudes. In 1954, under the guidance of the city's chief architect, M. Bulatov, a meticulous analysis of Tashkent's master plan was undertaken, concomitant with expansion of the city's territory to 20,000 hectares. This period witnessed the construction of areas of mass housing based on standardised designs for multi-storey dwellings, each tailored to specific circumstances.[1] A scrutiny of the architecture from this time reveals a palpable grandeur and expressive aesthetic. This period heralded the establishment of expansive and imposing thoroughfares that encapsulated a distinctly European style. Initially, construction of residential districts exhibited monotonous layouts based on a limited repertoire of building types. Starting in 1958, however, the adoption of the standardised Series 310 facilitated economical and efficient construction processes.

A pivotal transformation in the city's structural composition resulted from the inception of the Chilanzar district in 1956.[2] This phase marked a shift from imposing thoroughfares towards a holistic and integrative planning approach for residential complexes, with emphasis placed on micro-districts. In 1955 a governmental decree titled 'On Eliminating Excesses in Design and Construction' prompted a re-evaluation of orientation in architecture,[3] instigating an all-encompassing impetus toward use of industrial methods and implementation of standardised designs. The process of urban reconstruction in Uzbekistan did not unfold in isolation, separately from other events and influences. Instead, it was embedded in a broader pattern shaped by the Soviet regime. As one of the Soviet Union's constituent republics, Uzbekistan adhered to architectural and planning trends dictated by central policymakers.

A competition in 1962, organised by the Union of Architects of Uzbekistan and the Department of Architecture and Construction of the Uzbek Soviet Socialist Republic (UzSSR) and aimed at refining standardised residential building designs, ushered in alterations to architectural and planning solutions and the augmentation of apartment types with open balconies. 1964 witnessed the commencement

1   Askarov, Shukur, *Genezis Arkhitekturi Uzbekistana* [Genesis of the architecture of Uzbekistan] (Tashkent: San'at, 2014), p. 135.

2   Kadyrova, Tolkinoy, *Arkhitektura Sovetskogo Uzbekistana* [Architecture of the Soviet Uzbekistan] (Moscow: Stroyizdat, 1987), p. 88.

3   Central Committee of the CPSU, 'Resolution of the Committee of Ministers on the Elimination of Redundancies in Design and Construction', *Zakonodatelstvo v SSSR* [Legislation in the USSR], 4 November 1955, <https://www.libussr.ru/doc_ussr/ussr_5043.htm>, accessed 8 January 2024.

of large-panel residential building construction, characterised by an emphasis on colour and façade texture to mitigate the monotony of urban development.[4]

The calamitous earthquake of April 1966, which ravaged over 2.5 million square metres of housing, provoked a watershed moment in urban planning. Through the concerted efforts of the Soviet republics and local builders, 3.2 million square metres of housing were erected between 1966 and 1968, surpassing the losses incurred from the earthquake.[5] Workers from various regions of the Soviet Union invested significant efforts in construction of residential units. These achievements were underpinned by the establishment of an industrial construction base and widespread adoption of standardised designs.[6]

Transformation, privatisation, and urban planning challenges in the Chilanzar district – the path from Soviet legacy to the modern period

The micro-districts in Chilanzar were originally autonomous settlements with diverse social functions. The builders from the various USSR republics had a degree of freedom to vary layouts, based on modifications of the nationwide Series I-310.[7] The projects built by the Soviet republics differed mostly in the construction materials used. This was due to the fact that each republic sent construction trains to Uzbekistan. The trains brought to Tashkent bricklayers, plasterers, assemblers, engineers, and technicians, as well as the equipment, tools, and materials they needed. The residential districts shared a common infrastructure, including schools, kindergartens, state pharmacies, grocery stores, bakeries, and clinics, as well as cultural and recreational areas, parks, green spaces for leisure, and green boulevards (Fig. 1).[8]

One of the most distinctive features of housing construction in this district is the inclusion of commemorative inscriptions and mosaics on building façades or as individual stelae – elements left by construction brigades from various cities in the former Soviet Union.[9] Gifts from each country, these inscriptions have become a kind of heritage, imparting a special and memorable character to the district (Figs. 2, 3).

Externally, these structures look unpretentious. The unassuming architecture deserves attention as an example of a quick solution to the problem of how to build affordable industrial housing. A large-scale

---

4 Kadyrova, Tolkinoy, *Arkhitektura Sovetskogo Uzbekistana* [Architecture of the Soviet Uzbekistan] (Moscow: Stroyizdat, 1987), p. 165.

5 Arkhangelskiy, V., 'Khroniki 1969: Podvigu tri goda' [Chronicles 1969: three years of valour], in Arkhangelskiy, V. A. (ed.), *Tashkent – gorod bratststva* [Tashkent is the city of brotherhood] (Tashkent: Central Committee of the Communist Party of Uzbekistan, 1969), pp. 260–279, here: p. 273.

6 Kadyrova, Tolkinoy, Babiyevskiy, Konstantin, *Arkhitektura Sovetskogo Uzbekistana* [Architecture of the Soviet Uzbekistan] (Moscow: izdatelstvo literature po stroitelstvu, 1972), p. 38.

7 Askarov, Shukur, *Arkhitektura Uzbekistana i stran SNG* [Architecture of Uzbekistan and CIS countries] (Tashkent: San'at, 2012), p. 85.

8 Jordan, Jens Werner, Meier, Hans-Rudolf, Will, Thomas (eds.), *Baudenkmale in Taschkent: Beiträge zu einer Denkmaltopographie* (Dresden: THELEM Universitätsverlag, 2022), p. 47.

9 Titarenko, A., 'V bratstve nasha sila' [In brotherhood is our strength], in Arkhangelskiy, V. A. (ed.), *Tashkent – gorod bratststva* [Tashkent is the city of brotherhood] (Tashkent: Central Committee of the Communist Party of Uzbekistan, 1969), pp. 77–96, here p. 88.

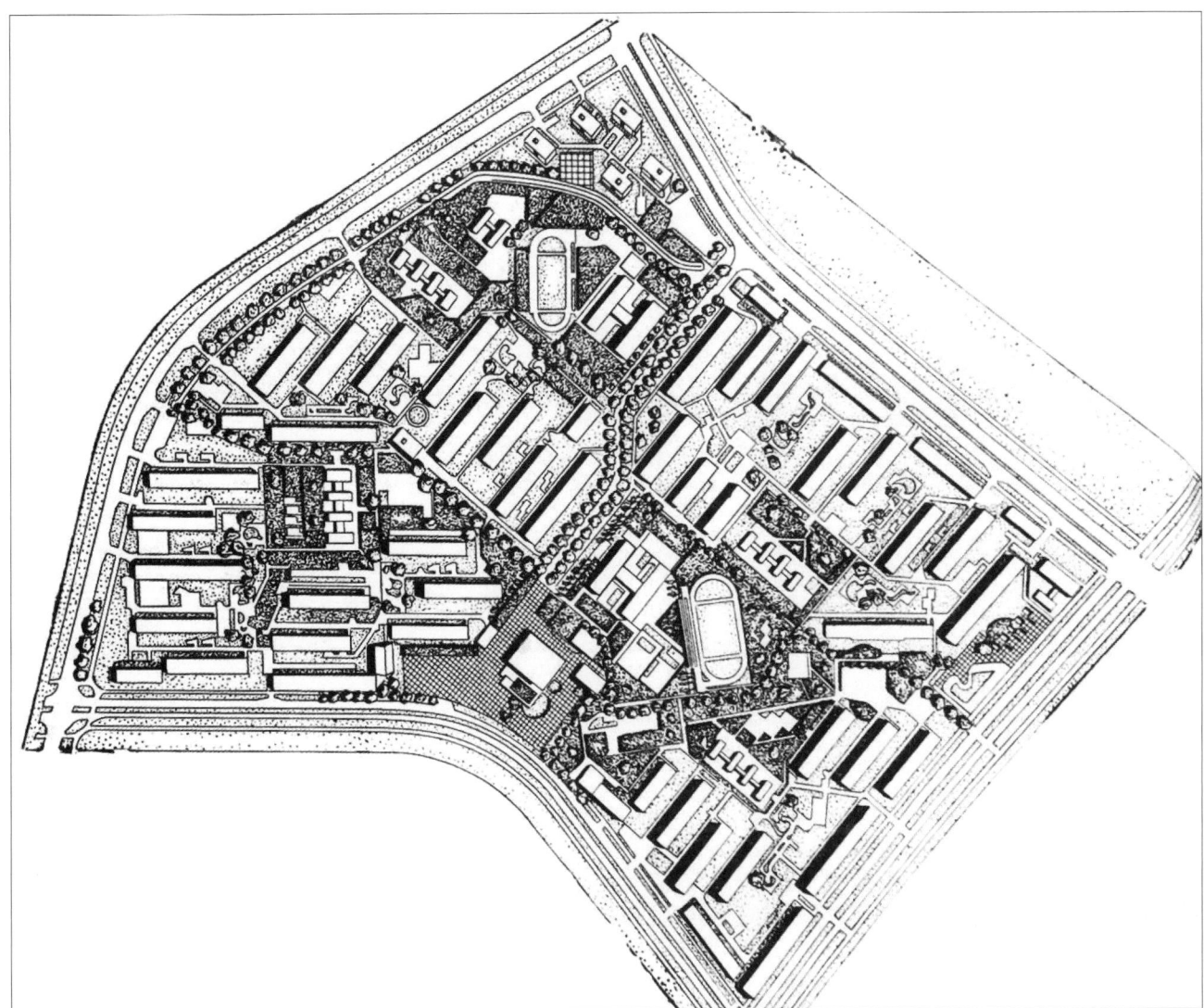

Figure 1:
Chilanzar, residential district in Tashkent,
site plan of Micro-district B-23.
Source: Tolkinoy Kadyrova, Konstantin Babiyevskiy, *Architecture of the Soviet Uzbekistan* (Moscow: izdatelstvo literature po stroitel'stvu, 1972), p. 42

Figure 2:
13th quarter, Chilanzar, inscription on the front of a house.
Photo: I. Glauberzon, V. Sirotkin, in
V. A. Arkhangelskiy (ed.), *Tashkent – Gorod bratststva* [Tashkent: city of brotherhood] (Tashkent: Central Committee of the Communist Party of Uzbekistan, 1969)

housing experiment was implemented in a very short time, underlining the effectiveness of this architectural approach. The simplicity of appearance does not diminish this method's impact in addressing the challenge of providing affordable housing.

However, the intensive expansion and commercialisation of Tashkent over the past 30 years, driven by the construction of new residential complexes by private enterprises, has resulted in transformation of the Chilanzar district and its evolution into a commercial sector.

In Uzbekistan, as in all post-socialist countries, at the beginning of the independence period a series of laws were adopted that primarily addressed property-related issues. In October 1990 Uzbekistan introduced the 'Law on Decentralisation and Privatisation' and the 'Law on Property', which, for the first time in a Soviet republic, introduced the concept of private ownership into practice through legislation. Private ownership was defined as the right to own, use, and dispose of assets with the aim of generating income.[10]

Chilanzar had formed as a district in the second half of the twentieth century under the administrative and financial management of state bodies.[11] This system had operated within the framework of a nationwide economic model in which the state had controlled and directed all aspects of the economy. The impact on residential areas was significant, leading to certain characteristics and features in their structure and functioning. State ownership of housing and centralised maintenance of residential buildings

10   Statement of the Supreme Council, 'Law of the Republic of Uzbekistan No. 152-XII on Property in the Republic of Uzbekistan', *LexUZ*, 31 October 1990, <https://lex.uz/docs/111455>, accessed 8 January 2024.

11   Filonovich, M. I., *Tashkent: zarojdeniye i razvitiye goroda i gorodskoy kulturi* [Tashkent: birth and development of the city and urban culture], (Tashkent: Fan of the Uzbek SSR, 1983).

Figure 3:
24th quarter, Chilanzar. Inscription on the front of a house.
Photo: Dona Kulmatova, 2023

had limited residents' autonomy in making decisions regarding their living conditions. Due to the absence of the possibility of individual or private ownership of flats in multi-storey buildings, residential units had effectively and legally belonged to the state. Citizens had had the right to free residence in these apartments but had been unable to acquire them through purchase. The only form of transaction permitted had been exchanges, including exchanges between residents of apartments situated in different geographical regions.

Uzbekistan's acquisition of independence launched the privatisation of state housing: apartments were now transferred to the ownership of their inhabitants on favourable terms. For example, participants and veterans of the war, pensioners, as well as teachers, researchers, educators, and cultural figures received property free of charge. In 1995, after the country started using the Uzbekistani sum as its national currency and eliminated its dependence on Russia, a new decree was passed 'On the Initiation and Promotion of Private Entrepreneurship'. This legal act became a starting point for the development of private entrepreneurship in the country, based on attracting investments and creating favourable conditions for market growth.[12]

These legislative changes proved particularly significant for the Chilanzar district. They served as the initial impetus for the emergence of new small retail points and the opening of new markets with private enterprises in this area. The new business opportunities created by these changes have facilitated the emergence of retail and service businesses in Chilanzar.

Since 1999 the government has taken measures to promote small and medium-sized enterprises and the development of the private sector. However, the adequacy and effectiveness of these measures are undermined by issues of consistency and commitment. Measures related to private sector development lack a coherent strategy or vision for the role of the private sector in the national economy.[13] With the increasing involvement of citizens in entrepreneurial activities, there has been a widespread transformation of residential into non-residential premises and mass allocation of vacant urban areas for various commercial purposes, often in contravention of the historically established urban structure. A consequence has been the conversion of a great number of residential units on ground floors into commercial premises with shopping arcades, catering facilities, and commercial services (beauty salons, tailoring studios, travel agencies, and the like). The lack of protection for architectural designs

12 Chernomorova, T. V., 'Uzbekistan: Svoy put privatizatsii' [Uzbekistan: its path to privatisation], in Vinogradov, V. A. (ed.), *Privatisatsiya v Rossii i drugikh stranakh SNG. Sbornik obzorov* [Privatisation in Russia and other CIS countries: Collection of reviews] (Moscow: INION RAN, 2003) pp. 185–206, here: pp. 191, 193.

13 Bakayeva, Sabina, 'How Much Is Allowed: Rights and Interests of Tenants in the Seizure Zone', *Gazeta.uz*, 20 November 2020, <https://www.gazeta.uz/ru/2020/11/20/interview/>, accessed 5 January 2024.

leads to changes in the external appearance of buildings, devaluing the initially dominant artistic and aesthetic principles originally conceived by the creators of the buildings, through the unrestricted conversion of dwelling units for commercial purposes.

The urban environment is constantly transforming under the influence of societal development. The evolution of society brings about changes in the organisation of the urban environment, its aesthetic values, and its functionality. In the case of the Chilanzar district, urban development has led to a reconsideration of land use and a shift in functions, subsequently resulting in alterations to the area's architecture. However, the new construction disregards historical traditions nad has replaced a significant part of the urban structure with an unorganised and chaotic approach, incorporating innovative forms that are incompatible with the historical significance of the urban district. Architectural disharmony, leading to the formation of an inconsistent and aesthetically discordant urban landscape, is due to the absence of architectural planning and a lack of consideration for regulatory standards in the field of urban planning.

The Urban Planning Code of the Republic of Uzbekistan has its contradictions. Many urban planning laws were adopted during the Soviet era, and the urban planning legislation itself determines how to build but does not specify what it is unacceptable to build. The absence of the concept of territorial zoning in legislation to define types of permitted land use necessitates more detailed land zoning. The abstract concept of 'land category' does not contribute to the preservation of a quality environment and provokes conflicts of interest between residents and businesses.[14] Additionally, there are no laws limiting the quota for the number of establishments of a certain profile in residential areas, leading to infringement of citizens' rights to a favourable natural environment, free from trade and crowds, especially in areas designated for recreation for families and children. The attractiveness of secondary service and entertainment sectors for transient visitors creates a conflict with the interests of residents in residential areas.

Contemporary dynamics of migration and societal changes

During the formation of an independent state and the implementation of economic reforms, Uzbekistan underwent a period of complex transition accompanied by migration. In the early 1990s the most prominent migration flows in the Commonwealth of Independent

14   National Legislative Database, 'Land Code of the Republic of Uzbekistan', *LexUZ*, 30 April 1998, <https://lex.uz/docs/149947>, accessed 10 January 2024.

States were driven by the return of repatriates. External migration in the post-Soviet era has been predominantly characterised by the movement of ethnic groups back to their historical homelands, giving an ethnic hue to external emigration flow. Here Russian-speaking groups have predominated.

Migration ties between Uzbekistan and Russia, dating back to the pre-Revolutionary period, have strengthened and expanded over time. For many decades Russia has played a key role in the external migration processes of the Uzbekistani population. In the early 1990s annual migration flows varied between 60,000 and 140,000 people, with more than half of the total emigrants heading to Russia. By the end of the 1990s the migration potential of various ethnic groups had significantly diminished. Over 15 years the number of Russians, Ukrainians, and Tatars in Uzbekistan had substantially decreased. Estimates indicate that by 1999 the impact of the decline in the population of Russians, Ukrainians, Jews, and Tatars had been significant. More than 48 per cent of the total emigration from Uzbekistan is attributed to the capital region of Tashkent. Migration processes not only affect the overall population but also the ethnic composition of the regions. The period from 1996 to 1999 is identified as the period with the highest population outflow from the country, according to the State Committee on Statistics of the Republic of Uzbekistan. Since the early 2000s there has been an increase in internal migration, with populations moving from the regions to the capital.[15]

The majority of the population in Chilanzar district was once composed of Russians and other ethnic groups, primarily represented by residents from the European part of the former Soviet Union. Despite the complexities of modern laws on registration of residency, the primary direction of internal migration remains movement from the regions to the capital. The institution of registration, by which residents register at a specific address, is an outdated legacy of the Soviet era. While in many developed countries registration of the population is considered a routine formality, in Uzbekistan registration not only carries legal significance but also creates an invisible border, separating the capital, Tashkent, and the regions of Uzbekistan.[16]

Over the years of independence the Cabinet of Ministers has passed various resolutions, imposing sanctions and restrictions on the right of Uzbek citizens to apply for registration in the capital. For example, in 2012 the Cabinet of Ministers approved regulations governing the procedures for permanent and temporary registration and for

15 Maksakova, Lyudmila, 'Uzbekistan in the System of International Migrations', in Zayonchikovskaya, J. A., and Vitkovskaya, G. S. (eds.), *Post-Soviet Transformations: Reflection in Migrations* (Moscow: Adamant, 2009), pp. 323–349.

16 Hojaqizi, Guliatir, 'Citizenship and Ethnicity: Old Propiska and New Citizenship in Post-Soviet Uzbekistan', *Inner Asia*, vol. 10, No. 2 (2008), pp. 305–322, here: p. 306.

17 Resolution of the Cabinet of Ministers, No. 41, 'Order of Permanent and Temporary Residence Registration in Tashkent and Tashkent Region', *Norma*, 16 February 2012, <https://www.norma.uz/novoe_v_zakonodatelstve/ustanovlen_poryadok_postoyannoy_i_vremennoy_propiski_v_tashkente_i_tashkentskoy_oblasti>, accessed 5 January 2024.

18 Bakhtiyor Ergashev, Bakhtiyor, Bunyod Avliokulov, Bunyod, *Urbanizatsiya v tsentral'noy Azii: vizovi, problemi i perspektivi* [Urbanization in Central Asia: challenges, problems and prospects], analytical report, (Tashkent: Centre for Economic Research, 2013), p. 31.

citizens of the Republic of Uzbekistan to register their residence.[17] According to these provisions, permanent registration is granted to citizens who own property in the city of Tashkent and the Tashkent region that was acquired before this law came into force. However, the acquisition of real estate in Tashkent remains essentially inaccessible to individuals without registration.

Despite the legal difficulties faced by citizens under the existing legislation, there has been a considerable influx of people migrating from the regions to the city of Tashkent, particularly to the Chilanzar district. According to statistical agencies in Central Asian countries, Tashkent's population growth over the past ten years is 13.6 per cent.[18] Originally geared towards the middle-class segment, Chilanzar continues to attract people with lower income levels by providing affordable housing options. This district has become an appealing destination for relocation, offering those seeking to live in the capital the opportunity to acquire housing in a spacious residential area at comparatively low prices.

The mass migration of families has led to an increased demand for ground-floor properties: people prefer proximity to the ground, which offers them opportunities for expansion and appropriation of additional space. In conditions of limited financial resources, there is a phenomenon of encroachment into public spaces, where personal space is extended at the expense of publicly accessible areas. An analogy with established traditions in Uzbek families, in which the development of a second family creates a need for expanded space and hence additional construction on existing territory, may explain this phenomenon in the context of Chilanzar. In this district this phenomenon occurs due to privatisation and appropriation of public spaces, such as the corridors in the gallery buildings that are characteristic of the region. Examples include annexation of balconies and staircases, and extensions to the façades of buildings.

Future prospects

The transformation of Chilanzar district is a multifaceted process influenced by legislative changes, economic reforms, and migration dynamics. Ensuring sustainable development in the future will require the government to adhere to a clear strategy for the development of the private sector and the resolution of urban planning issues. As the district evolves, it is crucial to balance economic growth, preservation of architectural heritage, and the well-being of residents. The historical transformations, the impact of legislative changes, and the dynamics of migration form a complex kaleidoscope of factors shaping how this district looks today.

Given this topic's relevance, special attention should be paid to developing coherent urban planning strategies and resolving real-estate conflicts. The expansion of the private sector and support for entrepreneurship should be accompanied by clear measures to ensure sustainable social and economic well-being for residents.

This study can serve as a starting point for a deeper understanding of the interplay between urban planning, economic development, and sociocultural changes in urban communities. Further research in this area may shed light on optimal development strategies for districts, taking into account variables that contribute to the formation of the modern urban landscape.

References

Arkhangelskiy, V., 'Khroniki 1969: Podvigu tri goda' [Chronicles 1969: three years of heroism], in Arkhangel'skiy, V. A. (ed.), *Tashkent – gorod bratststva* [Tashkent: city of brotherhood] (Tashkent: Central Committee of the Communist Party of Uzbekistan, 1969), pp. 260–279, here: p. 273.

Askarov, Shukur, *Arkhitektura Uzbekistana i stran SNG* [Architecture of Uzbekistan and CIS countries] (Tashkent: San'at, 2012), p. 85.

Askarov, Shukur, *Genezis Arkhitekturi Uzbekistana* [Genesis of the architecture of Uzbekistan] (Tashkent: San'at, 2014), p. 135.

Bakayeva, Sabina, 'How Much is Allowed: Rights and Interests of Tenants in the Seizure Zone', *Gazeta.uz*, 20 November 2020, <https://www.gazeta.uz/ru/2020/11/20/interview/>, accessed 5 January 2024.

Central Committee of the CPSU, 'Resolution of the Committee of Ministers on the Elimination of Redundancies in Design and Construction', *Zakonodatel'stvo v SSSR* [Legislation in the USSR], 4 November 1955, <https://www.libussr.ru/doc_ussr/ussr_5043.htm>, accessed 8 January 2024.

Chernomorova, T. V., 'Uzbekistan: Svoy put' privatizatsii' [Uzbekistan: its path to privatization], in Vinogradov, V. A. (ed.), *Privatisatsiya v Rossii i drugikh stranakh SNG. Sbornik Obyorov* [Privatisation in Russia and other CIS countries: a collection of reviews] (Moscow: INION RAN, 2003) pp. 185–206, here: pp. 191, 193.

Ergashev, Bakhtiyor, Avliokulov, Bunyod, *Urbanizatsiya v tsentral'noy Azii: vizovi, problemi i perspektivi* [Urbanization in Central Asia: challenges, problems and prospects], analytical report (Tashkent: Centre for Economic Research, 2013), p. 31.

Filonovich, M. I., *Tashkent: zarozhdenie i razvitiye goroda i gorodskoy kul'turi* [Tashkent: birth and development of the city and urban culture] (Tashkent: Fan of the Uzbek SSR, 1983).

Hojaqizi, Guliatir, 'Citizenship and Ethnicity: Old Propiska and New Citizenship in Post-Soviet Uzbekistan', *Inner Asia*, vol. 10, No. 2 (2008), pp. 305–322, here: p. 306.

Jordan, Jens Werner, Meier, Hans-Rudolf, Will, Thomas, *Baudenkmale in Taschkent: Beiträge zu einer Denkmaltopographie* (Dresden: THELEM Universitätsverlag, 2022), p. 47.

Kadyrova, Tolkinoy, *Arkhitektura Sovetskogo Uzbekistana* [Architecture of the Soviet Uzbekistan] (Moscow: Stroyizdat, 1987), pp. 88, 165.

Kadyrova, Tolkinoy, Babiyevskiy, Konstantin, *Arkhitektura Sovetskogo Uzbekistana* [Architecture of the Soviet Uzbekistan] (Moscow: izdatelstvo literature po stroitelstvu, 1972), p. 38.

Maksakova, Lyudmila, 'Uzbekistan in the System of International Migrations' in Zayonchikovskaya, J. A., and Vitkovskaya, G. S. (eds.), *Post-Soviet Transformations: Reflection in Migrations* (Moscow: Adamant, 2009), pp. 323–349.

National Legislative Database, 'Land Code of the Republic of Uzbekistan', *LexUZ*, 30 April 1998. <https://lex.uz/docs/149947>, accessed 10 January 2024.

Resolution of the Cabinet of Ministers, No. 41, 'Order of Permanent and Temporary Residence Registration in Tashkent and Tashkent region', *Norma*, 16 February 2012, <https://www.norma.uz/novoe_v_zakonodatelstve/ustanovlen_poryadok_postoyannoy_i_vremennoy_propiski_v_tashkente_i_tashkentskoy_oblasti>, accessed 5 January 2024.

Statement of the Supreme Council, 'Law of the Republic of Uzbekistan No. 152-XII on Property in the Republic of Uzbekistan', *LexUZ*, 31 October 1990, <https://lex.uz/docs/111455>, accessed 8 January 2024.

Titarenko, A., 'V bratstve nasha sila' [In brotherhood is our strength] in Arkhangelskiy, V. A. (ed.), *Tashkent – gorod bratststva* [Tashkent: city of brotherhood] (Tashkent: Central Committee of the Communist Party of Uzbekistan, 1969), pp. 77–96, here: p. 88.

03

Dubki micro-district in Taganrog, Russia.
The missing social dimension in urban development and heritage-making

Elena Batunova and Elena Chernysheva

– How do you like living in this district?
– Fine. If we don't call it 'bad'.[1]

Dubki: setting the scene

'The village of Cheryomushki gave its name to Moscow's world-famous new buildings in the southwest of our capital. Now, almost every Soviet city has its own "Cheryomushki"': this comment opens what may be the most famous Soviet film, *Irony of Fate* [Ironiya sud'by].

In 1956 Moscow's Cheryomushki became the first experimental site for mass housing construction in the USSR and the prototype for the future image of a typical Soviet city. The operetta *Moscow, Cheryomushki*, written by Dmitri Shostakovich, and the feature film *Cheryomushki*, released in 1962, popularised the new micro-district. 'Cheryomushki' became a common name designating the first micro-districts of *khrushchevkas* in many Soviet cities. Under Khrushchev's housing reform, these residential areas became symbols of a period of mass housing construction that was unparalleled in human history. They are known worldwide for their visual monotony, lack of distinctive characteristics, monofunctionality, and greyness. Pervading the entire expanse of the former Soviet Union, these areas of housing seldom find a place in urban heritage narratives because they lack a crucial necessary value: rarity.[2]

The residential area of Dubki in Taganrog, examined in this chapter, represents the 'Cheryomushki' type of micro-district. It was constructed in the 1960s in the north-eastern part of Taganrog near the industrial enterprise 'Krasnyy kotelshchik' as a housing area for the plant's workers. The district did not differ much from its twins in many other peripheral cities around the Soviet Union. It has all the typical characteristics of a 'Khrushchev' district: a free plan, absence of transport inside the residential area, educational facilities located within walking distance of the houses where pupils live, five-storey buildings of simple design, minimal living space, and tiny apartments. The material of the walls – red brick – is the only decorative element. Despite its apparent ordinariness, Dubki is rooted in a rich and layered urban landscape with a traceable history that reaches back to the Bronze Age. This heritage, spanning multiple epochs, has not only influenced the current urban structure but also gained partial institutional recognition in the initial years following the dissolution of the USSR. The 1990s were a crucial period for production of cultural heritage in Taganrog. Experts in heritage protection implemented

---

[1] Interview with a resident of Dubki; male, 65 years old, living in Dubki since 1983 (30 August 2023).

[2] Heinich, Nathalie, 'The Making of Cultural Heritage', *The Nordic Journal of Aesthetics*, vol. 22, No. 40–41, June 2011, pp. 119–128, <doi:10.7146/nja.v22i40-41.5203>.

Figure 1:
Alley of Immortality (left) and workers' dormitory (right) in Dubki, Taganrog.
Photos: Bolotov Mikhail, March 2023

pioneering practices in the city. Numerous monuments were listed in this period.³ Taganrog itself acquired the status of historical settlement. Today it is one of 41 historical settlements in Russia listed by the federal government.⁴

Most practices of heritage recognition and protection in Taganrog are incomplete due to the lack of resources and capacities, gaps in legislation, or bad governance. However, the existing heritage engages numerous stakeholders in discussions about urban transformation and increases the location's attractiveness for development projects. In the interim, a walk through Dubki gives little impression of the valuable historical landscape. Instead, it provides a picture of a troubled area and what can be an unpleasant experience. This area is not homogeneous. The relatively nice-looking houses surrounded by the well-kept trees in Dubki's central part contrast with the dilapidated, crack-ridden houses on the periphery.

Considering this context, our research aims to address the following questions:
1. What values do various urban development and heritage-making stakeholders attribute to Dubki micro-district?
2. Does the Dubki residential area hold potential for institutional recognition as a part of the urban heritage?

3   Interview with Voloshinova, Lyubov Feoktistovna; architect-restorer, local historian, and a state expert of the Ministry of Culture of the Russian Federation on cultural heritage sites (1 June 2023).

4   'List of Historical Settlements in the Regions of the Russian Federation' [in Russian], 2010, *Rossiyskaya Gazeta*, <https://rg.ru/documents/2010/09/29/istor-posel-dok.html>, accessed 10 September 2023.

The research methodology encompassed a diverse set of methods. Direct observations of Dubki's territory and photographic documentation were undertaken in April and August 2023. This allowed for a visual assessment of the area's upkeep, utilisation, and transformations. The study also looked at an extensive collection of regulatory documents concerning urban planning, land use, housing management, and heritage preservation. This included federal and regional legislation as well as the city's general plan, master plan, zoning regulations, and documentation on heritage recognition and conservation. Official databases from institutions overseeing the use and maintenance of real estate were scrutinised to gain insights into housing typology, ownership structures, and management paradigms.

Interviews were conducted with key stakeholders, such as planners and experts in heritage preservation. These interviews elucidated ambiguities in the regulatory documents and shed light on Dubki's development trajectory. Furthermore, five semi-structured interviews with residents and one interview with a representative of a local housing management company yielded insights into daily life in the area, local perceptions, prevailing maintenance challenges, and visions for the future. Analysis of real estate advertisements, a supplementary source of information, offered another lens through which to evaluate the residential area's characteristics.

This text is organised along a timeline from the period when the first traces of civilisation were recognised in the area up to the present day. The aim is to explore the legacies of the past that contribute to present-day heritage-making and its evaluation and perception by different stakeholders.

An ancient whisper

According to official data published by the Russian Ministry of Culture, the Rostov region is the richest in Russia in terms of archaeological sites. In 2021 there were 8152 listed archaeological sites and objects, according to the register kept by the federal Ministry of Culture; this represents 15 per cent of all archaeological sites in Russia.[5] The region's history is woven into the long and complicated history of the development of human presence in southern Russia, which has always been a crossroads of cultural migrations between Europe and Asia.[6] Palaeolithic monuments, the remains of ancient Albanian and Greek settlements, medieval Genoese fortresses, and traces of the Great Silk Road are relics of the region's history. The

5   These numbers do not include the archaeological heritage of the annexed territory of Crimea listed by the Russian Ministry of Culture.

6   Batunova, Elena, Cocaj, Rilind, Sokoli, Zana, and Kuma, Shohei, 'A Socialist Built Legacy in a Small Shrinking City: The Case of Zernograd, Southern Russia', *Territorio*, vol. 91, 2020, pp. 97–106, <https://doi.org/10.3280/TR2019-091010>.

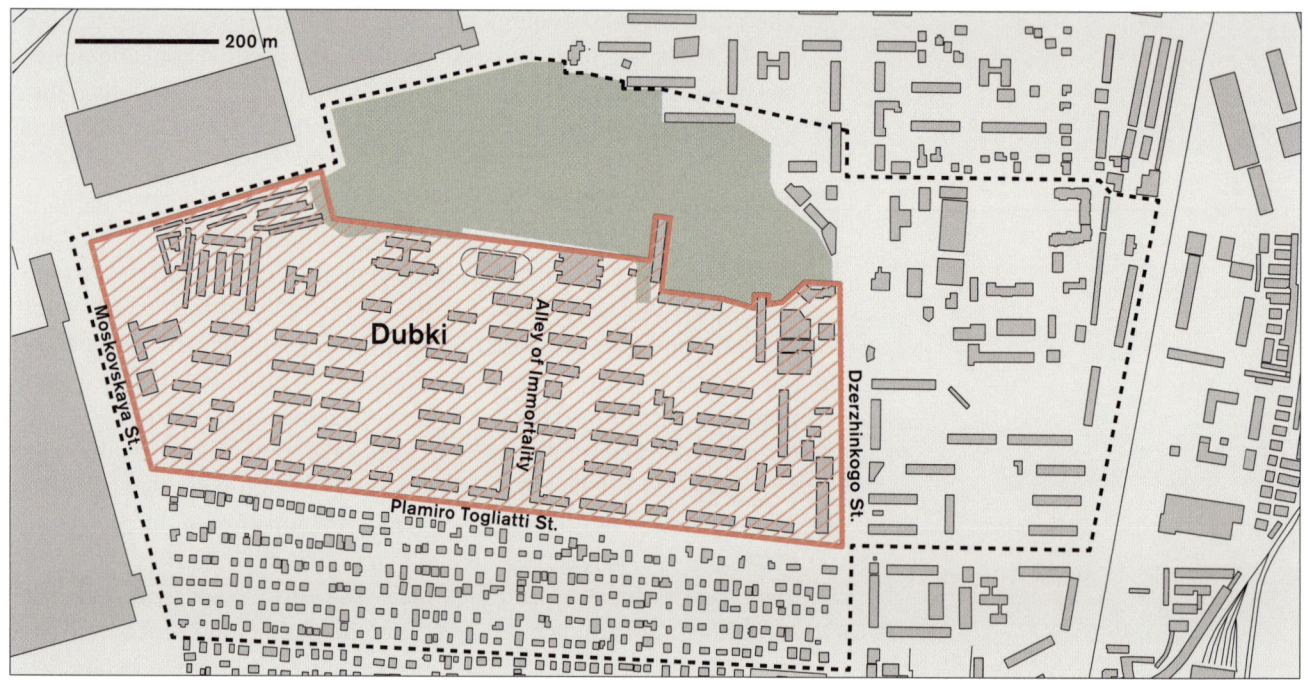

Figure 2:
Relative locations of the Dubki micro-district and archaeological sites.[10]

- - - United zone for the protection of two archaeological sites: Dubki and Petrovsky rampart

Source: Elena Batunova, based on OSM cartography

diverse kingdoms, cultures, and tribes that have settled here did not leave many untouched symbols of urban culture on the ground,[7] but have bequeathed a notable archaeological heritage. According to the regional register of listed monuments, Taganrog has 22 listed sites of federal significance and two newly identified sites. Local planning and zoning documents provide information on 30 archaeological sites in Taganrog. Discrepancies in title and documentation regarding cultural heritage are typical in Russia. In the Rostov region the heritage lists were compiled in the 1990s, mainly based on archival materials without inventories or field surveys.[8]

'The settlement of Dubki' is an archaeological site in Taganrog listed in the regional register under 'identified archaeological sites'. Taganrog's general plan and zoning documents (land use and development regulations) define its territory. The presence of the partly recognised archaeological site means that an archaeological study of the territory is required as a preliminary step in any construction within the site's boundaries. Moreover, construction attracts the attention of experts and activists in heritage preservation. They monitor the building or landscaping works in the area and foster public discussion about its development.[9]

[7] Kirichenko, Yevgeniya I. (ed.), Gradostroitel'stvo Rossii serediny XIX – nachala XX veka [Urban planning in Russia in the mid-nineteenth and early twentieth centuries], vol. 3 (Moscow: Progress-Traditsiia, 2010).

[8] Interview with Kozhin, Alexander Olegovich; head of the Rostov regional branch of VOOPiK [All-Russian Society for the Protection of Historical and Cultural Monuments] (15 November 2023).

[9] Olkhovskaya, Marina, 'Arkheologi i istoriki Taganroga b'yut trevogu: povrezhden kul'turnyy sloy poseleniya «Dubki»' [Archaeologists and historians of Taganrog are sounding the alarm: the cultural layer of the Dubki settlement has been damaged]. Bloknot Taganrog, 7 June 2022, <https://bloknot-taganrog.ru/news/arkheologi-i-istoriki-taganroga-byut-trevogu-povre?ysclid=lndjod1v it965059414>, accessed 10 September 2023.

In the shadow of the tsar's vision

The name 'Dubki' refers to the more recent history of Taganrog's founding by Peter the Great in 1698. He started by constructing the Trinity Fortress on Cape Tagan-Rog and the first Russian naval base here. The city was part of the numerous fortifications that formed a line of defence in the Russian confrontation with the Ottoman Empire. Tsar Peter I intended to gain total control of the Sea of Azov and to give two cities – Azov and Taganrog – the same role in the south that Petersburg and Kronstadt would later receive in the north.[11] According to legend, Peter the Great planted the first oak trees in the steppe to have material with which to build a fleet in the future. A document from 1701 records that he ordered the planting of oak trees and willows around Taganrog.[12] The name of today's surviving grove, 'Dubki', means 'young oak trees'.[13] Even though the very first trees have not survived until today, Dubki Grove in Taganrog is the oldest forest plantation in southern Russia.

Dubki micro-district was built next to the grove on the outer side of the corridor connecting Pavlovskaya and Cherepakh fortresses. This defensive line coincides with Palmiro Tolyatti Street, which forms the micro-district's south border.

The Dubki grove greatly impacts the development of the micro-district and its perception, plans, and use. Local people positively value closeness to the grove, which has a citywide significance. In 2006 the Dubki grove became a specially protected natural area (SPNA) of regional significance under the responsibility of the Ministry of Natural Resources and Ecology of the Rostov Region. A decree emphasises its historical, environmental, educational, and aesthetic importance.[14] The grove's status protects it from destruction.[15] As a protected natural area, Dubki Grove generates many social activities that attract bottom-up active participation and financial support from state actors.[16]

Foreign flames, industrial dawn

The rise of coal and iron mining in Donbas and the evolution of related industries gave a new impulse to the region's development. At the end of the nineteenth century the south of imperial Russia became a space of international cooperation with the conspicuous presence of European and US industries. Taganrog's commercial seaport played a significant role in the city's internationalisation. For instance, the durum wheat produced in southern Russia and Ukraine and exported to Italy and the United States through the port of Taganrog became known worldwide under the name 'Taganrog'.[17] The seaport, a railway, proximity to rich mineral deposits, and foreign investments transformed Taganrog into a major industrial centre. In terms of degree of concentration of production and workers at its largest enterprises, at the beginning of the twentieth century Taganrog was one of the leading cities in the entire Russian Empire.[18]

In the coastal area of Taganrog several factories were built by European companies – predominantly by Belgian enterprises.[19] Albert Louis Georges Nève, a prominent Belgian industrialist and mechanical engineer at the University of Liege, was a council member in Taganrog from 1902 forwards.[20] He founded the Russo-Belgian joint-stock company and the Taganrog Boiler-Making Works Albert Neve, Vilde and Co in 1896.[21] This joint-stock company also launched and operated a tannery and metallurgical and machine-building plants in Taganrog. For these purposes it bought vast tracts of land in the north-eastern part of the city and became owner of most of Taganrog's industrial enterprises.

In 1918, after the October Revolution, the Soviet Union nationalised the Taganrog Boiler-Making Works, as it did all other industrial enterprises in the city. The following years of hunger and reduced production at the largest factories caused an outflow of workers to the countryside and the mothballing of the city's most important enterprises. The boiler-making works did not operate between 1922 and 1925. In 1925 it was given a new name, which it still uses today – Krasny Kotelshchik (literally, 'Red Boilermaker').[22] In the pre-socialist period the boiler-making works produced low-power boilers of various types, including steamship and locomotive boilers. During the socialist period the plant began producing advanced boiler equipment, including high-pressure boilers, equipment for nuclear power plants, and steam generators.[23]

This intensive industrial development shaped Taganrog's cityscape. Production, utility, and storage areas occupy 21 per cent of the city's territory.[24] The enterprises needed to house the numerous workers who came to Taganrog; the Dubki micro-district became one such residential area.

The dominance of industries and the secondary role of housing in urban planning before and during the socialist period determined the quality of housing and resulted in residual financing of housing maintenance. It also defined the range of housing

17 Nicola, Fernanda G., and Scaccia, Gino, 'It's All About the Pasta: Protectionism, Liberalisation, and the Challenge for Quality and Sustainability of Made in Italy', *FIU Law Review*, vol. 14, No. 3, 2021, pp. 479–520, <https://ecollections.law.fiu.edu/lawreview/vol14/iss3/7>.

18 Pronshtein, Alexander P. *Taganrog*, (Rostov-on-Don: Rostov Book Publishing House, 1977).

19 Fox, Robert (ed.), *Technological Change: Methods and Themes in the History of Technology*, (Amsterdam: Harwood Academic, 1996).

20 Namazova, Alla S., "Guide des documents relatifs à l'histoire de Belgique conservés dans les archives des *institutions publiques de Moscou (1778–1940)*", *Bulletin de la Commission royale d'histoire*, Académie royale de Belgique, vol. 171, 2005, pp. 273–370.

21 *Krasnyy Kotel'shchik. Istoriya Taganrogskogo kotlostroitel'nogo zavoda (v dokumentakh i vospominaniyakh). 1917–1967 gg.* [Krasnyy Kotel'shchik: History of the Taganrog boiler-making plant (in documents and memoirs); 1917–1967] (Rostovskoye knizhnoye izdatel'stvo [Rostov book publishing house], 1967).

22 Andreenko, S. A., Bondarenko, G. M., Donskova, L. A., Emelyanov, S. N., Konopleva, E. P., Ryzhov, V. P., Skrynnikova, L. I., Timoshenko, V. I., and Shelukhina, E. B., *Taganrog: entsiklopediya* [Taganrog: Encyclopedia] (Taganrog: Anton, 2008).

23 Website of the 'Krasny Kotelshchik' boiler-making works <https://tkz.su/company/history/>, accessed 15 September 2023.

24 The general plan of the municipality 'City of Taganrog', approved by the decision of the City Duma of the City of Taganrog dated December 27, 2019, No. 49 'On amendments to the decision of the City Duma of the City of Taganrog', dated 25 December 2008, No. 753 'On approval of the general plan of the municipal formation of the City of Taganrog for the period to 2028'.

Figure 3:
Locations of the Dubki micro-district and the Krasny Kotelshchik plant.
Source: Elena Batunova, based on OSM cartography

types found in Dubki, where a large part of the housing consists of workers' dormitories.

The personal stories of Dubki residents who were interviewed are linked to the history of the Taganrog Boiler-Making Works. The intervieees or their parents received apartments here as workers at Krasny Kotelshchik.

Bricks of the proletariat: a Soviet promise

While the construction of industrial sites took place in the pre-socialist period, the industrial enterprises' workers became the main force in the revolutionary changes that occurred in Taganrog. The harbingers of the October Revolution and workers' protests are commemorated in the Dubki grove.[25] In 1992 the regional government recognised the Dubki grove as an object of cultural heritage of regional significance; the grove was the site of the first *mayovkas* (May Days).[26] In 2020 this remarkable site was designated a 'protected object'.[27] The many turbulent years following the October Revolution concluded with the end of the Second World War. The following period saw the next wave of the city's industrialisation and resurgence, accompanied by mass construction of housing.

Dubki micro-district was designed by the Rostov Regional Design Institute 'Rostoblproekt (1937–1964) for 15,000 people.[28] Its planners characterised it as a 'simple project, without any pretensions'.[29] Severe resource shortages in the post-war period made it impossible to build high-quality housing.[30,31,32] One of our respondents, an 85-year-old woman,[33] was a crane operator during the construction of Dubki. Claiming that she 'built all the buildings of Dubki', she explained that housing quality diminished from the district's central planning axis to its periphery. Today this is a conspicuous difference.

But Dubki had all the necessary facilities. It still has two schools and four kindergartens. Good infrastructure, transport connections, social amenities, and greenery are the main legacies of the socialist period and are highly valued by local residents and real estate agencies.[34] The Alley of Immortality forms Dubki's central planning axis. Initially established in the Dubki grove in 1969, it was moved to the micro-district in 1985, becoming its symbolic public space. A memorial plaque on a boulder on the alley has the following text: '*Alley of Immortality. In this alley, under the chestnut trees, the soil of the hero cities of Moscow, Leningrad, Volgograd, Sevastopol, Odesa, Kyiv, the heroic Brest Fortress, and other places of military*

[25] Andreenko, S. A., Bondarenko, G. M., Donskova, L. A., Emelyanov, S. N., Konopleva, E. P., Ryzhov, V. P., Skrynnikova, L. I., Timoshenko, V. I., and Shelukhina, E. B., *Taganrog: entsiklopediya* [Taganrog: Encyclopedia] (Taganrog: Anton, 2008).

[26] Decision of the Minor Council of Rostov Regional Council of People's Deputies, dated 18 November 1992, No. 301.

[27] Resolution of the Committee for the Protection of Cultural Heritage Objects of Rostov Region, dated 28 August 2020, No. 20/01-01/2947 'On approval of the subject of protection of a cultural heritage site of regional significance (remarkable place) "The place of the oak grove – the place of the first Mayovkas (May Days)" at the address: Rostov region, Taganrog city, residential micro-district "Dubki", between Dzerzhinsky Street and Moskrovskaya Street'.

[28] Artyushkina, Tatyana A., Iz istorii gradostroitel'stva Taganroga: vek XX. Vekhi Taganroga: istoriko-literaturnyy al'manakh: 2011 [From the history of the construction of Taganrog: twentieth century. Milestones of Taganrog: historical and literary almanac: 2011] (Taganrog: Lukomorye, 2011).

[29] Interview with an urban planner from Rostov-on-Don (anonymous) (21 September 2023).

[30] Ermakov, P. 'Protiv izlishestv v stroitel'stve' [Against excesses in construction], *Taganrogskaya Pravda*, 26 November 1955.

[31] Grodsky, A. 'Stroit' deshevo i udobno' [Build cheaply and conveniently], *Taganrogskaya Pravda*, 13 November 1955. No. 226.

[32] Chaptsev, I., 'Nekotorye voprosy stroitel'stva Taganroga' [Some issues in the construction of Taganrog], *Taganrogskaya Pravda*, 29 June 1960.

[33] Interview with a female resident of Dubki, 85 years old (anonymous) (28 August 2023).

[34] Analysis of interviews with residents and announcement on websites of real estate agencies.

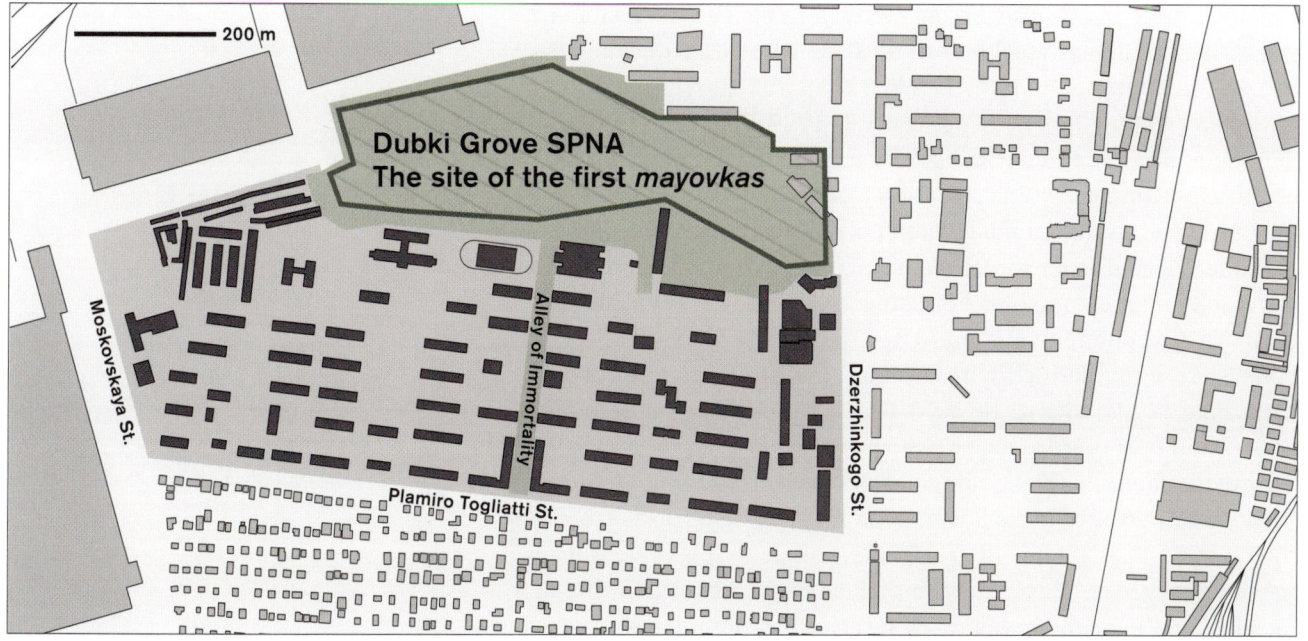

Figure 4:
Dubki Grove – a remarkable place of regional significance: the site of the first *mayovkas* (May Days) and the Alley of Immortality.
Source: Elena Batunova, based on OSM cartography

35 Pautova, Daria, 'Alleya bessmertiya bomzhey i alkashey' v Taganroge [Alley of Immortality of homeless people and drunks in Taganrog], *Bloknot Taganrog*, 25 August 2020, <https://bloknot-taganrog.ru/news/alleya-bessmertiya-bomzhey-i-alkashey-v-taganroge->, accessed 10 September 2023.

36 'Nochlezhka v Taganroge: zakrytiye radi progressa?' [The overnight shelter in Taganrog: closure for the sake of progress?], *RO.TODAY*, 17 January 2023, <https://ro.today/18766-nochlezhka-v-taganroge-zakrytie-radi-progressa.html>, accessed 10 September 2023.

37 Katz, Katarina, 'Labour in Transition: Women and Men in Taganrog, Russia', *Research Papers in Economics* 2002:1, Stockholm University, Department of Economics, 2001.

38 Gustafsson, Björn, and Nivorozhkina, Ludmila, 'Changes in Russian Poverty During Transition as Assessed from Microdata from the City of Taganrog', *Economics of Transition*, vol. 12, No. 4, 2004, pp. 747–776, <https://doi.org/10.1111/j.0967-0750.2004.00201.x>.

glory is preserved. The feat of the people in the Great Patriotic War is immortal! This Alley was founded in October 1969. Restored in August 2007.'

The Alley of Immortality does not have heritage status. However, it is maintained better than many recognised monuments because of the federal policy of patriotic education and the cult of the 'Holy War'. At the same time, the alley was for several years a space of conflict and fear. For an extended period it was occupied by homeless and drunk people who were users of a social shelter located in the micro-district.[35] After numerous complaints from locals, the shelter was finally closed by the local authorities, who, however, failed to provide any alternative solution for the homeless people.[36]

Crumbling walls, rising hopes?

At the end of the socialist period and the first decade after the dissolution of the USSR, the regional industrial sector underwent dramatic transformation. The sharp decline of the military-industrial sector, which dominated Taganrog, caused a drop in wages that was more pronounced in the city than in Russia as a whole.[37] A substantial percentage of the working-age population fell into poverty.[38] Taganrog became one of Russia's shrinking cities (a category which currently constitutes 70 per cent of Russian cities). Its population declined from 291,622 inhabitants in 1989 to 242,327 in 2023, after plunging by more than 49,000 – about 17 per cent – in 1989 alone.[39]

Economic decline and shrinkage often result in degradation of the urban environment.[40] The situation is usually worse in the case of peripheral cities of secondary importance that have suffered for an extended period from shortages of financial resources and authority. Dubki is an example of a housing area that initially provided a temporary economic solution. After decades of construction, the houses were maintained with minimal investment and effort. The turbulent 1990s with their wild privatisation left the communal spaces and courtyards 'ownerless' and neglected.

'Disgusting houses', 'Everything needs to be torn down to hell here', 'Renovate? Better to use a box of dynamite': these phrases from our interviews illustrate how its residents commonly perceive the area in which they live.[41] Residents complained of cracks in the walls, poor façades, and poor maintenance of interior communal areas, uncontrolled alterations by new owners who have privatised rooms and apartments, and poor technical infrastructure.

Another critical issue mentioned by all interviewees (including a representative of a housing management company) was the marginalised population living in several workers' dormitory buildings. Words often used by different respondents to describe these social groups include 'contingent' and even 'human waste'. The respondents pronounced those words with an expression of negative feeling – contempt, disgust, shame, or pity.

[39] Rosstat. Russian Federal State Statistics Service website, <http://www.gks.ru>, accessed 10 September 2023.

[40] Batunova, Elena, 'Urban Shrinkage, Aging, and Economic Change', in Filho, Walter Leal, Azul, Anabela Marisa, Brandli, Luciana, Özuyar, Pinar Gökçin, Wall, Tony (eds.), *Sustainable Cities and Communities*, *Encyclopedia of the UN Sustainable Development Goals*, (Cham: Springer, 2021), <https://doi.org/10.1007/978-3-319-71061-7_102-1>.

[41] Series of interviews with residents of Dubki (August 2023).

Figure 5:
Shared spaces in the houses of Dubki.
Photos: Batunova Ekaterina, August 2023

Figure 6:
A man in front of a house entrance in Dubki.
Photo: Bolotov Mikhail, March 2023

42 Analysis of real estate announcements on three websites (accessed 13 September 2023): https://rostov-na-donu.domclick.ru/; https://rostov.cian.ru/; https://www.avito.ru/.

43 Aleksandr, Bezmenov, 'Gubernator: Valentina Matvienko vzyala «pod opeku» Taganrog' [Governor: Valentina Matvienko took Taganrog 'under guardianship'], IA «*DON 24*», 5 April 2021, <https://don24.ru/rubric/politika/gubernator-valentina-matvienko-vzyala-pod-opeku-taganrog.html>, accessed 12 September 2023.

Negative feelings predominated in the description of the micro-district by its residents and external observers alike. Aspects positively rated by the residents included the area's location, transport infrastructure, greenery, and social facilities. The same positive aspects are mentioned in most real estate advertisements, which sometimes characterise the site as 'prestigious' due to these factors.[42] However, people clearly expressed their feelings of being abandoned and ignored by the state.

Recently, federal government officials began to show interest in the area.[43] With the support of Valentina Matvienko, the chairwoman of Russia's Federation Council, several important projects have been implemented in Taganrog, including modernisation of the tram network. Matvienko's particular focus on history and tourism resulted in attention being paid to beautifying and improving Dubki Grove. However, the landscaping and upgrading work implemented in the grove using federal money caused irritation and resentment among the micro-district's residents. They use words such as 'wasted money', 'useless', and 'money laundering' to describe the improvement measures undertaken near their crumbling houses.

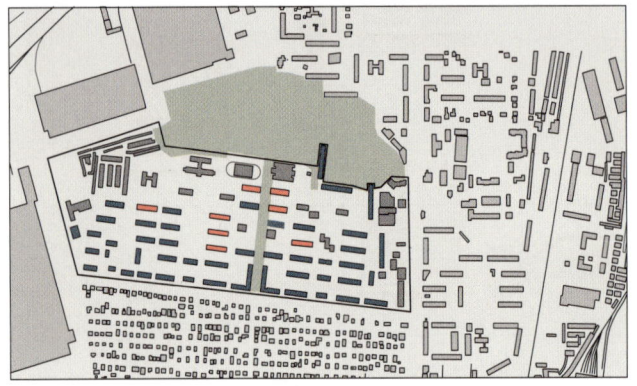 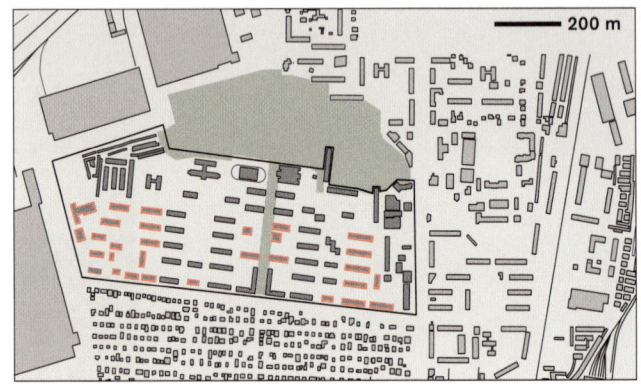

In 2023, under the auspices of the federal government and using national financial resources, the master plan for the city of Taganrog was developed. This document is a novelty in Russian urban planning practice, which is not regulated by existing legislation. Contrary to western practice, in Russia today master plans are imposed from the top down. The Taganrog master plan identified four priority strategic areas for future development. The Dubki micro-district is one of these four, defined for the local 'renovation' programme as an example of the transfer of Moscow practices to the regions.[44]

Surprisingly, the Dubki renovation project involves partial demolition of the buildings in Dubki but will preserve most of the workers' dormitories, which are notable for having the worst physical and social conditions. The project specifies various objectives to be achieved, such as increasing the number of square metres of housing, increasing density, and increasing population growth. It says nothing about social issues, poverty, and 'contingencies'.

Conclusion

Dubki micro-district in Taganrog, an ordinary residential area from the Khrushchev period, is embedded in a rich and multilayered historical landscape. The area's legacy involves archaeological remains, natural heritage, historical urban structure, and memorial sites which are wholly or partly recognised as valuable by the state institutions. Our main findings demonstrate that this place's history has shaped the residential area in the past, is impacting its use and development in the present, and can contribute to determining its future. The legacies of the past seem to be essential assets of the area for a variety of

Figure 7:
Left: housing types in Dubki: workers' dormitories and apartment buildings. Right: buildings to be demolished under the Taganrog master plan.

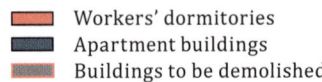

Workers' dormitories
Apartment buildings
Buildings to be demolished

Source: Elena Batunova, based on OSM cartography

[44] Zupan, Daniela, Smirnova, Vera, and Zadorian, Amanda, 'Governing Through *Stolichnaya Praktika*: Housing Renovation from Moscow to the Regions', *Geoforum*, vol. 120, 2021, pp. 155–164, <https://doi.org/10.1016/j.geoforum.2021.01.008>.

stakeholders: they are described positively by residents, are emphasised by real estate agencies as the area's main advantages, and attract developers and policymakers at different levels.

At the same time our research suggests that there is a notable contradiction between past and current urban planning and heritage-making practices in Dubki, on the one hand, and its residents' expectations on the other. In Taganrog, as in many other places, the decisions about what heritage designations should be created and protected are based on values that have been favoured by influential segments of society.[45] As principal heritage guardian, the state determines rules, develops policies, provides financial support, experts, and techniques, monitors compliance with the regulations, and punishes violations.[46]

For residents, housing is valuable when it meets their needs. The modernisation of residential buildings directly influences housing's most important value – its economic value.[47] As in most other Russian cities, residents of Dubki became owners without having to pay any debt associated with their homes,[48] but these means did not lead to the creation of effective ownership. The absence of capital and access to it transformed the new property from a potential resource into a burden with a negative return.[49] Marginalised populations inhabiting poor housing stock and workers' dormitories were unable to become agents of change in urban development.

Long-term underfunding of residential areas during the socialist period, ineffective private ownership, and accelerating centralisation in post-socialist Russia have widened the gap between decision-making and people's expectations. This has led to a negative evaluation of everyday life in Dubki by its residents and a rejection of government decisions made about the territory. Feelings of disappointment, resentment, and abandonment accompany the assessment of changes taking place in and around the territory.

The implemented urban projects and approved plans for Dubki's future development do indeed emphasise the value of the area's institutionalised heritage. However, its social component – the residents of Dubki themselves – is entirely ignored by both urban planning and heritage-making processes. Our limited research points to an untapped field of knowledge about local needs, perceptions, and values. It seems that the accumulated desperation of the local population due to feelings of neglect and stigmatisation has prevented them developing a sense of belonging and has become an obstacle to the bottom-up appreciation of the district's value by its everyday users.

---

45 Poulios, Ioannis, 'Moving Beyond a Values-Based Approach to Heritage Conservation', *Conservation and Management of Archaeological Sites*, vol. 12, No. 2, 2010, pp. 170–185, <DOI:10.1179/175355210X12792909186539>.

46 De Clippele, Marie-Sophie, 'Does the Law Determine What Heritage to Remember?', *International Journal for the Semiotics of Law*, vol. 34, 2021, pp. 623–656, <https://doi.org/10.1007/s11196-020-09811-9>.

47 Gibson, Lisanne, and Pendlebury, John, *Valuing Historic Environments*, (Farnham UK: Taylor & Francis, 2009).

48 Attwood, Lynne, 'Privatisation of Housing in Post-Soviet Russia: A New Understanding of Home?', *Europe-Asia Studies*, vol. 64, No. 5, 2012, pp. 903–928, <https://doi.org/10.1080/09668136.2012.681243>.

49 Verdery, Katherine, *The Vanishing Hectare: Property and Value in Postsocialist Transylvania*, Culture & Society After Socialism (Ithaca: Cornell University Press, 2003).

04

Microrayon No. 41 in Kamensk-Uralsky, Russia. Sparkles of heritage-making in the realm of inertia, ignorance, and dismay in the Brezhnev legacy

Albina Davletshina and Ivan Bushlanov

Historical development

Microrayon No. 41 in Kamensk-Uralsky is situated in front of Buynovsky Garden and is bounded by Kamenskaya, Kalinina, Oktyabrskaya, and Suvorova streets. Unfortunately, there are no specific records from Kamenskaya Street to facilitate detailed tracing of historical facts relating to the district's design and construction. According to the recollections of old-timers, development of this micro-district began in the 1960s in accordance with the principle of *samstroy* ('DIY construction') on the southeast side of the district. It was initiated and led by workers at the state-owned reinforced-concrete factory Stroy Montazh Konstrukt.

Local historians and community researchers tell us that Microrayon 41 was designed in the late 1960s / early 1970s by the local state construction company Trest UAS but was subsequently partially transformed (Fig. 2). The majority of residential areas here were built in the 1970s. By 1990 there were two schools, six kindergartens, and a children's hospital in the district (Fig. 1). After 1993 no new residential buildings were built. The only significant architectural changes took place in the 2010s: the Mandarin shopping centre was built southwest of the initial Microrayon No. 41, the Yuzhnyy shopping centre was reconstructed, and several commercial buildings were erected (Fig. 3).

The research area under consideration here is bounded by Kamenskaya, Kalinina, Oktyabrskaya, and Chelyabinskaya streets.

Figure 1:
Area of research, shown on the general plan of the district from the early 1960s.

- Initial project area at end of 1960s
- Research area

Source: archive of the Museum of Ural Aluminium Plant (UAZ)

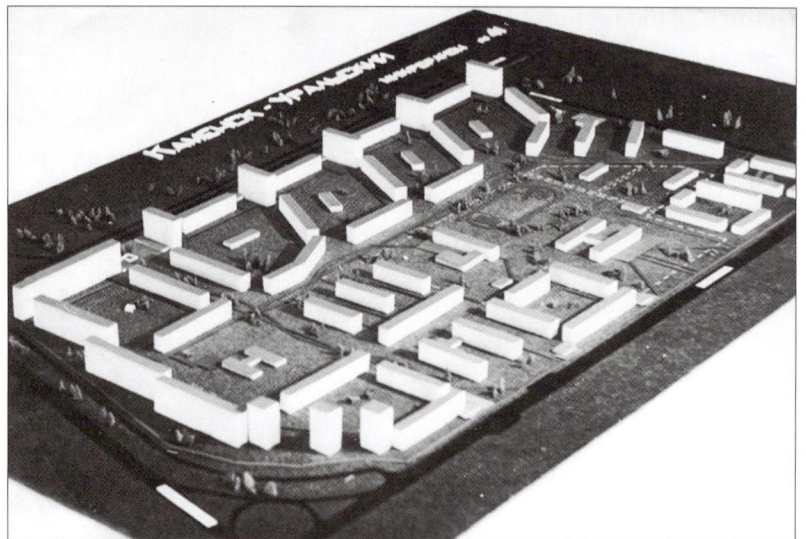

Figure 2:
Model of the master plan of Microrayon No. 41.
Source: archive of Ivan Bushlanov

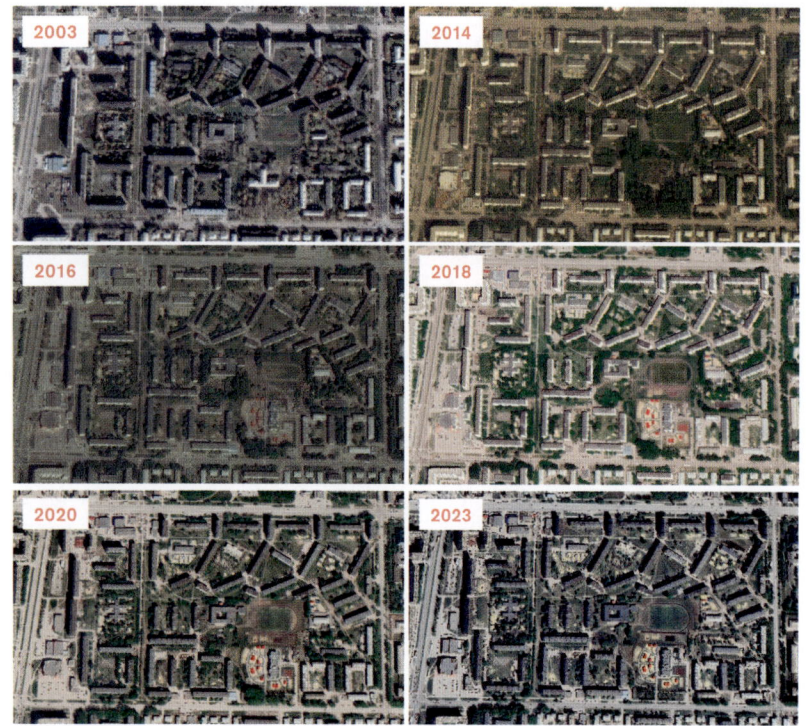

Figure 3:
Transformation of the research area.
Source: Google Earth Pro satellite view, changes by years, compiled by Albina Davletshina

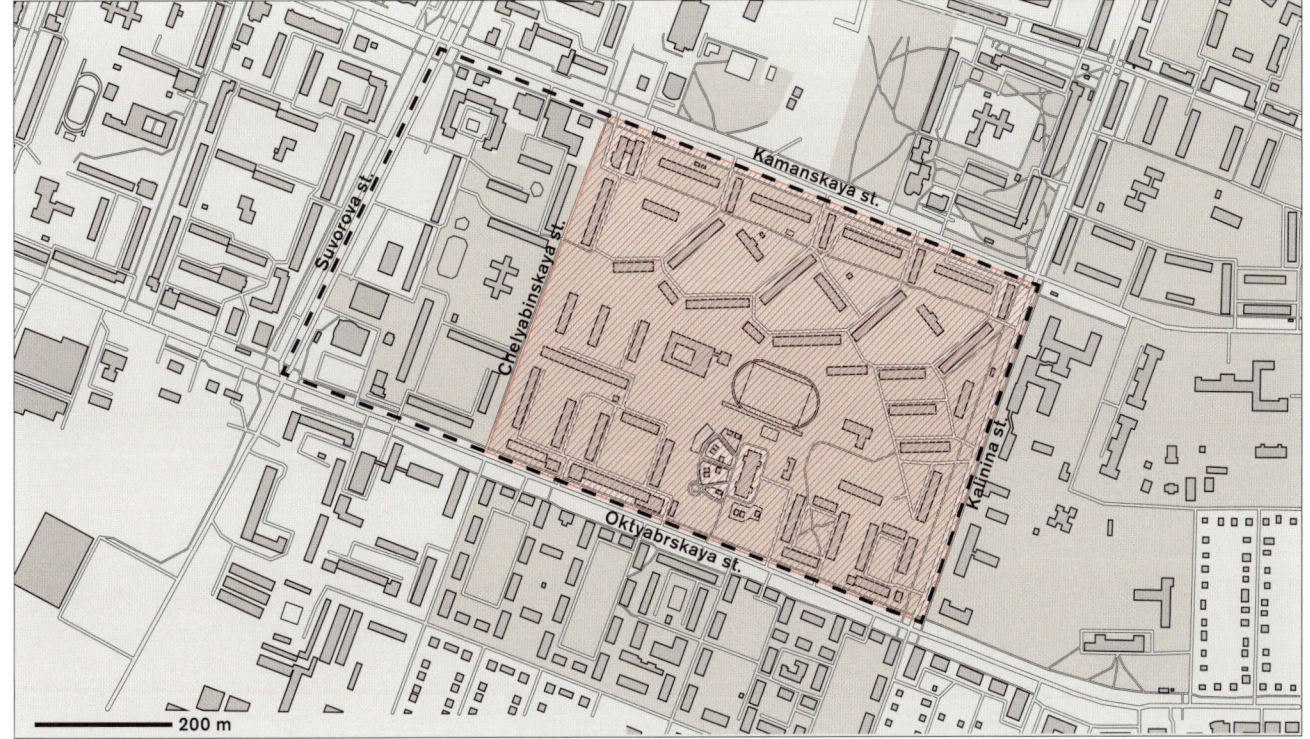

Figure 4:
The research area.

[- -] Research area
[////] Initial project area (1960s)

Source: prepared by Albina Davletshina

In the northwest part of the district retail functions were developed at the end of the 1980s, and by the 1990s, according to locals, this area in the west had been nicknamed *Torgovnik*, a Russian slang word for 'trading place'. Now, the Russian service Yandex Maps identifies these two parts of the microrayon as *Torgovyy Tsentr* ('Shopping Centre') and the 41st Quarter. This means that the area to the west had by the 1990s already started to acquire its own separate identity. This was followed by spatial and architectural changes (Fig. 3; note the southwest corner). Seemingly more interesting from the point of view of preserved architectural authenticity and historical integrity, the territory of the microrayon to the east of Chelyabinskaya Street, the micro-district's main body, consists of buildings erected in the 1970s and early 1980s (Fig. 4). There have bee only two significant interventions in the built environment in the research area: School No. 28 was demolished in 2013, and a three-storey kindergarten building was subsequently erected in its place.

Another element of spatial identity and authenticity in the appearance of Microrayon No. 41 is the visual character of the research area.

This is defined by five nine-storey residential buildings of concrete-panel construction aligned along the main road of Kamenskaya Street. The buildings' side façades are adorned with decorative marble aggregate embedded in the concrete panels (Fig. 5). Alas, apart from the five decorated side façades of the nine-storey buildings, there is nothing unique in this micro-district.

In order to understand ongoing processes and the reasons behind them, we examined the actors involved and how they interact with each other. Nine interviews were conducted with seven residents, one representative from the management company, and a local heritage activist and resident. Supportive material for the analyses included legal documents such as laws, strategies, and programmes,[1] the public cadastral map, and open-source governmental data from the Ministry of Housing and Communal Services. One may summarise these interviews as follows: while some interviewees struggled due to the absence of a chairperson, others focused more on battles over building maintenance (financial situations involving control and scarcity of resources or overall issues of communication with different actors).

Elements of path dependency: inertia and fear of responsibility

Following the start of Russia's all-out war in Ukraine, European academia intensified discussion regarding the necessity of abandoning terms such as 'post-socialist' or 'post-Soviet' when speaking of the countries of the former Soviet Union. However, can we say that the process of path dependency has been overcome and past processes have largely been finalised? Or are we still able to trace dependencies on institutional, social, and economic orders that tend to repeat similar patterns of logic from past legacies,[2,3] even in countries where there has been a dramatic change of regime?[4]

For 75 years the state provided solutions at all stages of a person's life: childcare, education, obligatory job placements after graduation from educational institutions, and distribution of housing. In the context of our article, the housing system provided ready-made technocratic solutions in the majority of situations; the entire structure of formal institutions was under state control: from design and construction of residential buildings to their operation, management, and maintenance, everything was run and decided by state mechanisms. This was a process where mechanisms were clear and defined and, most importantly, the role of inhabitants in this entire process was

1 The Law of the Sverdlovsk Region, 'Об обеспечении проведения капитального ремонта общего имущества в многоквартирных домах на территории Свердловской области' [On ensuring the overhaul of common property in apartment buildings in the Sverdlovsk region], 19 December 2013, No. 127-OZ.
Decree of the Government of the Sverdlovsk Region, 'Об утверждении Стратегии развития жилищно-коммунального хозяйства Свердловской области до 2035 года' [On Approval of the Strategy for the Development of Housing and Communal Services of the Sverdlovsk Region until 2035], 21 February 2019, No. 110-PP.
Decree of the Government of the Sverdlovsk Region, 'Об утверждении государственной программы Свердловской области Формирование современной городской среды на территории Свердловской области на 2018–2022 годы' [On Approval of the State Programme of the Sverdlovsk Region 'Formation of a modern urban environment on the territory of the Sverdlovsk region for 2018–2027'], 31 October 2017, No. 805-PP.
Жилищный кодекс Российской Федерации [Housing code of the Russian Federation], 29 December 2004, No. 188-FZ.

2 Auzan, Alexander, 'Revolutions and Evolutions in Russia: In Search of a Solution to the Path Dependence Problem', *Russian Journal of Economics*, vol. 3, No. 4, 2017, pp. 336–347, here: p. 342.

3 Gel'man, Vladimir, *The Politics of Bad Governance in Contemporary Russia* (University of Michigan Press, 2022), p. 31.

4 Mussagulova, Assel, 'Newly Independent, Path Dependent: The Impact of the Soviet Past on Innovation in Post-Soviet States', *Asia Pacific Journal of Public Administration*, vol. 43, No. 6, 2020, pp. 1–19, here: p. 12.

Figure 5:
The intersection of Kalinina and Kamenskaya streets, with a perspective view along Kamenskaya. Below the panoramic photo are images of each side façade along Kamenskaya Street: (a) Kalinina 48; (b) Kamenskaya 57; (c) Kamenskaya 63; (d) Kamenskaya 67; and (e) Kamenskaya 77.
Photos: Google Street View, compiled by Albina Davletshina

limited: they referred their problems to state instiutions, and funding for construction and maintenance also came from public sources. This form of governance – a parental attitude towards citizens, sometimes referred to as a 'nanny state', in which the state dictates how its citizens should address basic needs – shaped several generations of Soviet citizens. Public surveys conducted by the Levada Centre in 2001 and 1990 show that a majority of respondents, around 60–70 per cent, expect the state to take care of its citizens as a default mode. We perceived a similar way of thinking among our interlocutors, some of whom were expecting someone else to solve their problems. But there are also general complaints from active residents that other people wait for someone else to solve problems even when their participation is required by law. This can be considered as a social layer of path dependency of thinking in society.

Russia's current housing sector cannot be defined as a nanny state any longer, at least not in the same way. The rules of the game changed after privatisation, when property rights were placed in the hands of inhabitants of multi-apartment residential buildings. For instance, in our case study, according to analysis of the cadastral map of the Russian Federation, entire residential plots have already undergone a land allocation process and, further, have been privatised by owners of apartments in housing blocks. The ownership of residential land and buildings is held in full by each multi-apartment residential building which is in the shared ownership of its residents (Fig. 6).

Through housing reform and the introduction of a new housing codex in 2005, the state has obliged property owners to choose one of three forms of property management for their building: homeowner associations, management organisations, and direct management by property owners.[5] In our case study area, property owners have chosen, or, more accurately, inherited, a form of management organisation – a management company (MC) named 'KuDEZ' – that holds a monopoly in Kamensk-Uralsky, controlling 85 per cent of the city's housing management market. This company oversees approximately 1500 multi-apartment residential building. The term 'inherited' has been used advisedly, as KuDEZ is a legacy of the Soviet housing system. Following the collapse of the USSR, it was transformed from a state enterprise into a private one, maintaining the same organisational structure as in Soviet times. This continuity includes utilising the same operational mechanisms, albeit with a shift from public funding to resources collected from property owners. This introduces an additional dimension to the institutional path dependency.

[5] Жилищный кодекс Российской Федерации [Housing code of the Russian Federation'], 29 December 2004, No. 188-FZ.

Spatial transformation under the social lens

In 2017 the 'Comfortable Urban Environment' programme was introduced as part of 'Formation of a Comfortable Urban Environment', a federal project that was part of the 'Housing and Urban Environment' national project. This programme included the 'Courtyards Renovation' sub-programme, aimed at revitalising private courtyards in residential districts. Property owners were required to cover 20 per cent of the costs, with the remaining 80 per cent being funded by public sources at the federal, regional, and municipal levels, with the municipal authority as coordinator. The programme functioned as a tool for reshaping residential areas into a so-called 'comfortable urban environment', involving stages such as mandated design and participatory mechanisms that involved residents from design to project implementation. The initial requirement for participation in the programme involved securing consensus among residents willing to contribute 20 per cent of the funding. In an attempt to initiate this process, a proactive resident from a five-storey, six-entrance building on Kamenskaya Street assumed leadership for the complex, which comprises six houses with a total of 457 apartments. Despite the endeavours made by this proactive resident, she encountered challenges at a community meeting she organised, which saw the participation of 50 residents, or slightly less than 10 per cent of inhabitants. After the meeting, the attendees

Figure 6 (right page):
Distribution of territorial property rights over the research area.
Source: Analyses prepared by Albina Davletshina, based on the public cadastral map of the Russian Federation

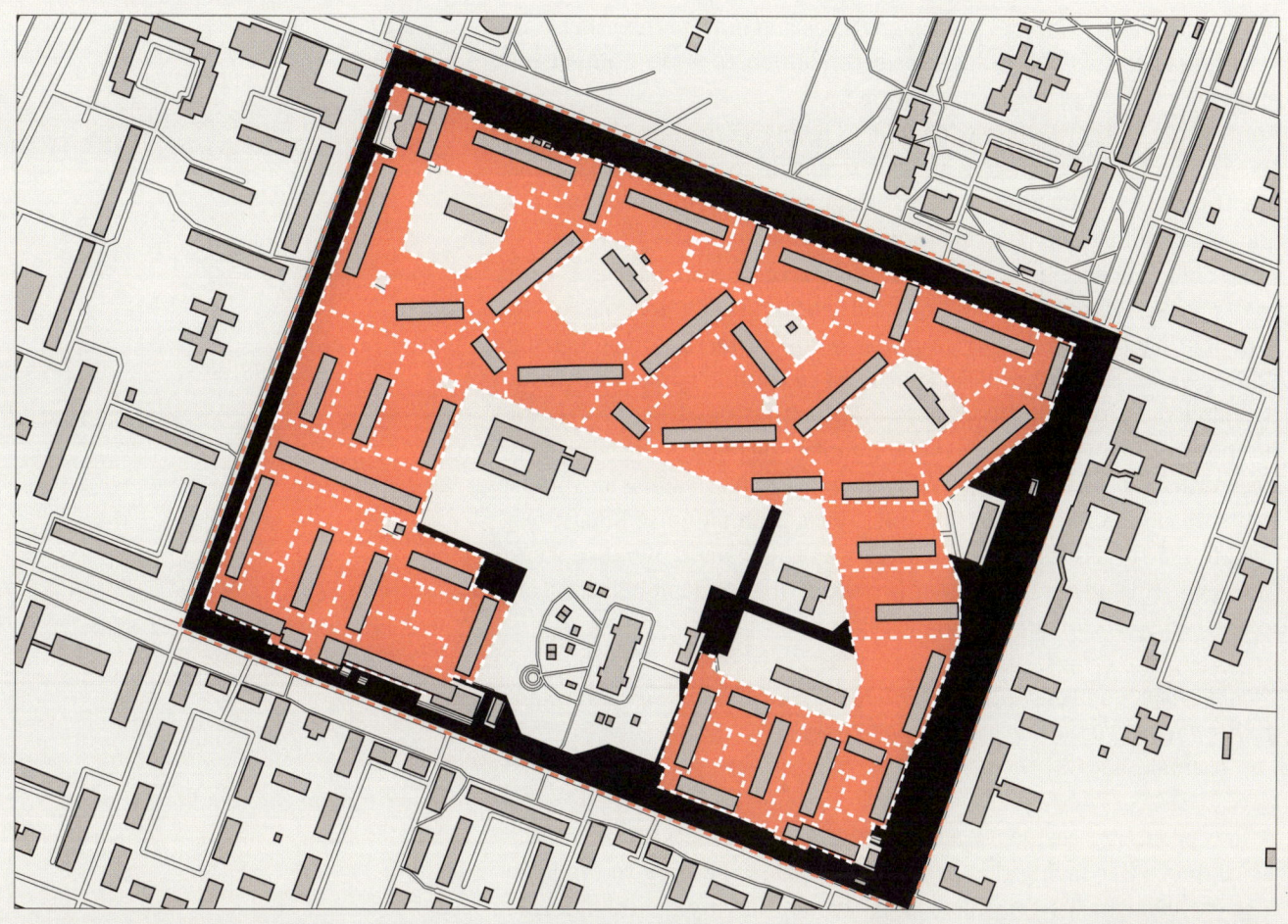

Property plots   Undefined / public properties   Other defined property plots

04 Microrayon No. 41 in Kamensk-Uralsky, Russia

lacked the enthusiasm to collect signatures and initiate the process of selecting heads of households – the second important prerequisite for applying to the improvement programme.

Confronted with the passivity of her fellow residents, the proactive resident decided to give up on attempting to apply again for the 'Comfortable Urban Environment' programme and instead concentrated her efforts on her own house, even though she was not the owner of her apartment. In 2023 she took steps to elect a 'formal' head of the house, who agreed to be officially recognised in documents but remains inactive. A similar situation unfolded in the neighbouring house, where the former head continued to fulfil her role informally, avoiding the bureaucratic process of collecting signatures to renew her powers. In another house in the complex the head of the house has been officially elected but remains unapproachable, leaving most residents unaware of her status and role. These examples also illustrate a certain fear of assuming responsibility, even for one's own property. Moreover, this deviant behaviour provoked further demobilisation, as expressed by one of our interviewees:

'"Fight alone, and you'll achieve nothing," as they say. I tried to put together a team, but no one was willing to help.'
   (Female, age 35)

A few proactive residents may make modest efforts to move forward, but, after facing this deep level of passivity, they too tend to lose enthusiasm. This problem is driven not only by the inhabitants themselves but also by the passivity and formality of bureaucratic processes that often respond to problems with non-committal replies (*otpiski*), as our respondents among the proactive inhabitants highlighted several times:

'Yes, I have had a lot of 'otpiski' like this, you know, from everywhere: from the administration, from KuDEZ, and from the housing unit and other communal services.'
   (Female, age 35)

The issue of owners' passivity appears as a leitmotif in legal documents at different levels in Russia on the topic of housing management and urban space. However, what we can see from the legal documents and their implementation on the ground is that the state machinery is also characterised by inertia and technocratic imitation of active work that does not correspond with reality. For instance, Task Three of 'The

Strategy for the Development of Housing and Communal Services of Sverdlovsk Region until 2035' is to reduce the number of cities with unfavourable urban environments and to increase the urban environment quality index and the share of citizens involved in solving issues of urban environment development. This is to be achieved by increasing the role and responsibility of owners of premises in apartment buildings in managing the real estate that they own.

The 'Formation of a Modern Urban Environment on the Territory of Sverdlovsk Region in 2018–2027' programme highlights the specific importance of citizens' involvement is. Goal No. 1 is to increase the level of involvement of interested citizens and organisations in the implementation of measures to improve the territorial conditions of settlements in the Sverdlovsk region.

At all levels federal and regional programmes and strategies emphasise citizen involvement as a core element in the formation of future responsible property owners. However, with regard to other parameters, what they mean, and how they are to be applied, the only parameter mentioned by these programmes is the quantitative performance indicator in the regional programme for 2023, according to which the rate of involvement among inhabitants in the process of design and decision-making has to be 30 per cent, which obliges design of a participatory nature.

In reality even those respondents who are actively engaged inhabitants are not aware of the participatory aspect of the design stage, and even they express uncertainty about their rights to provide input on the design. That means they are not aware that, based on legal procedure and with a 1/5 (20 per cent) financial share, they have the right to a design contribution. Only one respondent was aware that the municipality has to consider their opinion, but this still cannot be called a clear understanding of the participatory design process. One of the interviewees explained that participation is limited only to the role of chairperson of a house and only through confirmation by his or her signature under the design project:

'A council is convened in the administration, and the head of the house approves all these paths, everything that was in this territory. Why is everyone silent?'
   (Female, age 40).

The Russian state continues to preserve the legacy of the Soviet planned economic managerial system by integrating fashionable key performance indicators as an evaluative tool for the management system rather than for governance. This technocratic and numeric approach reveals a path dependency within the institutional setting as an element of the overall system of deliberately bad governance.[6] It is one where the state prioritises showcasing results through numerical metrics and relies on a strictly formal bureaucratic approach, instead of examining what is happening in the core of the processes or focusing on political governance.

Communication nightmares and ignorance

The interviews we conducted revealed a series of communication challenges among different actors. A major issue was the vicious circle of poor communication, leading to mistrust, misunderstandings, conflicts, and overall passivity among inhabitants. Inhabitants themselves displayed high levels of passivity, hindering the establishment of the quorum needed for majority decision-making. Furthermore, disrespectful communication was noted from all sides. For example, the former head of a housing unit (HU), the local representative of the MC, was repeatedly mentioned by our interviewees as a source of negative experiences. This representative had recently been replaced with a new person. During our interview, the new head of the HU highlighted the significant problem of a high level of aggression in communications with residents, which makes constructive dialogue nearly impossible. This is also illustrated by our conversations with residents, who used very strong expressions such as the following:

'I behave arrogantly; I shout. I'm ready to take further action – because either you get crushed or you crush them. That's how things happen around here.'
  (Female, age 40).

'Yes, it's just you have to give her a good shake. You have to frighten her.'
  (Female, age 84).

The head of the HU also explained that increasing the involvement of residents in the process of maintaining and improving housing stock would not add to the HU's overall management problems but, on the contrary, considerably improve things. If, for example, residents were to become more motivated, HU employees would not have to collect signatures for improvement works.

[6] Gel'man, Vladimir, *The Politics of Bad Governance in Contemporary Russia* (University of Michigan Press, 2022), p. 15.

Overall, there is a conspicuous lack of understanding or a high level of misinformation about the legal mechanisms behind various issues, both among active residents and among the HU staff who generally deal with regular residents. For instance, the head of the HU frequently encounters misunderstandings where residents falsely assume that the MC is responsible for the capital renovation of buildings. In reality this responsibility falls under the jurisdiction of another institution, the State Fund for Major Repairs, which determines when and which parts of the building will undergo the renovation process. Furthermore, residents are often unaware that they have the right to take the funds they have already accumulated for their houses and establish a separate account so as to manage this money and oversee the related processes themselves. Another common misunderstanding concerns the role of the member of the city duma (council) in matters related to territory and building issues. In such cases residents frequently turn to their city deputy to address housing issues, even though this falls outside the member's scope. When acting as intermediaries between residents and MCs, members of the city duma simply refer residents' complaints to the MC. Only then are issues resolved.

Our interviews reveal that after three decades of a market economy, a significant percentage of residents lack awareness of the fundamental legal and financial mechanisms available to them to improve the living conditions in their homes and neighbourhoods. This ignorance contributes to another layer of social path dependency, distinct from the concept of a nanny state. To comprehend the complexity of the situation, we need to explore alternative elements. A pervasive level of passivity among residents emerged as a consistent theme in our research. Our interlocutors unanimously emphasised residents' inertia: many residents express reluctance to take proactive steps, even concerning property-related issues. As one of our senior interviewees said,

'Nobody, nobody needs anything here. Everyone goes to their hut and hides there.'
    (Female, age 79).

This social behaviour can be characterised as escapism and inertia, rooted in weariness that is a response to futile efforts and an expectation that others will initiate action. This phenomenon aligns with Hirschman's theoretical framework of Exit-Voice-Loyalty,[7] further developed by urban studies scholars into the Exit-Voice-Loyalty-Neglect model.[8] This model adopts a socio-psychological perspective on

[7] Hirschman, Albert O., *Exit, Voice, and Loyalty: Response to Decline in Firms, Organizations, and States* (Cambridge, MA: Harvard University Press, 1970), p. 55.

[8] Dowding, Keith, and John, Peter, *Exits, Voices and Social Investment: Citizens' Reaction to Public Services* (Cambridge University Press, 2012), p. 56.

human behaviour, suggesting that neglect, combined with loyalty and 'internal migration' (retreat within oneself), represents a fertile area for further exploration in our research.

Community formation through heritage-making: the Podyezd 'Podyezd' art project and its renovation

A local initiative is stimulating another approach. A community formation has started taking care of the community's space by emphasising positive features and developments. This provides a kind of role model and potential inspiration for others to act through the process of heritage-making. Microrayon No. 41 does not have any state-authorised cultural heritage or area status and may generally be considered a typical example of Brezhnev's mass housing legacy. However, a group of young people aged 16 to 24 are making efforts to create a distinctive historical and creative profile for the neighbourhood, offering their unique perspective on the social history of Russia's Soviet past and its present. The art space *podyezd 'Podyezd'* (the Russian word *podyezd* literally means 'entrance', but in the Russian context refers to the combination of an entrance and staircases in a building) is an independent, self-financed art project located in a five-storey residential building with six entrances. Initiated by the local heritage activist Ivan Bushlanov in 2020, the Podyezd art project began as a casual effort to freshen up the paint on a staircase's walls. Subsequently, it expanded as other artists joined in, and a social media call for paint and materials generated unexpected attention. Despite a mixed reaction in the city, news about the transformation of an ordinary *podyezd* into a museum / art gallery spread across online groups with millions of subscribers and through federal and regional media, including TV. Activists created a social network group on the Russia website VK, showcasing ongoing work and launching a crowdfunding campaign for funds and materials. The once-green walls of the staircases have been repainted white and embellished with interactive objects from the Soviet era sourced from scrapyards. According to participants in the project, 'the easiest way to reflect current problems is through the prism of the past.'

In 2021 the housing MC initiated renovations in the building where the Podyezd art project is situated. The MC's decision to renovate prompted plans to remove the existing artworks. In response, the artists, aiming to preserve the artworks, outlined stylistic preferences based on conceptual ideas and set out certain constraints for the MC. The head of the HU requested activists to document the need for repairs and to gather signatures from all tenants, including non-owner residents. After collecting signatures, the head of the HU informed the activists that the contractor was unwilling to comply. It was only after social media posts about the MC's intention to destroy the art project that the company publicly expressed its support for the residents' opinions and a willingness to meet their demands. Despite this, behind the scenes, the representative of the MC continued to behave disrespectfully, while the contractor decided to make concessions.

Following cosmetic renovations by the MC, the project was able to carry on, with participants using their own money to buy materials. Over three years there has been an observable shift in residents' attitudes towards the activists' efforts, marked by an increase in positive comments. This change is attributed to the white colour scheme, improved work quality, and enhanced publicity. This project has not only influenced residents' opinions but also helped build a community, fostering communication among residents of the building.

Conclusions

The overarching pattern observed in the study underscores a challenging dynamic: the absence of proactive engagement from HUs, coupled with pervasive passivity among property owners. This symbiotic relationship between management inaction and resident apathy creates a discouraging cycle of fighting windmills. Breaking free from this cycle will require concerted efforts from both stakeholder groups to overcome tensions and foster a more dynamic and responsive community.

Despite the numerous obstacles, some positive trends are also emerging, such as HUs' efforts to collaborate with engaged residents to secure municipal subsidies for courtyard renovation. The story of Podyezd illustrates that persistence and resource mobilisation pays dividends – demonstrating that despite certain constraints, a limited group of people can bring about positive change and create a basis for self-governance in the future.

Drawing broad conclusions about an entire micro-district from a limited number (nine) of qualitative interviews is challenging. The scope of our research has necessarily been limited, meaning that it can only be regarded as a qualitative illustration of certain observed patterns. However, heritage-making is a unique situation that can only be effectively analysed through a qualitative approach, given the absence of similar cases in the district and the city as a whole.

05

Khimmash neighbourhood in Sverdlovsk-Yekaterinburg, Russia. The Soviet palace: from social hub to remnant of the past and back again

Polina Gundarina

Soviet clubs, or houses of culture (*doma kultury*) – distant relatives of the 'people's houses' (*narodnye doma* in Russian) in the Russian Empire – underwent a remarkable transformation during their almost 75-year history in the USSR. Heralded by early Soviet Avantgarde architects from the early 1920s as 'social power plants' and 'radically new building types',[1] by the late 1980s they had become a routinised part of the everyday Soviet urban landscape. Their extent was astonishing: there were over 90,000 such buildings in the Soviet Union, the majority of which were standardised designs built after World War II. The common narrative is that by the time of the dissolution of the Soviet Union, given that the majority of these clubs were firmly associated with propaganda, they had largely lost their role as community centres and were rejected by local residents.[2]

Palaces in transition

After 1991 the transition to market economies and the subsequent deindustrialisation of the regions disrupted financial support for the clubs and palaces, support which had largely been provided by factories and trade unions through social policy funds. Nevertheless, as of 2023, more than 40,000 former Soviet clubs remain open and operational in Russia alone.[3] In the absence of a centralised renovation programme and impetus for reevaluation of the symbolic significance of this Soviet infrastructure, many clubs rely on modest municipal funding or income from renting out their premises. Despite the unfavourable conditions, many former Soviet houses of culture still serve as social hubs for communities, especially in smaller urban or rural areas.

The Khimmash neighbourhood on the outskirts of Yekaterinburg is one such case. An industrial district, and the district furthest from the city centre of Yekaterinburg (called 'Sverdlovsk' during the Soviet era), Khimmash was actively built up around the developing chemical plant after the war. The district was conceived as a socialist city, a specific type of settlement situated near the factory to accommodate its workers and their families, and was built on the territory of a previous industrial settlement from the late eighteenth century.[4] The history of the district's development is not only a fairly typical story of urban industrialisation following World War II, but also reveals specific situations in which the memories of locals are closely tied to the standardised architectural environment consisting of prefabricated housing and infrastructure. The transformation of the

---

1 Bokov, Anna, 'Soviet Workers' Clubs: Lessons from the Social Condensers', *The Journal of Architecture*, vol. 22, No. 3, pp. 403–436, here: p. 410.

2 See, for example: White, Anne, *De-Stalinization and the House of Culture: Declining State Control Over Leisure in the USSR, Poland, and Hungary, 1953–1989* (London: Taylor & Francis, 1990).

3 Boyev, Alexey, and Naugolnova, Daria, *Identichnost' v tipovom* [Identity in the Typical] (Ekaterinburg: Tatlin, 2019) p. 13.

4 See Korepanov, N., Dumchikov, A., and Pimenova, K., *Khimmash: vdol' i poperek* [Khimmash: every nook and cranny] (Yekaterinburg: AO Format, 2022).

Figure 1:
The Khimmash district and the Uralkhimmash plant in 1974, seen on a satellite image of the city of Sverdlovsk.
Source: US Geological Survey
<earthexplorer.usgs.gov>

Khimmash Palace of Culture, a significant community centre in both the Soviet and post-Soviet eras, highlights the transmission of enduring values of entertainment and leisure among the local population. It also plays out as a history of deindustrialisation, private interests, and the struggle to preserve a post-war modernist building.

Palaces of culture and Soviet architectural modernism

Mass construction of standardised palaces (*dvortsy*) or houses of culture (*doma kultury*, 'DKs' for short) took place in Soviet cities after the war as part of Nikita Khrushchev's reforms of the construction industry. The reforms rejected use of one-off designs and architectural 'excesses' and aimed to change the mode of architectural production to faster, larger-scale, on-site installation of prefabricated parts in order to provide every Soviet family with an apartment. Palaces of culture, now integrated into the cultural infrastructure of the newly built *mikrorayony* (micro-districts), were to be located within walking distance of housing complexes in the neighbourhood."⁵

The replication of a single design blueprint was not a novel concept in these reforms for Soviet palaces and houses of culture. Notably, the

5   Stroitel'nyye normy i tekhnicheskie usloviya proektirovaniya zdaniy klubov, SN 44-59 [Construction standards and technical conditions for the design of club buildings, Building norms 44-59]. *Kontsortsium Kodeks*, 1 May 1959, <https://docs.cntd.ru/document/1200064745>, accessed 3 November 2023.

Figure 2:
Moscow Children's Creative Activity Palace (Palace of Pioneers), 1959–1963, architects: V. S. Egorev, V. S. Kubasov, F. A. Novikov, I. A. Pokrovskiy, and M. N. Khajakyan; engineer: Yu. I. Ionov.
Photo: Sergey Norin, Creative Commons Attribution 2.0 Generic

architect Yakov Kornfeld (1896–1962), an alumnus of VKHUTEMAS and a prominent theoretician of the design and construction of palaces of culture from the 1930s forwards, produced a widely reproduced design for a workers' club in 1947. This *tipovoy proekt* (standardised design) for a club with a capacity of 500 people was used throughout the USSR, from cities such as Konotop in Ukraine to Kemerovo in Russia. Another popular design, by the prolific architect Konstantin Bartashevich (1906–1991), featured columns with variable decorative elements, enfilades in the front yards, pediments, and spacious interiors for shows and spectacles. These late Stalinist architectural projects still reflected the urban design paradigm of the time, but their realisation over the course of the 1950s signalled changing attitudes, with a rejection or minimisation of decorative elements.

After Khrushchev's reforms in the late 1950s, however, designs for palaces of culture underwent a significant transformation. The new approach prioritised functional spaces by increasing the number of rooms and reducing stage and audience sizes. This entailed a rejection of 'excessive' decorative elements, such as columns and ornaments. Instead, the focus was on easier assembly, embracing straightforward forms, a more equitable division of rooms and concert halls, and the

use of glass and wider overlays. This architectural approach was not only characteristic of the era in the Soviet Union but also resonated with contemporary trends in western architecture.[6]
The architect Feliks Novikov (1927–2022), credited with coining the term *sovmod*, or Soviet modernism, identifies three symbolic eras of Soviet architecture associated with 'palaces'. These include the Palace of Labour competition project in the early 1920s as a reflection of the Avant-garde thinking of the early Soviet architects, the Palace of Soviets competition project in the 1930s as a reflection of the strict vertical power relations of the Stalinist era, and the Palace of Pioneers in Moscow (1958–1962), a building co-authored by Novikov himself, as a reflection of the fresh, modernist paradigm.[7] The Palace of Pioneers marked a turning point in the approach to public architecture, a new kind of palace in the Soviet Union.

The Khimmash district and its club: from forest to palace

The district of Khimmash took shape on the site of the industrial Lower Iset Settlement Plant, which started operating in the late eighteenth century.[8] In the twentieth century this area's development received a new impulse. 1930 brought the start of one of the priority projects of the first Soviet five-year plan, about one and a half kilometres from the dam of the former Lower Iset Plant and approximately 12 kilometres from Sverdlovsk: construction of the Ural Chemical Machinery Plant (Uralkhimmash) from scratch in the midst of a pine forest.[9] As recalled by Ivan Noskov, a veteran worker at the plant, the first construction workers were housed in the nearby homes of local residents. The first semi-basement barracks were constructed in 1932–1933; intended as a temporary solution, they ended up serving for many years.[10]
The living conditions during construction of the Uralkhimmash plant and of a nearby district are described by witnesses as deeply unsanitary, cold, and marked by hunger. Despite the fact that the plant was planned as one of the key facilities of Soviet industrialisation under the first five-year plan (1928–1932), its construction was mothballed a couple of years after its commencement.[11] The impetus for further development of the area came during World War II and was associated with another plant, the Bolshevik Kyiv Machine-Building Plant, which was evacuated to the region in 1941.
As recalled by Valeryan Kurganov, the director of the evacuated Bolshevik plant, when his factory and workers were evacuated to

6 Chepkunova, I., Steltsova Iu., et al. *Pionery sovetskogo modernizma: arkhitektura i gradostroitel'stvo* [Pioneers of Soviet Modernism: Architecture and Urban Planning] (Moscow: Kuchkovo pole, 2019), p. 191.

7 Novikov, Feliks, *Obrazy sovetskoy arkhitektury* [Images of Soviet architecture] (Moscow: Kuchkovo pole, 2021).

8 Solonina, Nadezhda, 'Vyyavleniye istoriko-arkhitekturnogo potentsiala istoricheskoy promyshlennoy territorii pri razrabotke arkhitekturnogo proekta' [Identification of historical-architectural potential of a historical industrial territory during the development of an architectural project], Arkhitekton, December 2021, <https://archvuz.ru/2021_4/1/>, accessed 8 November 2023.

9 Ibid.

10 Davydov, I., *Shagi Khimmasha* [The steps of Khimmash] (Yekaterinburg: Vneshtorgizdat, 1992), pp. 41–43.

11 Ibid., p. 43.

Figure 3:
View of the Nizhne-Isetsky plant between 1930 and 1939.
Source: 1723.ru, uploaded by chist

12   Kurganov, Vlaeryan, *Tak rozhdalsya Uralkhimmash...* [How Uralkhimmash was born...] (Sverdlovsk: Sredne-Uralskoye book publishing, 1973, <http://fort-himmash.narod.ru/RozdHim/>, accessed 3 November 2023.

13   Ibid.

Sverdlovsk to the site of the Uralkhimmash plant, which was then under construction, both the plant and the surrounding settlement were underdeveloped:

'Conditions were much worse [than in Sverdlovsk], on the outskirts of the city …. A single-track dead-end railroad from Koltsovo Station, a disused garage building … and two empty barracks – that was all that existed in this area … There was no electricity, heat, water, sewerage. The entire plant area only had an unloading platform. That's all that sounded so impressive in official documents – Uralkhimmash.'[12]

But the evacuation efforts, combined with the urgent need for rapid growth in production to meet demands at the front, meant that significant work lay ahead for the evacuees. Kurganov, appointed director of Uralkhimmash, was joined by trains arriving in Sverdlovsk with people and equipment not only from the evacuated city of Kyiv, but also from other regions across the USSR.[13] Newcomers were housed in tents; some lived in the barracks from the 1930s; and some were offered accommodation in the private homes of locals. During the war years the population of Khimmash was continually changing due to the constant turnover of personnel, including as a result of periodic conscription to the Red Army and the arrival of new construction workers and other evacuees from Belarus, Western Ukraine, and Central Asia. The Khimmash district was created during these years in what was a challenging and unfamiliar environment for many resettlers. It involved demanding physical labour on construction sites, the constant preparation of resources, and a persistent shortage of food. Despite the difficulties, the population was slowly growing, and the new residents and their families soon needed essential everyday services. The first kindergarten had been established immediately after the evacuation, and by 1943 the first trolleybus line in Sverdlovsk linked the Khimmash district (then still called Nizhne-Isetsk) with the city.[14] Around the same time, the first factory club appeared: the predecessor of the future Khimmash Palace of Culture. This first proto-club was located in the ruined and abandoned church of the Kazan Icon of the Mother of God, closed in 1935, and regularly held film screenings, hobby groups, and concerts with the participation of artists from theatres in Sverdlovsk.[15] After the end of the war, it was almost two decades before a proper palace of culture was built in the neighbourhood.

Rare photographs from the late 1940s and early 1950s depict a turning point in the history of this neighbourhood. It was at this time that proper residential complexes were constructed, replacing temporary barracks with four- and five-storey buildings. Prospekt Griboyedova, Khimmash's main urban axis, was laid out in the early 1950s. Soon ensembles of residential and public buildings in the Stalinist Neoclassical style appeared along this avenue, stretching from the Uralkhimmash Factory entrance to ulitsa Borodina; they occupied approximately half of the main avenue. The other half of prospekt Griboyedova, however, illustrates a shift in Soviet urban planning: it was here, at the beginning of this street, that some of the district's first panel buildings appeared. Photographs from the mid-1960s show the Ekran Cinema, which opened in 1966 at one end of the avenue, standing on a site which has yet to be landscaped and beside a road which has yet to be paved. Despite the completion of the cinema building, this area remained undeveloped and almost rural; it was only by the late 2000s that the area behind the cinema was built up with high-rise housing. On the neighbouring ulitsa Profsoyuznaya new panel buildings coexisted with private wooden houses until the mid-1960s, with additional panel housing only appearing in the 1980s.

With the implementation of reforms in the architectural and construction sectors, standardised panel buildings, mostly five-storey, quickly became prevalent in Khimmash. As Yury Korovin, the chief engineer of the city's capital construction department in the 1960s, recalled: 'prefabricated panel construction was on the rise

14 Ibid.

15 Ibid.

16 Interview with Yury Korovin, 2019, <https://on.soundcloud.com/wfhux>, accessed 8 November 2023.

17 *Perechen' tipovykh* proektov TP-3 RSFSR [List of standardised projects by Project Institute No. 5], s.v. 'Series 169-129' (Moscow: Gosstroy RSFSR, 1959).

…. This was marvellous, that houses could be erected in the space of a month. This was the Khimmash *sotsgorod* [socialist town].'[16] But the growing socialist town of Khimmash lacked infrastructure. In 1967 the Khimmash Palace of Culture, officially called 'the Palace of Culture of the 50th Anniversary of the October Revolution' opened, and in 1973, the Kristal swimming pool was added.

The design project used for construction of the Khimmash Palace of Culture in Sverdlovsk is one of the most common types of club building realised in the Soviet Union in the late 1960s and 1970s. This project resembles the 169–129 series developed in 1959 by Project Institute No. 5, which belonged to the Ministry of Building of the RSFSR.[17] Adaptations to the local climate and landscape were made by architects from Sverdlovskgrazhdanproekt, the local design bureau. One of the first standardised design projects offered by the state, the project had three floors and an 800-seat auditorium. According to open sources, similar projects with minor adaptations were implemented in various other Soviet cities, including the DK Taras Shevchenko in Melitopol, Ukraine; the DK Khimikov in Barnaul, Russia; and the DK Yunatstva in Grodno, Belarus.

The new palace of culture marked the beginning of prospekt Griboyedova, its pristine white structure visible from afar in this still sparsely developed district. Gradually evolving into the centre of community life, the palace became the new home for all artistic initiatives from the former factory club. Its spatial placement reflects its symbolic significance: the square surrounding the palace served as a gathering space for events and children's games; the palace of culture was within convenient walking distance of all houses along the main avenue. Margarita Sozonova, a local resident, witnessed the palace's inauguration:

'The palace of culture was opened on 5 November 1967 – at that time the entire Khimmash [district] celebrated for three whole days, and the event was unforgettable. It was built jointly by the NIIKhimmash and Uralkhimmash enterprises and immediately became the recreational centre of the entire settlement. The palace was built on an empty space: there were private houses around, where we used to play as children … The palace was needed because the district was quite isolated; transportation was only possible with the help of the first trolleybus. The Uralkhimmash plant highly valued its personnel and set about developing infrastructure … Where the parking lot is now [in front of the palace], they used to build an ice town in winter. On 31 December the entire Khimmash went there to celebrate

Figure 4:
Construction of the 50th Anniversary of the October Revolution Palace of Culture.
Photo: V. M. Malkov (1965–1967). Courtesy of the Museum of the History of Yekaterinburg

the New Year ... I remember well that the decline of the palace began in 1993, after perestroika. I lived abroad for three years, and upon my return, I did not immediately understand what had happened. New Year's was approaching; I was riding the trolleybus and passing the palace. A woman sitting next to me, looking out of the window, suddenly said to the whole trolleybus, "You won't be able to look at it without tears." And when I looked, it was horrifying: no beautiful Christmas tree, no ice town. That's when it all began.'[18]

The post-Soviet condition of Khimmash: industrial symbol and post-Soviet resilience

The official Soviet narrative about Sverdlovsk focused on the rupture between pre-Revolutionary Yekaterinburg and the contemporary city as 'industrial capital'.[19] Uralkhimmash played an important role in this narrative. The factory was one of the 'industrial giants' of Soviet Sverdlovsk, a surety for the city's claim to the title of 'industrial capital'. Soviet guides and monographs about Sverdlovsk highlighted Khimmash as a young district with a 'glorious, heroic history' and 'one of the best-landscaped districts in the city.'[20] The written history of Khimmash omitted the challenges of construction, hunger, and disorganisation in the 1930s and early 1940s, focusing on portraying the district as an ever-expanding *sotsgorod*. Its physical distance from the city centre contributed to the perception of Khimmash as a city within a city. A limited influx from the city ensured the stability of Khimmash's population, fostering a sense of community loyalty and resilience.

18 Novikova, Sasha, 'Ya zhivu na Khimmashe, gde protestuyut protiv snosa DK' [I live at Khimmash, where they're protesting against the demolition of the Palace of Culture] *The Village*, 15 March 2018, <https://www.the-village.ru/city/where/305417-himmash-4-life>, accessed 6 November 2023.

19 Panov, P., Oblik Sverdlovska segodnya [The image of Sverdlovsk today] in *Sverdlovsk v nastoyaschem i budushchem* [Sverdlovsk in the present and the past] (Sverdlovsk: Sverdlovsk book publishing house, 1958), <http://www.1723.ru/read/books/sverdlovsk-1958/sverdlovsk-1958.htm>, accessed 3 November 2023.

20 Berdnikov, N., *Gorod v dvukh izmereniyakh* [The city in two dimensions] (Sverdlovsk: Sredne-Uralskoye book publishing, 1979), <http://www.1723.ru/read/books/city2.htm>, accessed 3 November 2023.

Figure 5:
Khimmash Palace of Culture, ca. 1980.
Source: Materials from the photo archive of SverdNIIKhimmash. Published in Arduanov, M., *Put k priznaniyu* [On the way to recognition] (Moscow: UMEMO RAN, 2002) <https://elib.biblioatom.ru/text/put-k-priznaniyu_2002/> accessed 3 November 2023

21 'Khrushchevki i brezhnevki v Yekaterinburge podesheveli na 5-6 protsentov' [Khrushchevki and brezhnevki in Yekaterinburg have fallen in price by 5-6 per cent], *Expert-Ural*, 11 October 2007, <https://expert-ural.com/news/hrushevki-i-brezhnevki-v-ekaterinburge-podesheveli.html>, accessed 18 November 2023.

22 'Kompaniya Atomstroykompleks k letu 2025 goda postroit na Khimmashe 17 tys. kv. metrov zhil'ya '[Atomstroycomplex will build 17 thousand square metres of housing in Khimmash by summer 2025] UralBiznesKonsalting, 8 August 2023, <https://urbc.ru/1068122290-kompaniya-atomstroykompleks-k-letu-2025-goda-postroit-na-himmashe-17-tys-kv-metrov-zhilya.html>, accessed 19 November 2023.

23 Author's interview with E. Sh. and E. S., urban activists and researchers. April 2022.

24 Politkovskaya, Anna, 'Saga Sverdlovskaya. Chisto konkretnaya. Chto stoit za nedavnimi sobytiyami na kombinate Uralkhimmash v Ekaterinburge?' [The Sverdlovsk saga. A very special story. What is behind the recent events at the Uralkhimmash plant in Ekaterinburg?], *Novaya gazeta*, 25 September 2000.

25 Kolesnikov, Andrey, 'Uralkhimmash vzyat Mirom' [Uralkhimmash taken by 'Mir'], *Kommersant*, 19 September 2000, <https://www.kommersant.ru/doc/158277>, accessed 18 November 2023.

The composition of housing in the Khimmash district has also remained relatively stable from the Soviet to the post-Soviet years. During the Soviet era the Uralkhimmash plant was the main client for housing complexes. The most active phase of construction was in the 1960s and 1970s, when most of the housing that exists in Khimmash today was built. The coexistence of private wooden houses and panel buildings persisted for a long time, however, and some pre-Revolutionary structures are also still intact, such as the 1840s building of the Lower Iset Administration. In the 1990s only a few housing projects were completed, and mass construction of new housing in Khimmash only started in the late 2000s. During the mid-2000s the housing market in Khimmash stagnated as *khrushchevkas* (Khrushchev-era houses) and *brezhnevkas* (Brezhnev-era houses) were the least marketable type of housing.[21] In recent years, with the formation of plans to develop a new micro-district, Severny Khimmash, the situation has changed slightly.[22] But, according to Yekaterinburg activists, the city's residents find housing in Khimmash unattractive due to the poor environmental conditions and the distance from the city centre: those who live here either work at the plant or have lived there for generations.[23]

After 1991 Khimmash Palace of Culture remained the property of the Khimmash plant. In the early 2000s, however, the plant itself became a contested property.[24] News of an armed attempt to seize the factory in September 2000 spread across the country yet shocked no one: the struggle for industrial assets, which began after the collapse of the Soviet Union, unfolded most aggressively of all in industrial centres.[25] By the end of the 2010s the plant had become part of a large

Figure 6:
The Palace of Culture of the 50th Anniversary of the October Revolution in the 1960s–1970s.
Courtesy of the Museum of the History of Uralkhimmashplant

holding company, United Machine-Building Plants, which also consolidated other former Soviet enterprises in the Urals. Yet although the Khimmash plant maintained its role as a district-forming enterprise (*gradoobrazuyuschee predpriyatie* in Russian), at a smaller scale its involvement in social policies had diminished. Its infrastructural assets were privatised, exposing them to vulnerabilities, as happened with the Khimmash Palace of Culture.

Palace of culture: modernist heritage or typical community centre?

One of the consequences of post-Soviet deindustrialisation has been a shift of responsibility for public infrastructure away from industries. As a result, these infrastructural assets have often lingered in a state of ambiguity, lacking clear ownership or direction.
In the post-Soviet years the palace of culture in Khimmash followed the trajectory typical for most palaces that had belonged to Soviet factories. In 2004 it was officially renamed 'Khimmash' (officially the palace retained the name '50th Anniversary of October' but from the early years had been commonly known as 'DK Khimmash') and transferred into private ownership. Since 2004 the land and the building have been owned by Valery Saveliev, a member of the local parliament and owner of the development company AVS Group. In the Khimmash district the two buildings that were originally part of the Khimmash factory infrastructure, the palace of culture and the Kristal swimming pool, were privatised, becoming the property of the same company. 2018 brought the first news that both buildings were slated for demolition to make way for residential complexes.[26]

26 Govorkovskaya, Viktoriya, 'Valeriy Savel'yev poluchit ot administratsii Yekaterinburga 20 tys. zemli [Valery Savelyev will receive 20 thousand square-meters of land from the Yekaterinburg administration] *DK*, 24 October 2022, <https://www.dk.ru/news/237174802>, accessed 18 November 2023.

27 Zakhvatoshina, Oxana, Kak zhivet DK Khimmash, kotoryy spasli ot snosa [How lives the Khimmash Palace of Culture, which was saved from demolition] E1, 31 May 2019, <https://www.e1.ru/text/realty/2019/05/31/66108907/>, accessed 18 November 2023.

28 Fadeykov, Max, 'Snesem odnoznachno. AVS Group gotovitsya zamenit' khimmashevskiy DK na zhilyye vysotki' ['We will demolish it unequivocally.' AVS Group is preparing to replace the Khimmashev DK with residential high-rises], 30 January 2018, <https://uralpolit.ru/article/sverdl/30-01-2018/129854>, accessed 18 November 2023.

29 Author's interview with I. S., a co-organiser and leader of the civic protest (May 2022).

In the post-Soviet era Khimmash Palace of Culture continued to function as a recreation centre for children, funding itself by renting out rooms to small businesses or services. A local resident of Khimmash recounted that the owner 'used to support them [the organisers of children's events] for a long time, for which we are grateful ... About a year and a half ago [in 2018], they said they were going to demolish the palace of culture.'[27] By this time the palace was used for about 100 initiatives offering activities for kids and adults, such as dance, crafts, choir, and music. In May 2018 lease agreements between the organisers of these activities and the developers were not renewed, and AVS Group announced plans to demolish the palace of culture and build a residential complex in its place.[28] According to local activists, the owner had long intended to demolish the cultural centre, and deliberately neglected its need for renovation, waiting for it to fall into disrepair.[29] The building is indeed in poor condition today: no major repairs have been conducted since its opening in 1967, and visible signs of decay include deteriorating façades, structural defects, and crumbling mosaics.

Figure 7:
Nizhneisetsky Pond, view from Khimmash district.
Source: Vyacheslav Bukharov, 2 April 2023

After the news of the impending demolition came from the developers, a group of Khimmash residents formed an opposition group. Called 'Live, Our Khimmash Palace of Culture! (*Zhivi nash DK Khimmash!*)', the group largely consisted of parents whose children attended the facility. Pensioners, many of whom had either been involved in the construction of the palace or had participated in its activities during Soviet times, also joined the protest. The palace's functionality was a major driving force behind the protests: the planned spatial characteristics of the palace turned out to be a crucial motivation.[30]

The case of post-Soviet struggles in the Khimmash district is symptomatic of post-war Soviet heritage not only in Yekaterinburg but throughout Russia. Firstly, it highlights the developers' interest in densifying residential areas and the vulnerability of post-war 'everyday' standardised architecture to such efforts. Moreover, the value of post-war modernist architecture is not widely recognised in contemporary Russia, and most initiatives to study and popularise it come mainly from Moscow and concern iconic, exceptional buildings. In the case of Yekaterinburg local research has been conducted since the early 2000s to study and popularise Constructivist architecture, often referred to as the city's brand.[31] But Yekaterinburg activists were also among the first in the country to draw the attention of the public to the absence of post-war modernism in the discourse of heritage conservationists and, in general, to the need to recognise it as valuable heritage.[32] Simultaneously, the Khimmash case is not the most suitable for popularising such heritage as heritage discourse among activists still largely revolves around uniqueness as a prime value: according to local activists, Khimmash Palace of Culture is an example of 'primitive modernism', a typical and frequently repeated design implemented without the use of excessive details.[33] The district's location on the city map also plays a role: greater attention has been paid to the study and popularisation of the heritage of the Uralmash *sotsgorod* with its well-studied, accessible Constructivist architecture, while the condition of post-war industrial micro-districts has yet to be explored by researchers.

Secondly, the battles around Khimmash highlight the resilience of the post-war Soviet infrastructure. After active protests by local residents, both on social media and at public demonstrations, the city administration reached an agreement with AVS Group in mid-2018 to purchase the palace of culture site, with the promise to give the company another plot of land to build on. The minister of

30 Ibid.

31 Suchkov, Nikita, and Tsarikov, Alexander, 'Kak Yekaterinburg za 10 let stal stolitsey konstruktivizma' [How Ekaterinburg became the capital of Constructivism in 10 years], *Rambler*, 30 December 2019, <https://news.rambler.ru/other/43439877-kak-ekaterinburg-za-10-let-stal-stolitsey-konstruktivizma/>, accessed 18 November 2023.

32 Ivanova, Polina, A guide map to Soviet modernist buildings in Sverdlovsk-Yekaterinburg, <https://sov-modsvx.spread.name>, accessed 18 November 2023.

33 Author's interview with E. Sh. and E. S., urban activists and researchers (April 2022).

culture of Sverdlovsk Region also wrote an official letter, highlighting the high cultural value of the Khimmash Palace of Culture for the district, and the Institute of Modernism in Moscow provided a recommendation for its inclusion in the list of protected cultural and historical heritage. But there has been a recent new development: in November 2023 the palace of culture was closed again due to its failure to pass a fire-safety inspection. Since the property transfer procedure had been continually delayed since 2018 and because it was still privately owned at the time of the closure, the residents' initiative group again raised concerns. Despite the lack of repairs to the deteriorating building, the main attraction for local residents remains the palace's functionality: it currently serves as the primary and only centre for children's leisure activities in Khimmash. On 5 December 2023 Yevgeny Kuyvashev, the governor of Sverdlovsk Region, announced that an agreement had been reached with AVS Group and the palace of culture would be transferred to municipal ownership by January 2024.

Figure 8:
Griboedova Street and the square with the palace of culture in the near background.
Source: Vyacheslav Bukharov, 2 April 2023

Figure 9:
Khimmash Palace of Culture, April 2023.
Photos: CC BY-SA 4.0 Deed, Vyacheslav Bukharov

What can this case tell us about the preservation of post-war modernist heritage and its ability to fulfil community needs in the post-Soviet era? In the case of the Khimmash district and Khimmash Palace of Culture it is not architectural qualities but rather residents' attachment and memories that reflect the value of this heritage. The palace of culture has served as the focal point for various events in the lives of local residents, from Soviet parades and New Year celebrations to the post-Soviet variety of small businesses and community services. Both symbolically and spatially, the building and its surroundings remain a focus for collective memories and current life in the district.

Research into the community value of modernist architecture in Europe is gaining momentum, and the case of Khimmash in Yekaterinburg fits into a larger European narrative, alongside such exemplary cases as the Palace of Sports in Vilnius and Warsaw's

34 See Sokołowicz, Mariusz E., Nowakowska, Aleksandra, and Ciarkowski, Błażej, *The Ambiguous Legacy of Socialist Modernist Architecture in Central and Eastern Europe*, (Routledge, 2023); Sokołowicz, Mariusz E., and Zbigniew Przygodzki. 'The Value of Ambiguous Architecture in Cities. The Concept of a Valuation Method of 20th Century Post-Socialist Train Stations', *Cities* 104 (September 2020): 102786.

35 Popova, Polina. 'Zhiteli Khimmasha vzyalis' za vosstanovleniye zimnego sada vo Dvortse kultury' [Khimmash residents have started restoring the winter garden in the Palace of Culture], *Global City*, 24 January 2023. <https://globalcity.info/news/24/01/2023/48471>, accessed 18 November 2023.

modernist train stations.[34] The people of Khimmash not only continue to visit Khimmash Palace of Culture but are also engaged in its improvement: last winter, volunteers restored the palace's winter garden.[35] Further exploration of the motivation to maintain and protect such buildings could be fruitful for research beyond architectural history, including for political scientists seeking to understand civic dynamics in Russian society after the full-scale invasion of Ukraine in February 2022.

The plans for demolition by the private owner and the struggles to 'return' the palace to the city administration underscore the fragility of this mundane, standardised post-war Soviet architecture in the face of urban development interests. However, amidst this trend, the case of Khimmash also highlights the local community's resilience and powers of campaigning. Although this architectural project is not unique, its embeddedness in the spatial structure of the micro-district offers potential for adaptive reuse. The square around the palace of culture, once used for mass gatherings and winter festivities, now serves as a car park. The right design approach and availability of investment could see this open space transformed into a green area or a permanent children's playground. The central façade of the palace of culture, with its panoramic windows facing prospekt Griboyedova, overlooks this open space, which is currently filled with cars. A more creative use could be envisioned here. Moreover, the building has two entrances, but only the entrance facing prospekt Griboyedova is currently in use. Clearing the space in front could open up the building, making it more attractive to tenants and for use for creative activities. However, the main priority for the building now is to renovate and improve its accessibility for all residents.

In the years following the protest the Museum of the History of Yekaterinburg, together with a group of researchers and activists, published a guide on the history of this neighbourhood and held several exhibitions, highlighting the history of the factory and its settlement. Yekaterinburg, known for its preservationism and research into the city's Constructivist heritage, is also a pioneer in civic activism to protect post-war architecture in industrial districts. For now, the fate of Khimmash Palace of Culture is still to be decided by the city administration. But the significant attention that local residents have drawn to the threat of its demolition in both 2018 and 2023 provides hope that reuse and adaptation of this post-war modernist building will be possible.

References

Arduanov, M., *Put' k priznaniyu* [The path to recognition] (Moscow: UMEMO RAN, 2002), <https://elib.biblioatom.ru/text/put-k-priznaniyu_2002/>, accessed 3 November 2023.

Author's interview with E. Sh. and E. S., urban activists and researchers (May 2022).

Author's interview with I. S., the co-organiser and leader of the civic protest (May 2022).

Berdnikov, N., *Gorod v dvukh izmereniyakh* [The city in two dimensions] (Sverdlovsk: Sredne-Uralskoye book publishing, 1979), <http://www.1723.ru/read/books/city2.htm>, accessed 3 November 2023.

Bokov, Anna, 'Soviet Workers' Clubs: Lessons from Social Condensers', *The Journal of Architecture*, vol. 22, no. 3, pp. 403–436.

Boyev, Aleksey, and Naugolnova, Daria, *Identichnost' v tipovom* [Identity in the typical] (Ekaterinburg: Tatlin, 2019).

Budantseva, Tatiana, 'Modernist Heritage of Sverdlovsk Today', *Heritage at Risk* (Berlin: Hendrik Bäßler Verlag, 2007), pp. 90–95.

Chepkunova, I., Steltsova Iu., et al., *Pionery sovetskogo modernizma: arkhitektura i gradostroitel'stvo* [Pioneers of Soviet modernism: architecture and urban planning] (Moscow: Kuchkovo pole, 2019).

Davydov, I., *Shagi Khimmasha* [Steps of Khimmash] (Yekaterinburg: Vneshtorgizdat, 1992), p. 247.

Egerev, V., Kubasov, V., Novikov, F., Paluy, B., Pokrovskiy, I., Khazhakyan, M., and Ionov, Yu. *Moskovskiy Dvorets pionerov* [Moscow Pioneer's Palace] (Moscow: Stroyizdat, 1964).

Fadeykov, Max, 'Snesem odnoznachno. AVS Group gotovitsya zamenit' khimmashevskiy DK na zhilye vysotki' [We'll knock it down, for sure. AVS Group is preparing to replace the Khimmashev DK with residential high-rises], *Uralpolit*, 30 January 2018, <https://uralpolit.ru/article/sverdl/30-01-2018/129854>, accessed 18 November 2023.

Govorkovskaya, Viktoriya, 'Valeriy Savelyev poluchit ot administratsii Yekaterinburga 20 tys. zemli [Valery Savelyev will receive 20 thousand square metres of land from the Yekaterinburg administration], *DK*, 24 October 2022, <https://www.dk.ru/news/237174802>, accessed 18 November 2023.

Gundarina, Polina. 'One Past, One Future?', *moderneRegional*, 9 August 2023, <https://www.moderne-regional.de/portraet-one-past-one-future/>, 18 November 2023.

Kazakova, Olga, *Estetika ottepeli: novoe v arkhitekture, iskusstve, kul'ture* [Aesthetics of the thaw: the new in architecture, art, culture] (Moscow: ROSSPEN, 2013).

'Khrushchevki i brezhnevki v Yekaterinburge podesheveli na 5-6 protsentov' [Khrushchevki and brezhnevki in Yekaterinburg have fallen in price by 5–6 per cent] *Expert-Ural*, 11 October 2007, <https://expert-ural.com/news/hrusevki-i-brezhnevki-v-ekaterinburge-podesheveli.html>, accessed 18 November 2023.

'Kompaniya Atomstroykompleks k letu 2025 goda postroit na Khimmashe 17 tys. kv. metrov zhil'ya' [Atomstroycomplex will build 17 thousand square metres of housing in Khimmash by summer 2025], *UralBiznesKonsalting*, 8 August 2023, <https://urbc.ru/1068122290-kompaniya-atomstroykompleks-k-letu-2025-goda-postroit-na-himmashe-17-tys-kv-metrov-zhilya.html>, accessed 19 November 2023.

Kolesnikov, Andrey, Uralkhimmash vzyat Mirom' [Uralkhimmash grabbed by 'Mir'], *Kommersant*, 19 September 2000, <https://www.kommersant.ru/doc/158277>, accessed 18 November 2023.

Korepanov, N., Dumchikov, A., and Pimenova, K., *Khimmash: vdol' i poperek* [Khimmash: every nook and cranny] (Yekaterinburg: AO Format, 2022), pp. 260.

Kurganov, Valeryan, *Tak rozhdalsya Uralkhimmash…* [Thus Uralkhimmash was born…] (Sverdlovsk: Sredne-Uralskoye book publishing, 1973), <http://fort-himmash.narod.ru/RozdHim/, accessed 3 November 2023.

Novikov, Feliks, *Obrazy sovetskoy arkhitektury* [Images of Soviet architecture], (Moscow: Kuchkovo pole, 2021).

Novikova, Sasha, 'Ya zhivu na Khimmashe, gde protestuyut protiv snosa DK' [I live in Khimmash, where they are protesting against the demolition of the palace of culture] *The Village*, 15 March 2018, <https://www.the-village.ru/city/where/305417-himmash-4-life>, accessed 6 November 2023.

Panov, P., *Oblik Sverdlovska segodnya* [The image of Sverdlovsk today], *Sverdlovsk v nastoyaschem i budushchem* [Sverdlovsk in the present and the past] (Sverdlovsk, 1958), <http://www.1723.ru/read/books/sverdlovsk-1958/sverdlovsk-1958.htm>, accessed 3 November 2023.

Perechen' tipovykh proektov TP-3 RSFSR [List of standardised projects by Project Institute No. 5], s.v. 'Series 169-129' (Moscow: Gosstroy RSFSR, 1959).

Politkovskaya, Anna, 'Saga Sverdlovskaya. Chisto konkretnaya. Chto stoit za nedavnimi sobytiyami na kombinate Uralkhimmash v Yekaterinburge?' [The Sverdlovsk saga. A very specific story. What lies behind recent events at the Uralkhimmash plant in Ekaterinburg?], *Novaya gazeta*, 25 September 2000.

Popova, Polina. 'Zhiteli Khimmasha vzyalis' za vosstanovleniye zimnego sada vo Dvortse kultury' [Khimmash residents have started restoring the winter garden in the palace of culture], *Global City*, 24 January 2023, <https://globalcity.info/news/24/01/2023/48471>, accessed 18 November 2023.

Interview with Yury Korovin, *Proekt Yekaterinburg – gorod 7 rayonov* [Project 'Yekaterinburg: city of 7 districts'], <https://on.soundcloud.com/wfhux>, accessed 8 November 2023.

Sokołowicz, Mariusz E., Nowakowska, Aleksandra, and Ciarkowski, Błażej, *The Ambiguous Legacy of Socialist Modernist Architecture in Central and Eastern Europe* (London: Routledge, 2023), pp. 254.

Solonina, Nadezhda, 'Vyyavleniye istoriko-arkhitekturnogo potentsiala istoricheskoy promyshlennoy territorii pri rzarabotke arkhitekturnogo proyekta' [Identification of the historical-architectural potential of a historical industrial territory during the development of an architectural project], *Arkhitekton*, December 2021, <https://archvuz.ru/2021_4/1/>, accessed 8 November 2023.

Stroitel'nye normy i tekhnicheskie usloviya proektirovaniya zdaniy klubov, SN 44-59 [Construction standards and technical conditions for the design of club buildings, Building norms 44-59]. *Kontsortsium Kodeks*, 1 May 1959. <https://docs.cntd.ru/document/1200064745>, accessed 3 November 2023.

Suchkov, Nikita, and Tsarikov, Alexander, 'Kak Yekaterinburg za 10 let stal stolitsey konstruktivizma' [How in 10 years Ekaterinburg became the capital of constructivism], *Rambler*, 30 December 2019, <https://news.rambler.ru/other/43439877-kak-ekaterinburg-za-10-let-stal-stolitsey-konstruktivizma/>, accessed 18 November 2023.

Zakhvatoshina, Oksana, 'Kak zhivet DK Khimmash, kotoryy spasli ot snosa' [The life lived by Khimmash Palace of Culture after being saved from demolition] *E1*, 31 May 2019, <https://www.e1.ru/text/realty/2019/05/31/66108907/>, accessed 18 November 2023.

06

Lazdynai in Vilnius, Lithuania.
Creative touches in Soviet mass housing

Barbara Engel

Post-war housing is a remarkable phenomenon in the post-Soviet urban landscape, demonstrating a strong relationship between political power and modern planning theories.[1] What characterised Lithuanian post-war urbanisation was constant attempts by planners to find a local way to give the districts being designed a sense of uniqueness within the economic, ideological, and technical limits imposed by the centralised Soviet planning system.[2,3]

Lazdynai was built from 1967 to 1973 in response to massive population growth in Vilnius. During the time when the new district was being built, it was seen as a modern area with superior living conditions. Despite the rigid Soviet planning system, the planners managed to achieve substantial modifications. The specific urban composition and architectural details gave the area originality, and Lazdynai was perceived as unique in comparison to other districts of mass housing. In 1974 Lazdynai was awarded the Lenin Prize as the first mass housing district in history – and thus recognised as a symbol of Soviet planning and power. Today it is discussed from a complex perspective that encompasses both its spatial and functional performance and its relation to an unwanted system of former Soviet power.

Historical development

Similar to developments occurring throughout Europe at the time, the erection of mass housing in Lithuania was closely linked to socio-economic and demographic factors. Vilnius was facing rapid population growth after World War II. In 1945 the post-war Lithuanian capital had 110,000 inhabitants. By 1959 that number had more than doubled, to 236,000, and by 1979 Vilnius had nearly half a million inhabitants.[4] The massive urban expansion and increasing demand for housing made the city an excellent testing ground for architects and planners.[5]

Lazdynai is located in the north-western part of Vilnius, the Lithuanian capital. On its west, south, and east sides, its borders are defined by the course of the River Neris. Its site is characterised by hills and forests. The commission for the master plan for Lazdynai was awarded in 1962 to two Lithuanian architects: Vytautas Brėdikis and Vytautas Čekanauskas. The construction of the new district for 40,000 inhabitants on an area of 9.9 square kilometres began in 1967 on the site of the former village of Lazdynai and was completed in 1973. Brėdikis and Čekanauskas went on trips to Finland on two

---

[1] Belli, Nicola, 'From Construction to Deconstruction: The Heritage of Post-War Modern Mass Housing', *Architecture and Urban Planning*, vol. 16, No. 1, 2020, pp. 93–98, here: p. 96.

[2] Hess, Daniel Baldwin, and Tammaru, Tiit, 'Modernist Housing Estates in the Baltic Countries: Formation, Current Challenges and Future Prospects' in Hess, Daniel Baldwin, and Tammaru, Tiit (eds.) *Housing Estates in the Baltic Countries: The Legacy of Central Planning in Estonia, Latvia and Lithuania* (Cham: SpringerOpen, 2019), pp. 3–30, here: p. 8.

[3] Belli, Nicola, 'Postwar Modern Mass Housing in Europe: Anatomy of a Decline?' (doctoral dissertation, Kaunas University of Technology, 2022), p. 92.

[4] Drėmaitė, Marija: *Baltic Modernism: Architecture and Housing in Soviet Lithuania* (Berlin: DOM publishers, 2017), pp.158–159.

[5] Belli, Nicola, 'Postwar Modern Mass Housing in Europe: Anatomy of a Decline?' (doctoral dissertation, Kaunas University of Technology, 2022), p. 92.

1962: initial concept

1965–1977: first construction phase

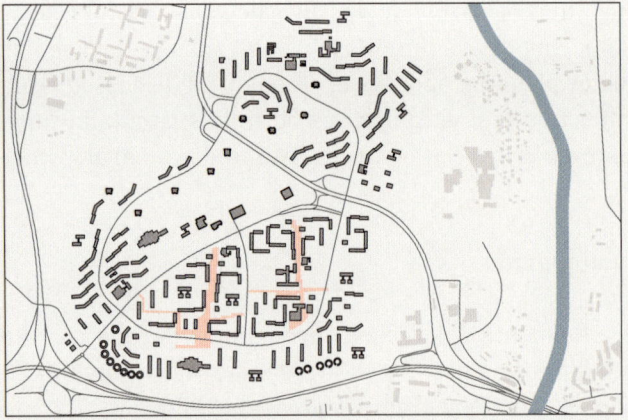
1981–1985: second construction phase

2023: transformation

Figure 1:
Phases of development.
Source: Julia Bakucz, Magdalena Hehnen, based on 'Vilnius gyvenamasis rajonas' by Vytautas Brédikis and on the master plan of 1967, by V. Balciunas, 1983, Drémaité, Marija, 'Baltic Countries, The Exceptional Design of Large Housing Sstates in the Baltic Countries' in Hess Daniel Baldwin, Tammaru Tiit (eds.) *Housing Estates in the Baltic Countires, The Legacy of Central Planning in Estonia, Latvia and Lithuania* (Springer Open, 2019), https://doi.org/10.1007/978-3-030-23392-1, pp. 71–93, here: p. 87.

occasions (in 1959 and in 1960) to exchange experiences.[6] They were also inspired by other foreign models, such as Vällinbgy and Farsta (both in Sweden) and Toulouse-Le-Mirail (France).[7] The architects' familiarity with other, particularly Nordic, residential designs led to housing with a more human scale than other Soviet mass housing complexes. The buildings were predominantly built between five and nine storeys high, and the design showed respect for surrounding nature.[8] Especially with the newly designed 12-storey buildings, this area stands out for its variety – not only in terms of building types, but also in its balanced and moderate building heights and density.

Urban patterns and building typologies

Lazdynai is composed of four microrayons and includes schools, nursery schools, basic facilities for sports, and shopping centres. The organisation of building plots according to the positioning of the buildings differs from other socialist estates that were built in the 1960s. Building heights and the sizes of the micro-districts and blocks were smaller than in a typical Soviet neighbourhood.

Greenery was one of the distinctive features of the district. The system of green spaces supported the relationship between the living environment and the landscape.[9] The forest, which at the time of construction was almost wild, could be easily reached in all directions. The harmony between the built environment and nature reflected the Scandinavian model that inspired the architects.[10] One could enjoy nature not only in the forest but also through one's windows, by looking at carefully maintained flower beds and rock gardens.[11] The trees – including lime trees and chestnuts – were also tended in a professional manner.[12]

The plan for Lazdynai represented an attempt to introduce a new element into Soviet urban space. The commercial centre was supposed to symbolise the hybrid nature of the late socialist society, where consumption and individual behaviour were of increasing importance.[13] However, access to products remained limited. The plan to build a commercial centre was not aimed at providing consumer goods but at representing a new lifestyle and new aesthetic codes.[14] Some links between public spaces were not implemented, such as the concept for the Lazdynai commercial and cultural centre as a part of the district centre, which proposed the integration of not only pedestrian streets but also transport.[15]

---

6   Maciuika, 'Baltic Shores, Western Winds: Lithuanian Architects and the Subversion of the Soviet Norm', *Centropa: A Journal of Central European Architecture and the Related Arts*, vol. 1, No. 2, 2001, pp. 108-116, here p. 112.

7   Drėmaitė, Marija: *Baltic Modernism: Architecture and Housing in Soviet Lithuania* (Berlin: DOM publishers, 2017), p. 172.

8   Rimkutė, Kristina, 'Soviet Mass Housing in Vilnius: Exploring the Consequences of the 1955 Housing Reform and the Rebellion Against Architectural Homogenisation', (doctoral dissertation, University of Edinburgh, 2014), p. 43.

9   See Nekrošius, Liutauras, 'Partially Realized Modernist Heritage of Vilnius' in Sołtysik, Maria Jolanta and Hirsch, Robert (eds.), *Modernism in Europe – Modernism in Gdynia: 20th Century Architecture Until the 1960s and its Preservation*, pp. 143–148, here: p. 145

10 See Drėmaitė. Marija 'Baltic Countries, The Exceptional Design of Large Housing Sstates in the Baltic Countries', Hess, Daniel Baldwin and Tammaru, Tiit (eds.) *Housing Estates in the Baltic Countires, The Legacy of Central Planning in Estonia, Latvia and Lithuania* (Springer Open, 2019), https://doi.org/10.1007/978-3-030-23392-1 pp. 71–93, here: pp. 83–84.

11 Janušauskaitė, Viltė, 'Lazdynai – A Constructed Spirit of Place?', *Archmuziejus*, 1 December 2018, <http://archmuziejus.lt/en/lietuviu-lazdynai-sukonstruota-vietos-dvasia/>, accessed 28 December 2023.

12 Ibid.

13 Šiupšinskas, M., and Lankots, E., 'Collectivist Ideals and Soviet Consumer Spaces: Mikrorayon Commecial Centres in Vilnius, Lithuania and Tallinn, Estonia', in Hess, Daniel Baldwin and Tammaru,Tiit (eds.), *Housing Estates in the Baltic Countries: The Legacy of Central Planning in Estonia, Latvia and Lithuania* (Cham: Springer Open 2019) pp. 301–320.

14 Belli, Nicola, 'Postwar Modern Mass Housing in Europe: Anatomy of a Decline?' (doctoral dissertation, Kaunas University of Technology, 2022), p. 95.

15 Nekrošius, Liutauras, 'Partially Realized Modernist Heritage of Vilnius' in Sołtysik, Maria Jolanta and Hirsch, Robert (eds.), *Modernism in Europe – Modernism in Gdynia: 20th Century Architecture Until the 1960s and its Preservation*, pp. 143–148, here p. 145.

Figure 2:
Aerial view of Lazdynai, 10 May 2021.
Source: Augustas Didzgalvis.jpg, https://upload.wikimedia.org/wikipedia/commons/d/d8/Lazdynai_by_Augustas_Didzgalvis.jpg?uselang=de, accessed 2 January 2024.

Figure 3:
Footprint of Lazdynai in its urban context.
Source: Julia Bakucz, Magdalena Hehnen, based on google maps

Figure 4:
Pedestrian area of Lazdynai.
Source: Barbara Engel, March 2023

Lazdynai was the first district in Lithuania to have clear separation of pedestrian and traffic flows. The transport system in each microrayon consists of one transit road and three internal streets. Pedestrian pathways ensure accessibility in the neighbourhood and link the houses to commercial and recreational centres, educational institutions, and public transport stops.[16] Cars are accommodated in semi-underground car parks located in the outer part of the district. Equally important was that this district is rich in elements of street furniture – from sculptures and benches to playgrounds for children. At the time Lazdynai was considered the most complete district in the republic.[17] Such a perception was extremely significant: given the constant lack of funds, residential districts often opened without social infrastructure or street furniture, whereas in Lazdynai paths were built, greenery was planted according to a plan of plant types, benches and outdoor lighting fixtures were installed, children's playgrounds and laundry drying facilities were built, and even artworks were erected – sculptures that have since become important aesthetic landmarks and accents in the neighbourhood.[18]

Lazdynai presents an urban morphology that differentiates it from the typical Soviet residential district because of its unusually dynamic silhouette, achieved through utilisation of the site's hilly relief. Instead of following the common practice of arranging housing along the contours of hills, some of the five-storey blocks are positioned directly on the slope of the hill. As if built on terraces,

16 Ibid.

17 Janušauskaitė, Viltė, 'Lazdynai – A Constructed Spirit of the Place?', *Archmuziejus*, 1 December 2018, <http://archmuziejus.lt/en/lietuviu-lazdynai-sukonstruota-vietos-dvasia/>, accessed 28 December 2023.

18 Ibid.

Figure 5:
Series-1-464 LI-building in Lazdynai.
Photo by Barbara Engel, March 2023

19   Rimkutė, Kristina, 'Soviet Mass Housing in Vilnius: Exploring the Consequences of the 1955 Housing Reform and the Rebellion Against Architectural Homogenisation' (doctoral dissertation, University of Edinburgh, 2014), p. 52.

20   Drémaité. Marija, 'Baltic Countries, The Exceptional Design of Large Housing Sstates in the Baltic Countries', Hess, Daniel Baldwin, Tammaru, Tiit (eds.) *Housing Estates in the Baltic Countires, The Legacy of Central Planning in Estonia, Latvia and Lithuania* (Springer Open, 2019), https://doi.org/10.1007/978-3-030-23392-1, pp. 71–93, here: p. 82.

21   Ibid.

they step downhill, creating dynamic lines with their silhouettes. The district also has five-storey blocks of a broken configuration that follow the natural contour lines, as well as rectangular nine-storey blocks and unique monolithic structures. All these different types of buildings are distributed across the landscape in a manner that shows respect for the surrounding nature; the blocks look as though they are rooted in the greenery of Lazdynai rather than dominating it.[19]

All the houses in this district were made at Vilnius House-Construction Combine. Until 1967 the houses made at the factory were from Series LT; subsequently, they were replaced with the more modern Series 1-464-LI (architects: B. Krūminis and others), known as 'the Lithuanian series'.[20] The designers managed to push the limits of Soviet planning standards, creating artistic variations of this prefabricated standardised series.

The Standard-Design Department at Vilnius Urban Construction Planning Institute developed 15 'improved' versions of the I-464-LI building series specifically for Lazdynai.[21]

Initially, there were eight types of this series of five- and nine-storey houses. This, however, did not satisfy the architects of this district, so they designed another seven types of house, the most distinctive of which were 'stepped' houses – with each section 'falling on the relief', which made it necessary to dismantle and reassemble the lifting cranes for each section – and two versions of the broken-plan

Figures 6 and 7:
Tower buildings in Lazdynai.
Photos by Barbara Engel, December 22 and March 23

22 Janušauskaitė, Viltė, 'Lazdynai – A Constructed Spirit of Place?', *Archmuziejus*, 1 December 2018. <http://archmuziejus.lt/en/lietuviu-lazdynai-sukonstruota-vietos-dvasia/>, accessed 28 December 2023.

23 Ibid.

24 Rimkutė, Kristina, 'Soviet Mass Housing in Vilnius: Exploring the Consequences of the 1955 Housing Reform and the Rebellion against Architectural Homogenisation' (doctoral dissertation, University of Edinburgh, 2014), p. 50.

25 Ibid., p. 49.

26 Ibid., p. 58.

27 Drėmaitė, Marija, *Baltic Modernism: Architecture and Housing in Soviet Lithuania* (Berlin: DOM Publishers, 2017), p.171.

five-storey types, which were necessary to give flexibility in response to the terrain. This was the first time that 12-storey tower blocks had been built in Lithuania; their only purpose was to implement the composition – it was recognised that constructing such a tall linear building was impractical.[22]

Nine types of five-storey buildings, three types of nine-storey buildings, and, for the first time, 12-storey towers were added to the standardised series. Due to the quite complex topography, the distances between buildings were designed to be greater than the standards of the time required.[23]

In addition to various creative ways of composing blocks inside the districts, a number of exterior detailing techniques were employed to differentiate the standardised housing. For example, the nine-storey blocks of Series 1-464-LI in Lazdynai can be distinguished from blocks of exactly the same series in other districts by the concrete screens that mark the vertical circulation axis in each structure. The first monolithic tower blocks started to appear in Lazdynai in the late 1970s. Designed by the architect Česlovas Mazūras and the engineer Jonas Rusteika, they have some typically Brutalist features. There are four apartments on each floor, mirrored along the axis that runs through the centre of the vertical circulation core.[24]

The design of these blocks differs considerably from the surrounding Series 1-464-LI: the balconies are significantly larger on the upper and lower floors, projecting outwards from the massive-looking core structures so as to create dynamic visual accents on what might otherwise be rather static vertical edifices.[25]

The creative use of colour was another important design tool that, along with decorative detailing, helped add character to these districts of Vilnius. Colour was introduced through miniature tiles that adhered to the exterior surface of the balconies.[26]

Apartments in Lazdynai exhibit improvements when compared to typical Soviet units – namely, larger balconies, a better-designed kitchen, more storage space, and separation of the toilet and bathroom. In accordance with Soviet standards, the buildings had only one-, two-, three- and four-room apartments. By the first half of the 1970s the average number of inhabitants per room was 1.43, which was considered a sign of convenience and comfort. Constituting 42.9 per cent of the units in Lazdynai, two-room apartments are the most common type of apartment; three-room apartments make up 33.3 per cent of units; one-room and four-room units constitute 13.3 per cent and 10.4 per cent respectively.[27]

Lazdynai evolved as a stylistically unified and original-looking urban entity because Lithuanian architects were obviously very much involved in the process of designing this residential district.[28] Instead of functioning as a strictly hierarchical institution that is detached from local realities, the mass-housing industry in Soviet Lithuania was, to a degree, receptive to the criticism and suggestions of local architects.[29] The relatively open dissemination of progressive building ideas in the local press and the incorporation of international ideas were significant factors in shaping the local architects' approach to modern housing.[30] Due to good personal relations with the directors of the factories making reinforced-concrete panels, the planners in Lazdynai were able to achieve substantial modifications in panel design.[31] Some of these directors genuinely cared about the appearance of their cities and wanted to improve living standards in their country. Encouraged by the architects' ideas, they modified some of the standardised panel designs to fit the architects' concepts.[32]

Lazdynai: the Soviet showcase model

The emergence of an unusually well thought-out design for a residential district in Lithuania was a particularly significant event in Soviet housing in the mid-1970s.[33] Mass housing from the mid-1960s onwards had come in for criticism from architects in the Soviet Union. Visual monotony was the main focus of their concerns, and they were beginning to take a stand against the repetitive replication of standardised concrete-panel systems.

At a time when Soviet mass housing was already facing criticism for visual monotony and low-quality construction, the planners of Lazdynai proved successful at integrating the natural and built environment and in creating a safe residential environment with pedestrian pathways, greenery, well-kept public spaces, and ample services. In this context Lazdynai conveniently reaffirmed the idea that it was indeed possible to build with artistic variation while using standardised elements. Furthermore, only widely available materials were used for the exterior and interior finishes at Lazdynai, allowing the cost of the district to remain on budget.[34]

Lazdynai won recognition from both delegations of specialists keen to adopt the 'know-how' and leading figures in the national Gosstroy agency. Communist Party leaders viewed the project as a 'model design', a pivotal example of Soviet-Lithuanian urbanism.[35] In 1974 Lazdynai was awarded the Lenin Prize for All-Union Architectural

28 Rimkutė, Kristina, 'Soviet Mass Housing in Vilnius: Exploring the Consequences of the 1955 Housing Reform and the Rebellion against Architectural Homogenisation' (doctoral dissertation, University of Edinburgh, 2014), pp. 59–60.

29 Ibid.

30 Ibid., p. 61.

31 Ibid., p. 69.

32 Ibid.

33 Ibid., pp. 43–44.

34 Ibid., pp. 43–44.

35 Drėmaitė, Marija, *Baltic Modernism: Architecture and housing in Soviet Lithuania* (Berlin: DOM publishers, 2017), p. 173.

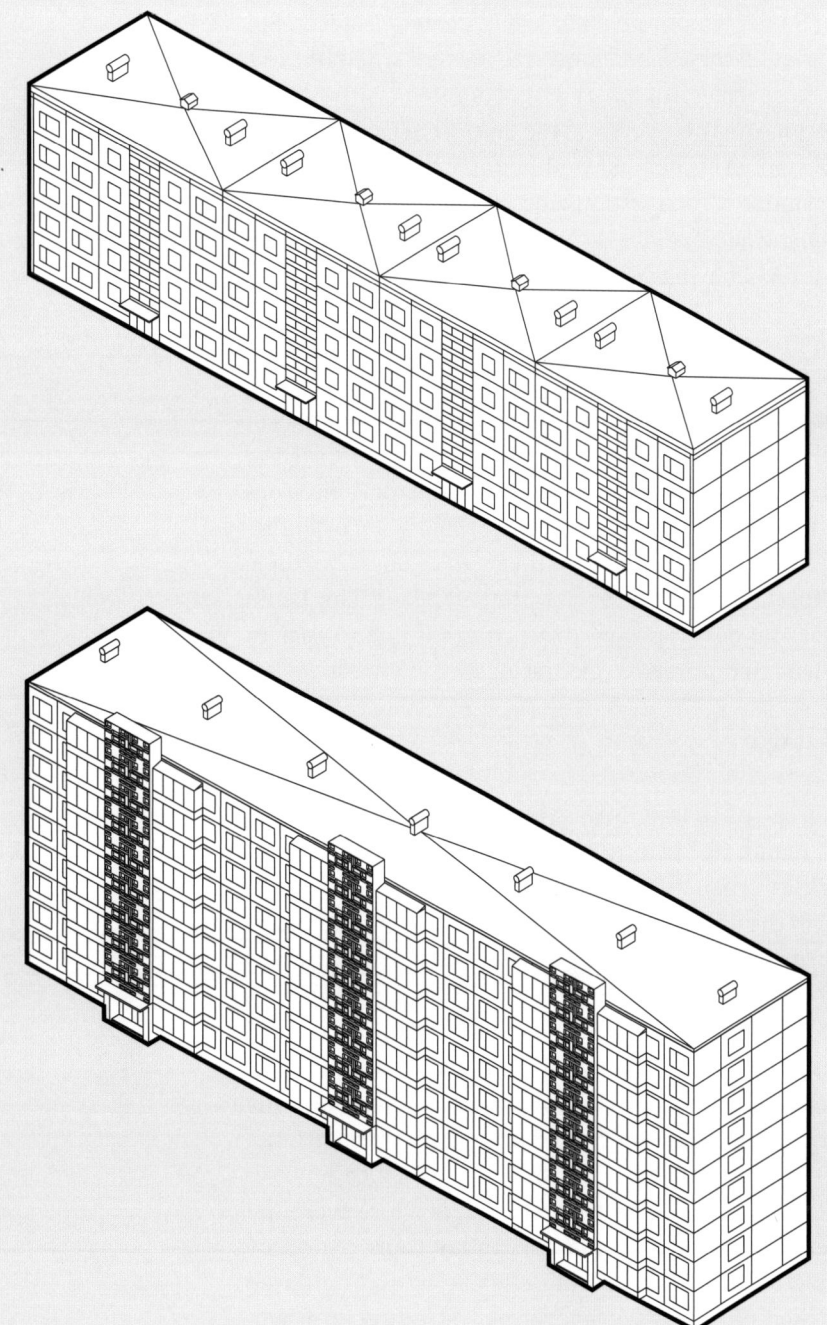

Figures 8 and 9:
Housing types
with five and nine storeys in Lazdynai.
Source: Julia Bakucz and Magdalena Hehnen,
based on google maps

Design, the highest Soviet honour given to urban design projects. For the first time in Soviet history, the Lenin Prize was awarded not to a single building but to a residential district. A commemorative stone was erected in Lazdynai on this occasion; the district became a model of Soviet housing, a symbol of socialist well-being.[36] In 1976 Lazdynai even received international recognition when it was featured on the cover of *Neue Wohngebiete Sozialistischer Länder,* an international survey of modern panel housing construction in the Eastern Bloc by Werner Rietdorf.[37]

The Lenin Prize and international attention demonstrated that post-war districts were central in discourses aimed at showcasing the outcomes of Soviet urbanism. Lazdynai demonstrated the success of its planners in exploiting the natural site, integrating the natural and built environment, and creating a high-quality residential environment. It achieved success and centrality in the discourse on architecture and urban planning. At the same time, the open celebration made Lazdynai a powerful instrument of Soviet propaganda.[38] The Lenin Prize demonstrated that Soviet power attached great importance to mass housing and was committed to celebrating its outcomes.

Post-socialist heritage

How is Lazdynai perceived today? How is this legacy of mass housing in Vilnius, the Lithuanian-Baltic interpretation of post-war modernism, evaluated? Soviet urban structures and architecture, although recognised as part of the national heritage, remain objects of controversy in Lithuania, provoking emotions that range from admiration and nostalgia to criticism and rejection.[39]

The collapse of the Soviet Union and the end of the socialist system in the 'satellite states' triggered the transition of an enormous amount of urban fabric in eastern Europe. The end of centralised planning gave rise to new forms of social and spatial organisation,[40] with the result that an increasing number of housing estates lost their initial attractiveness. The legacy of the past – districts which were developed as progressive neighbourhoods – is today represented by an ageing building stock with structural deficiencies and outdated housing types, in need of extensive renovation, including improvement of its spatial-structural organisation and orientation, redesign of its open spaces, and new mobility concepts and services.

In post-Soviet Lithuania districts of post-war mass housing continued to represent the social, political, and architectural values of the

36 Janušauskaitė, Viltė, 'Lazdynai – A Constructed Spirit of the Place?', *Archmuziejus*, 1 December 2018., <http://archmuziejus.lt/en/lietuviu-lazdynai-sukonstruota-vietos-dvasia/>, accessed 28 December 2023.

37 Belli, Nicola, 'Postwar Modern Mass Housing in Europe: Anatomy of a Decline?' (doctoral dissertation, Kaunas University of Technology, 2022), p. 97.

38 Ibid., p. 98.

39 Martignolles, Tanguy, 'Lithuania: the uncertain fate of Soviet architecture in Vilnius',*Regard sur l'Est*, 2 September 2022. <https://regard-est.com/lithuania-the-uncertain-fate-of-soviet-architecture-in-vilnius>, accessed 30 December 2023.

40 Dekker, van Kempen, Tosics, 2005.

post-war decades. After regaining independence in 1991, Lithuania de-Sovietised but did not choose to demolish Soviet buildings en masse; the economic transition imposed limits on the budgets allocated to urban renewal, and, due to a lack of funds, the vast majority of Soviet buildings were instead rehabilitated. Post-war neighbourhoods are generally associated with the Soviet era, a deeply 'disfavoured' and contested past in contemporary Lithuania.[41]

Since the end of the Soviet Union, Lazdynai has undergone transformations in its spatial configuration and organisation. The idea of preserving the interior of the district as a pedestrian zone proved unable to resist trends in contemporary development. The number of private vehicles has increased, and motorways have been built to facilitate inhabitants' mobility needs. But there are also trends for new, sustainable modes of transport. In 2018 the first official bike path was built around the etire district. A cycle path was also built parallel to the main transport axis. The total area of green space has not been drastically reduced and has escaped densification. In 2020 a new green axis was created to link to East Lazdynai Forest – a project that was already part of the 1965 master plan. A church was built, and on the site originally intended for a public centre buildings were erected for a variety of purposes, including housing.[42]

Today Lazdynai is listed as heritage of local significance. The protection status aims to keep the urban ensemble intact. The nine 17-storey buildings dominate the panorama and are therefore mentioned separately in the official listing document. In addition to the district-level heritage, five individual objects have protection status: three sculptures, a fountain, and Minties Gimnazija secondary school. Since residential buildings are listed separately, no restrictions are placed on renovation of façades. As a result, more and more houses are being individually renovated to improve their technical performance and living conditions. The black wooden windows in the district have been replaced with windows of coloured plastic. Decorative elements are now seen as a kind of rubbish – sculptures that were needed to compensate for the grey colour of the monotonous houses and their erection in a 'nowhere' setting. Characteristic of construction of the time, they have since lost their meaning.[43]

Large housing districts in post-Soviet cities are often perceived as massive urban representation of the unwanted years of communism and discussed using negative attributes such as greyness, monotony, large-scale, and poor public space. But there are inherent national complexities attached to the manifestations of Soviet mass housing

[41] Petrulis, Vaidas, 'Socialist Realism: Timeline in Lithuania', in *Socialist Realism and Socialist Modernism: World Heritage Proposals from Central and Eastern Europe*, ICOMOS-Hefte des Deutschen Nationalkomitees, vol. 58, 2013, pp. 90–94, here: p. 93.

[42] Nekrošius, Liutauras, 'Partially Realized Modernist Heritage of Vilnius', in Sołtysik, Maria Jolanta, and Hirsch, Robert (eds.), *Modernism in Europe – Modernism in Gdynia: 20th Century Architecture until the 1960s and its Preservation*, pp. 143–148, here: p. 145.

[43] Janušauskaitė, Viltė, 'Lazdynai – A Constructed Spirit of the Place?', *Archmuziejus*, 1 December 2018, <http://archmuziejus.lt/en/lietuviu-lazdynai-sukonstruota-vietos-dvasia/>, accessed 28 December 2023.

outside of Soviet Russia. The concept of socialist design did not produce a single, consistent aesthetic standard across the Soviet Union. Instead, cities in the former Soviet republics acquired a distinctive architectural appearance through a cohesive institutionalised logic and a series of complex planning procedures that had a negative impact on individual creativity and prevented fruitful communication between the lower and higher levels of the Soviet building industry. Flaws in this immense system of building, combined with support from the local authorities of various Soviet republics, allowed a modest degree of independence of expression in relation to distinctly national approaches to mass housing – such as in Lazdynai.[44] The geographical position of Vilnius – on the periphery of the Soviet Union – was favourable for allowing this country to be actively involved in a degree of cultural exchange between the eastern and western blocs. Today's discussion of values is difficult because, in addition to their functional, aesthetic, and social performance, these districts are always evaluated against the background of highly emotional perception. However, the creative touches added by the local architects in the spheres of planning and exterior detailing have undeniably increased Lazdynai's heritage value. Despite the changes and transformations that have already taken place, Lazdynai still retains its very specific spatial character. Although changes are happening slowly, efforts are needed in order that this precious heritage is not lost.

Lazdynai is an outstanding example of socialist housing, a landmark of Soviet planning in its Lithuanian interpretation. In this respect it is unique as a document of political, architectural, and cultural expression and of efforts that have to be made. Whether a nomination to the UNESCO World Heritage List is appropriate, as Lazdynai is unique heritage that is representative of twentieth-century mass housing, is something that needs to be discussed.[45] It would be an important step towards more active and successful conservation efforts on the national level. At the very least, a strong management plan is needed in order to guide this heritage towards a sustainable future, allowing for necessary adaptations to current needs while avoiding the gradual destruction of a valuable testament to modern heritage.

44 Rimkutė, Kristina, 'Soviet Mass Housing in Vilnius: Exploring the Consequences of the 1955 Housing Reform and the Rebellion against Architectural Homogenisation' (doctoral dissertation, University of Edinburgh, 2014), p. 63.

45 See Petrulis, Vaidas, 'Socialist Realism: Timeline in Lithuania' in *Socialist Realism and Socialist Modernism: World Heritage Proposals from Central and Eastern Europe*, ICOMOS-Hefte des Deutschen Nationalkomitees, vol. 58, 2013, pp. 90–94, here: p. 93.

References

Belli, Nicola, 'From Construction to Deconstruction: The Heritage of Post-War Modern Mass Housing', *Architecture and Urban Planning*, vol. 16, no. 1, 2020, pp. 93–98.

Belli, Nicola, 'Postwar Modern Mass Housing in Europe: Anatomy of a Decline?' (doctoral dissertation, Kaunas University of Technology, 2022).

Drémaité, Marija, 'Baltic Countries, The Exceptional Design of Large Housing Sstates in the Baltic Countries' in Hess Daniel Baldwin, Tammaru Tiit (eds.), *Housing Estates in the Baltic Countires, The Legacy of Central Planning in Estonia, Latvia and Lithuania* (Springer Open, 2019), https://doi.org/10.1007/978-3-030-23392-1, pp. 71–93.

Drémaité, Marija, *Baltic Modernism: Architecture and Housing in Soviet Lithuania* (Berlin: DOM publishers, 2017).

Hess, Daniel Baldwin, and Tammaru, Tiit, 'Modernist Housing Estates in the Baltic Countries: Formation, Current Challenges and Future Prospects', in Hess, Daniel Baldwin, and Tammaru, Tiit (eds.), *Housing Estates in the Baltic Countries: The Legacy of Central Planning in Estonia, Latvia and Lithuania* (Springer, 2019), pp. 3–30.

Janušauskaitė, Viltė, 'Lazdynai – A Constructed Spirit of the Place?', *Archmuziejus*, 1 December 2018, <http://archmuziejus.lt/en/lietuviu-lazdynai-sukonstruota-vietos-dvasia/>, accessed 28 December 2023.

van Kempen, Ronald, Dekker, Karien, Hall, Stephen, and Tosics, Iván, *Restructuring Large Housing Estates in Europe: Restructuring and Resistance Inside the Welfare Industry* (Bristol: Policy Press, University of Bristol, 2005).

Maciuika, 'Baltic Shores, Western Winds: Lithuanian Architects and the Subversion of the Soviet Norm', *Centropa: A Journal of Central European Architecture and the Related Arts*, vol. 1, no. 2, 2001, pp. 108–116.

Martignolles, Tanguy, 'Lithuania: The Uncertain Fate of Soviet Architecture in Vilnius', *Regard sur l'Est*, 2 September 2022, <https://regard-est.com/lithuania-the-uncertain-fate-of-soviet-architecture-in-vilnius>, accessed 30 December 2023.

Nekrošius, Liutauras, 'Partially Realized Modernist Heritage of Vilnius' in Sołtysik, Maria Jolanta, and Hirsch, Robert (eds.), *Modernism in Europe – Modernism in Gdynia: 20th Century Architecture until the 1960s and its Preservation*, pp. 143–148.

Petrulis, Vaidas, 'Socialist Realism: Timeline in Lithuania' in *Socialist Realism and Socialist Modernism: World Heritage Proposals from Central and Eastern Europe*, ICOMOS-Hefte des Deutschen Nationalkomitees, vol. 58, 2013, pp. 90–94.

Rimkutė, Kristina, 'Soviet Mass Housing in Vilnius: Exploring the Consequences of the 1955 Housing Reform and the Rebellion against Architectural Homogenisation' (doctoral dissertation, University of Edinburgh, 2014).

07

Olaine, Latvia.
Tacitly embracing the heritage of the Soviet monotown: social and infrastructural dynamics

Guido Sechi, Kārlis Lakševics, and Māris Bērziņš

1   Smith, Mark B., 'Faded Red Paradise: Welfare and the Soviet City After 1953', *Contemporary European History*, vol. 24, No. 4, 2015, pp. 597–615.

2   Sultson, Siim, 'Replacement of Urban Space: Estonian Post-war Town Planning Principles and Local Stalinist Industrial Towns', *Journal of Architecture and Urbanism*, vol. 40, No. 4, 2016, pp. 283–294.

3   Dabašinskienė, Ineta, 'Understanding the Post-Soviet Nuclear Locality Through Language Policy Orientations', *Journal of Baltic Studies*, vol. 53, no. 3, 2022, pp. 397–414.

4   Ķūle, Laila, 'Urban–Rural Interactions in Latvian Changing Policy and Practice Context', *European Planning Studies*, vol. 2, No. 4, 2014, pp. 758–774.

5   Drėmaitė, Marija, *Baltic Modernism: Architecture and Housing in Soviet Lithuania* (Berlin: DOM publishers, 2017).

6   Sultson, Siim, 'Estonian Urbanism 1935–1955: The Soviet-era Implementation of Pre-war Ambitions', *Planning Perspectives*, vol. 33, No. 3, 2018, pp. 385–409.

7   Cinis, Andis, Drėmaitė, Marija, and Kalm, Mart, 'Perfect Representations of Soviet Planned Space: Monoindustrial Towns in the Soviet Baltic Republics in the 1950s–1980s', *Scandinavian Journal of History*, vol. 33, No. 3, 2008, pp. 226–246.

The post-Stalinist Soviet monotown (single-enterprise town) shares with the *microrayon* ('micro-district') the characteristic of being one of the distinctive 'socialist spaces' devised by Soviet planners to implement the connection between urbanisation, industry, and welfare, which was one of the primary tenets of the Soviet developmental project and social contract.[1] The transitional trajectories of certain Soviet-era small monotowns in Latvia illustrate to some extent the common logic behind the two categories of settlement.

Planned mono-industrial settlements in the Baltic republics were nodes of large-scale Soviet industrial projects, which made them significantly different from traditional local small towns. Originally representing Stalinist industrial modernisation priorities,[2] from the Khrushchev 'thaw' onwards, these settlements – associated with the energy, chemical, and military industries – came to embody the promotion of a new socialist way of life and were portrayed as remarkable achievements of Soviet industrial policies.[3] Monotowns played a significant role in promoting industrialisation and the growth of local economies, bridging the urban–rural divide.[4] At the same time, they helped establish Soviet norms and unify the spatial environment, contributing to the integration of the Baltic republics into the broader Soviet planning system.[5]

After the collapse of the USSR, these settlements generally suffered, as elsewhere, from economic restructuring, industrial resizing, and shrinkage. Some, however, have managed to take advantage of their geographical proximity to major urban centres – particularly the capital city of Riga – and to their welfare and green infrastructure, which, to a certain extent, combines the advantages of both urban and rural settlements. A few monotowns have also managed to maintain their industrial capacity intact.

In the last few decades mono-industrial towns in the Baltic states have been the object of several studies focusing on the planning and construction of residential areas and related infrastructure.[6,7] However, less attention has been paid to the dynamics of social and infrastructural change and the associated issues of belonging, identity, and attitudes towards heritage.

Olaine (population 10,224 as of 2022), located in the Riga metropolitan area, 20 kilometres southwest of the capital, is the largest of Latvia's small monotowns and appears to be a particularly successful example of transition, having managed to capitalise on both its largely preserved industrial capacity and its favourable location. Our chapter combines in-depth, semi-structured interviews (conducted

Figure 1:
Map of Olaine, landmarks, and location

- Industrial zone
- Multi-storey housing estates
- Low-rise residential areas
- Urban green spaces and allotment gardens

Author: Jānis Krūmiņš

- Municipal buildings
- Libraries
- Education facilities
- House of culture
- Medical facilities
- Museums

in 2020–2023) with residents, administrative and political decision-makers, and cultural operators in Olaine with on-site observation and analysis of grey literature and official documents to assess (a) management of maintenance of housing and social infrastructure; and (b) the dynamics of community culture in a time of transition, with the aim of investigating the interplay between community dynamics and infrastructural development. We aim to shed light on the dynamic development of community culture and attitudes and the role of infrastructure, viewed not as a simple background but as a factor shaping social relations and culture.[8] At the same time we explore how an integrated understanding – and tacit embrace – of Soviet urban and industrial heritage has shaped a development vision encompassing both Fordist and post-Fordist elements, leading to the coexistence of traditional industrial and 'mobile' suburban culture.

[8] van der Straeten, Jonas and Obertreis, Julia, 'Technology, Temporality, and the Study of Central Asia: An Introduction', *Central Asian Survey*, vol. 41, No. 2, 2022, pp. 211–222.

Case study

The urban development of Olaine began with the establishment of a peat-extraction site in 1939, one year before Latvia was occupied by the Red Army and annexed by the USSR. Working and living conditions were difficult from the very beginning and were further exacerbated by World War II and the subsequent influx of forced labourers. Although penal colonies survived until the mid-1960s, housing and infrastructural conditions gradually improved from the early 1950s forwards. More significant development and demographic growth followed the establishment of chemical and pharmaceutical factories in accordance with a decision of the Council of Ministers of the USSR in 1958; this decision led to the transformation of the originally envisaged 'urban village' into a town. Following the construction of two large chemical plants in 1967, the settlement, which by then had 7000 inhabitants, received the status of town. The chemical-pharmaceutical factory, called 'Olaines ķīmiski farmaceitiskā rūpnīca' (Olaine chemical-pharmaceutical factory), started operating in 1972. Urban development proceeded at an even faster pace in the late 1970s and the 1980s but was interrupted by the collapse of the USSR. However, the main factory, renamed 'Olainfarm', was privatised as a joint-stock company and, after significant troubles in the 1990s, managed to re-emerge as a sector leader in Latvia and the Baltic region. Simultaneously, the town has seen a significant influx of suburbanites from Riga in the last two decades and is gradually becoming a residential satellite of the capital city.

Today Olaine municipality – consisting of the town and a rural parish – is among the wealthiest in Latvia; as of 2020, average salaries were comparable to those in the capital. Apart from Olainfarm, the most relevant industrial businesses are the chemical factory CrossChem and the seafood processing company Atlas Premium. While 39 per cent of the working population is employed in local industry, 50 per cent of residents commute to work in Riga and eight per cent work in other municipalities in the metropolitan area. Like all industrial towns in Latvia, Olaine is a multi-ethnic and de facto bilingual town, shaped by Soviet-era immigration from other parts of Latvia and other USSR republics, in particular the Latgale region and Belarus. Ethnic Russians constitute slightly the largest ethnic group among the population (41.5 per cent), while 40.3 per cent of residents are ethnic Latvians. The remainder are mainly Russian-speaking Belarusians and Ukrainians. There is also an ethnic Polish minority.

The territory of the town of Olaine has a surface area of 6.8 square kilometres. The residential area, built along the railway and highway connecting Riga to the city of Jelgava, has a linear structure. The town centre, where most of the administrative and public buildings are located, separates the 'old' district – including housing built from the 1950s to the early 1970s – from the 'new' district, built from the late 1970s onwards as a southwest extension. The green zone, which was expanded after 1991 to include forest areas within the town limits, consists of an extensive forest park, wild forest, swamps, and allotment gardens. The industrial zone is located in the north of the town and occupies approximately one-fifth of its territory. Nowadays, it contains the Olainfarm complex, other plants in the chemical-pharmaceutical sector, and an industrial park – created in 2000 – with production facilities, warehouses, and office buildings. Some of the industrial infrastructure has been abandoned.

Urban history

Olaine was established on the site of a rural village that was first mentioned in the early seventeenth century, located on the Riga–Jelgava road, on the historical border between Vidzeme Governorate (part of the Swedish Empire and then of the Russian Empire) and the Duchy of Courland and Semigallia (until the late eighteenth century a vassal state of the Polish-Lithuanian Commonwealth). Owing to its strategic location, the settlement has historically been a hub for trade and postal routes. In the mid-eighteenth century a post

Figure 2:
Design of department store in Olaine.
Source: *Cīņa* (newspaper), 1967. Archives of the National Library of Latvia

Figure 3:
Design for the nursing home of Olaine chemical plant (unrealised project).
Source: *Zinātne un Tehnika* (journal), 1978. Archives of the National Library of Latvia

9 Bellat, Fabien, *Tol'yatti. Rozhdeniye novogo goroda* [Tolyatti: Birth of a new city] (Ekaterinburg: Tatlin, 2014).

office was established in the village. In 1868 a station was built on a new railway connecting the Russian and German empires. The village was severely damaged during World War I but recovered in the 1920s and 1930s. Pre-Soviet buildings (the railway station, the post office, the school, a municipal house, and the church) continue to define the settlement's 'historical' centre.

For a period of 14 years after the peat-extraction site was established in 1939, the residents – peat-extraction workers and, after World War II, penal colony detainees – were housed in wooden barracks. Housing development started at a slow pace in 1953. Over seven years, professional builders and prisoners built eight two-storey residential buildings in the Stalinist Neoclassical style and some wooden dormitory-type buildings; a workers' club was also established, and basic water supply infrastructure was put in place. In the early 1960s the strategic decision to build chemical and pharmaceutical plants drove the shift from the 'industrial village' to the 'town' concept. The town plan followed the modernist planning guidelines adopted for planned industrial towns and cities in the USSR and elsewhere at the time.[9] The industrial zone was conceived as a large complex encompassing recreational buildings and other service facilities next to plants. Functional zoning envisaged separation of industrial and residential areas by means of a wide green sanitation zone. The micro-district

principle was applied to residential planning, and the residential areas were planned next to forest areas.[10,11] By 1965, 23 apartment buildings were operational. Eleven five-storey buildings were constructed between 1965 and 1967. In 1967, when Olaine received the status of town, the executive committee put the construction company Khimstroi in charge of the construction process. In the same year a cinema, a department store, and a catering complex were built. In the following years nine-storey panel buildings from Series 467 became the most common type of building. New developments occurred from 1972 to 1978, when buildings from the 104, 105, and 114 series – characterised by more comfortable layouts – were integrated into the Series-467 housing stock. The same year, a municipal library was established. In the late 1970s a start was made on construction of a new district, dominated by nine-storey buildings (Series 602, very similar to Series 467, but with balconies in place of loggias) and five-storey red-brick and concrete houses (Series 103, the only brick series in Latvia in the 1970s/1980s).[12] A park was created in the forest area in the second half of the decade. Improvements in common

10   Berdņikova, Anastasiya, 'Olaines pilsētas veidošanās un attīstības iespējas' [Genesis and development opportunities of Olaine town] (MSc dissertation, University of Latvia, Faculty of Geography and Earth Sciences, Department of Geography, 2013).

11   Buka, Olgerts and Volrāts, Uldis, *Pilsētbūvniecība [Urban construction]* (Riga: Zvaigzne, 1987).

12   Meuser, Philip, and Zadorin, Dmitrij, *Towards a Typology of Soviet Mass Housing: Prefabrication in the USSR 1955–1991* (Berlin: DOM publishers, 2015).

Examples of unrenovated Soviet housing.

Figure 4 (left page):
Late Soviet mass housing with one-room apartments (this building type was known as 'the small-family project'; a variant of Series 104).
Author: Kārlis Lakševics

Figure 5 (right):
Late Soviet mass housing (series 602).
Author: Guido Sechi

spaces, such as the construction of squares and benches in courtyards, were implemented in the 1970s. Nevertheless, population growth put pressure on the sewage-treatment system, water supply, and maintenance of housing stock. Construction of the new district proceeded intensively during the 1980s. In 1993, the district had 26 buildings containing 1396 apartments. However, planning issues that had affected maintenance and service development since the 1970s became even more acute in the following decade; housing quality started to decline again, and, by the early 1990s, construction was halted; several projects remained unfinished. In the end many recreational and service buildings envisaged for the industrial zone were never built. In 1990 the town council acknowledged that the rapid development of the industrial area had created environmental pollution problems, which led to a halt in industrial and infrastructural development. By then, the town had 95 apartment buildings. The only major intervention in the 1990s was improvement of the water-supply system, while the municipality struggled to provide maintenance amid economic and financial hardships. Recovery started in the early 2000s, when

Figure 6:
1950s two-storey house in
the Stalinist Neoclassical style.
Author: Kārlis Lakševics

Figure 7:
Example of unrenovated Soviet housing.
Detail of unrenovated late Soviet mass housing.
Author: Kārlis Lakševics

many unfinished projects were finally completed and the service infrastructure was substantially improved.[13]

13 Ribickis, Māris, Olaines būvniecības un infrastruktūras attīstība [Olaine construction and infrastructural development] (Olaine: History and Art Museum, 2020).

Community life, culture, and attitudes

While the 1990s saw significant industrial downsizing, several factories managed to survive. The town has largely retained its industrial identity as a source of pride, reflected in city branding initiatives and residents' narratives of their working lives. The paper 'Olaines būvniecības un infrastruktūras attīstība' (2020), a detailed history of the settlement's development since the establishment of the peat-extraction site in 1939 written by Māris Ribickis, a leading expert at Olaine History and War Museum, conveys a narrative of resilience and recovery in recent years. This is also supported by data on employment, which show a 38 per cent increase in jobs between 2011 and 2021. The persistence of the industrial economy is also reflected in the local community culture and the distinctive character of local politics. Olaine is one of the few Latvian municipalities governed by the Latvian Social Democratic Workers' Party (LSDSP), a historical party of the Latvian left, originally founded by local Mensheviks after World War I. Although the party has been a marginal political force in the country as a whole for the past 20 years, a recent partial recovery has seen it dominate the municipality's electoral landscape over the same period. The fact that the party – refounded in the 1990s as a mix of former social-democratic dissidents and 'reformed' communists – has roots not only among industrial

Figure 8:
Public spaces in Olaine.
Canal in Olaine town centre.
Author: Guido Sechi

Figure 9:
Public spaces in Olaine.
Olaine open-air market.
Author: Kārlis Lakševics

workers but also among Soviet industrial management is one of the likely factors behind this unusual tendency. Residents sometimes credit factory directors for trying to shelter workers during the hardships of the 1990s. Tellingly, the first Social Democratic mayor of Olaine in the early 2000s, Jānis Pavlovičs – whom many residents associate with the first stages of development and recovery after the 1990s – was the head of the local trade union in the 1970s. However, Social Democratic administrations have also been associated with active urban development since the 2000s (mostly driven by the EU's Cohesion Fund). The municipality's planning vision during these decades has, unusually for Latvia, been based on welfarist and developmentalist principles. This vision is reflected in the programmatic development strategy until 2040, in which neoliberal language emphasising local competitiveness – widespread in Latvian spatial planning discourse – is kept to a minimum, while there is a strong emphasis on expansion of social welfare measures, with strong echoes of Scandinavian social democratic corporatism. Although the welfarist language is partly transposed from the rhetoric of the EU Cohesion Fund, the discourse outlined in local official documents is significantly different from that prevalent in Latvian mainstream politics.

By conducting welfarist and developmentalist policies, the LSDSP administration has also managed to attract the votes of a large part of the Russian-speaking community, which would have otherwise been likely to support minority-interest parties. This has been a way to rebalance the ethnic polarisation and tensions that existed in the

Figure 10:
Public space in Olaine.
Detail of Olaine town centre.
Author: Kārlis Lakševics

late 1980s and the early 1990s between supporters of the national independence movement and Soviet sympathisers.

At the same time, Olainfarm engages in some initiatives that echo the welfare-provision responsibilities borne by companies in the Soviet era. However, these initiatives are framed in the contemporary language of corporate responsibility, and some of them may be regarded as tokenistic. Examples include a €50 donation for each newborn child in the town in the summer of 2023 and the commissioning of the construction of an Orthodox church.

However, socio-economic issues among town residents are far from irrelevant. Town administration officials mentioned the elderly and large families as the most financially fragile categories. Retired residents who have lived in the town for several decades have developed dense social ties that help them cope with financial and health-related hardships. Interpersonal networks are less dense for newcomers; however, people who have moved recently tend to develop a sense of attachment to place. Overall, attracting suburbanites by 'competing' with other municipalities is presented as a necessity to attract needed resources, but this influx in turn creates pressure on services and amenities.

The residents interviewed generally stated that interethnic tensions and divisions are very rare in the town today. Municipal officials believe that 'desegregated' leisure and cultural activities play an essential role – even more so in recent years as everyday life has become more atomised. For instance, 'bilingual' musical events are given priority whenever possible. Nevertheless, intra-community divides do exist, usually along lines relating to socio-economic status and

Figure 11:
Public space in Olaine.
Zemgales Street in Olaine town centre, with early Soviet mass housing (*khrushchevkas*) and Stalin-era Neoclassical housing.
Author: Guido Sechi

generational differences. Some residents complain that a segment of the community – those who still have ties to the local industry – are still 'stuck in Soviet times'. Although they do not usually elaborate on these statements, they seem to imply that certain categories of fellow residents reject urban development and modernisation. However, this 'rejection' is often due to financial constraints rather than cultural mindset. Some of these 'critical' residents describe the town as a 'dormitory district' without attractive qualities due to its Soviet industrial origins and heritage.

Housing and social infrastructure: heritage and development

Residents of Olaine appreciate Soviet heritage mostly in terms of planning and services rather than architecture. Both residents and policymakers emphasise the compactness/walkability and the relative completeness of the inherited infrastructure, on which post-1990 administrations have capitalised. With some exceptions, residents regard serialised housing as unassuming rather than bad; despite the town having a significant variety of types of mass housing, most residents barely differentiate between them and have not developed a discourse about the aesthetic qualities of these buildings. Nevertheless, residents state that some series have clearly shown more drawbacks than others with respect to material quality; silicate brick is regarded as superior as insulation to red brick. The attitude towards industrial and Soviet heritage is not expressed explicitly in official documents. Although only a few pre-Soviet sites and buildings are listed as

Examples of renovated Soviet mass housing.

Figure 12 (left):
Renovated late-Soviet brick mass housing (Series 103).
Author: Kārlis Lakševics

Figure 13 (centre):
Renovated early-Soviet mass housing.
Author: Kārlis Lakševics

Figure 14 (right):
Renovated early-Soviet mass housing with new children's playground.
Author: Kārlis Lakševics

'historical heritage', the development strategy states that Soviet-era buildings and infrastructure may be considered for such a designation 'in the future', emphasising dynamic continuity over rejection, in line with the administration's developmentalist discourse.

At all levels, however, Soviet residential buildings are not considered 'heritage', and while renovation projects may sometimes show a spirit of 'homage' to the original design projects, this is not systematic and happens only on a project-by-project basis. At the same time, demolition proposals have not been discussed.

Housing renovation based on EU funds has been one of the key policies of municipal administration in recent years. The LSDSP programme for the (successful) 2017 elections outlined generous subsidies for housing renovation and interest on loans, plus a 90 per cent reduction in property tax for residents of renovated buildings. As of August 2023, 33 buildings (23.5 per cent of the multi-apartment housing stock) had been renovated, indicating a higher rate than in many other urban areas in Latvia. While in other Latvian towns the renovation process is generally decentralised – the loans to cover renovation costs are taken out by homeowner associations that are often created solely for this purpose – in Olaine, the municipal maintenance company takes out the loan, and only one homeowner association was active at the time of writing. However, residents have taken the initiative to start the process in all renovation projects.

Overall, the residents interviewed gave a positive assessment of the housing renovation process. In contrast with the 'decentralisation' arguments proposed by policymakers in other towns, centralisation of the process is seen as complementary to grassroots initiatives rather than a hampering factor. Moreover, residents do not criticise the authorities for 'offloading responsibilities', as often happens in urban areas where homeowner associations are at the centre of the renovation process. The residents interviewed also stressed the importance of information and dialogue in successfully overcoming mistrust between authorities and residents – one of the major problems affecting municipality-led renovation in other towns in Latvia. Criticisms, if any, focus on the authorities' lack of vision and concepts for renovation – that is, on a lack of long-term and systematic decision-making. For example, the rapid rise of renovation projects in the past few years has created debates on whether municipal aesthetic guidelines should exist for these projects, as colours and balcony designs used in renovating apartment buildings in the same series have varied widely.

Some residents also lament that problems related to housing quality – such as bad insulation – have not been solved by renovation. However, members of the town administration with responsibility for maintenance mostly call this a 'myth' deriving from a single unfortunate case of renovation.

At the same time, development of public infrastructure and public spaces is regarded by residents as part of the same development process and is evaluated positively. Public spaces appear to have been well maintained and developed in the last 20 years thanks to the effective management of EU Cohesion Fund money. Spaces and amenities have been improved (modernised) by expanding and renovating Soviet-era infrastructure. However, some complain about the municipal administration's failure to consult and involve residents when planning new public spaces and buildings; others disagree with the transfer of some amenities and functions to the nearby village of Jaunolaine (the administrative centre of the municipality's rural parish, framed as a 'less deserving' settlement due to its lack of industrial history and activity). Some mention that while welfare services and amenities are adequate, green spaces still require improvement. Other complaints reflect the impact of broader tendencies and policies, from spatial polarisation to 'gentrification': some residents lament the lack of services and amenities that are concentrated in Riga – a reminder of Olaine's relatively peripheral status – whereas others complain about hypothetical plans to get rid of traditional spaces, such as replacing the open-air market with a 'modern' supermarket. In any case, the active development of the townscape and social infrastructure has had a positive impact on residents' attachment to place; many describe the town as 'clean', 'safe', and 'family-friendly'. Combined with the town's closeness to Riga and Jelgava, these qualities are also attractive to newcomers. However, some residents complain of a lack of support for further infrastructural renovation and development on the part of other residents, who they see as 'stuck in Soviet times'.

Conclusions

Unlike the dominant neoliberal discourse – which tends to emphasise decentralised decision-making in infrastructural maintenance, particularly with regard to housing – the integrated approach to housing renovation employed by the municipal administration of Olaine seems to be successful among its residents and to have a beneficial impact on their involvement in 'grassroots' activities. Building on the planning and infrastructural heritage of the recent past as an 'integrated' set of resources has allowed the town not only to retain and capitalise upon its industrial infrastructure, but also, as in other small monotowns, to attract and accommodate suburbanites looking for a convenient residential location with urban-standard infrastructure. Thus, consideration of Olaine's experience could be an opportunity to redefine discourses and strategies at the national level. At the same time, the local 'welfarist' model operates under vastly different conditions from those of the twentieth-century welfare state. The town planning vision devised for Olaine in the 1960s was ambitious but was partially hampered by a number of factors: the excessive focus on quantitative results and exaggerated targets of central planning,[14] the economic crisis of the late USSR, and the harshness of the transition in the 1990s. The first two factors accounted for the low quality of some of the built housing stock and the delayed provision of service infrastructure and amenities, particularly in the late Soviet years. The latter led to the neglect of maintenance and welfare services and put the survival of industry at serious risk. The preservation of industry and welfare infrastructure was a remarkable achievement. However, this success is still inscribed within the broader context of neoliberalisation and austerity, which requires the embrace of the logic of competition to attract suburbanites in order to obtain the necessary resources for further development and maintenance. This creates, at least in the short term, additional pressure on services and infrastructure, as well as potential tensions with the local, tight-knit community culture and thereby poses further challenges for the municipality.

Finally, the tensions between and among residents over decision-making in public spaces, allocation of resources and services in the municipality, and priorities of development seem to imply there is no lack of divisions in the community, where socio-economic differences certainly play a role. We argue that the development vision of the Olaine administration incorporates a tacit (and somehow

[14] Smith, Mark B., *Property of Communists: The Urban Housing Program from Stalin to Khrushchev* (DeKalb, IL: University of Northern Illinois Press, 2010).

ambiguous) embrace of the Soviet planning heritage, building upon an integrated understanding of infrastructural development by adjusting, but not distorting, its original goals and improving its outcomes. From the point of view of this understanding, 'Soviet heritage' is not just a set of architectural or spatial objects considered individually but a 'scaffold' based on 'infrastructural thinking' that can be both extended and partially repurposed.[15] This can explain both the retention of a centralised approach to housing renovation while simultaneously 'opening up' to bottom-up initiatives and the incremental approach to the improvement and revitalisation of common and public spaces.

However, it is not only urban design and planning that constitute this heritage but also social relations and community life.[16] At this level, suburbanisation may create a challenge. Nevertheless, municipal authorities seem to be aware that initiatives – and, above all, common spaces and services – are needed to 'integrate' newcomers and to avoid or reduce new intra-community divides (just as they have been useful in the past to defuse interethnic tensions). At the same time, demographic expansion beyond the town limits – into the rural part of Olaine municipality – may be an opportunity rather than a burden, leading to an extension of the network of welfare infrastructure and services beyond the town limits, thereby reducing urban–rural inequalities. Whatever the objective constraints the national economy provides to developmental ambitions, this balanced approach – acknowledging the central role of urban industrial culture in development but extending the outreach of urban services beyond it – can help manage current transformations for the better.

Finally, it may be argued that the survival of the industrial infrastructure and culture – something that not all monotowns in Latvia have managed to retain – has been a crucial factor in fostering the developmental vision discussed above. The infrastructural framework – including housing, public spaces, and welfare and transport services – can certainly also be used and repurposed in partially or fully de-industrialised contexts, but its social and cultural content is inevitably different,[17] and this can have significant consequences, particularly concerning development and renovation as structurally coherent rather than fragmented decision-making processes. In such contexts it is unlikely that Olaine's 'non-neoliberal' approach to heritage and development can be reproduced.

15 Zarecor, Kimberly Ellen, 'What Was so Socialist About the Socialist City? Second World Urbanity in Europe', *Journal of Urban History*, vol. 44, No. 1, 2018, pp. 95–117.

16 Bocharnikova, Daria, and Harris, Steven E., 'Second World Urbanity: Infrastructures of Utopia and Really Existing Socialism', *Journal of Urban History*, vol. 44, No. 1, 2018, pp. 3–8.

17 Lakševics, Kārlis, Sechi, Guido, Zeiļa, Regita and Bērziņš, Māris, 'Between Adaptation and Alienation: Socio-Infrastructural Dynamics in Two Small Latvian Monotowns', unpublished paper (under review).

08

Purvciems microrayon in Riga, Latvia.
Unravelling the inherited residential patchwork

Marina Sapunova and Ekaterina Gladkova

Tracing the spatial evolution of the Purvciems microrayon in the broader context of Riga's development

One of the 58 urban districts in modern-day Riga, Purvciems belongs to the districts of mass housing, or *microrayons*, constructed in Riga from the late 1950s to the early 1990s (Fig. 1). Compared to other mass housing districts, Purvciems covers quite a large area – 501.7 hectares; it is one of the two most densely populated areas (along with Pļavnieki), with 109.79 people per hectare.[1] As of 2021, 55,022 people resided here.[2] However, this is one area where mass housing was constructed not on undeveloped land but on the site of a village with low-rise buildings. In addition to the 1955 city master plan, a 'red-line plan' (a plan showing the boundaries of planned streets) was developed for Purvciems,[3] envisioning an entirely new layout accommodating high-rise housing. Subsequently, in 1964, based on the 1955 red-line plan, a planning project for Purvciems was developed, encompassing building plans, engineering communications, transportation, building types, and more.[4] Nevertheless, during the implementation phase, the developers had to deviate significantly from the initial plan – the 1955 red-line plan – and the ideas developed in 1964. The street structure that we see in the area today largely took shape before the 1950s. The construction plan had to be significantly adapted to fit this existing structure and pre-existing houses (Fig. 2).

On a broader scale, the development of mass housing districts in cities under the Soviet regime followed a similar trend.[5] While some microrayons were built on the sites of villages, preserving at least the street grid (e.g. Chulkovo in Tula), many underwent complete transformations in layout and street configuration (e.g. Novye Cheryomushki in Moscow). The 'modernisation' and infrastructural improvement of rural areas also had another aspect – erasure of the memory of the original place, its way of life, and its social composition.[6] A different situation unfolded in Purvciems, where single-family houses from the former village, the two- to three-storey housing from the first post–World-War-II years, and the primary street grid became part of the developing district. The typological diversity of construction from different periods became a characteristic and complex feature of the Purvciems district.

The district's name is derived from the Latvian *Hausmana purvs* ('Hausman swamp'); 'Purvciems' literally translates as 'swamp village'. This toponym goes back to the seventeenth and eighteenth

---

1   City Population, s.v. 'Purvciems – Quarter in Riga City', 1 January 2021, <https://citypopulation.de/en/latvia/rigacity/LV113992__purvciems/>, accessed 15 December 2023.

2   Ibid.

3   Latvijas Arhitektūras muzeja fondos, Red lines plan map, Purvciems planning project, 1955, p. 2.

4   Latvijas Arhitektūras muzeja fondos, Poyasnitel'naya zapiska k proyektu detal'noy planirovki 'Purvciems', [Explanatory note to the detailed planning project], vols. 1–2, 1964.

5   Drėmaitė, Marija, *Baltic Modernism: Architecture and Housing in Soviet Lithuania* (Berlin: DOM publishers, 2017).

6   Crawford, Christina E., *Spatial Revolution: Architecture and Planning in the Early Soviet Union* (Ithaca, NY: Cornell University Press, 2022).

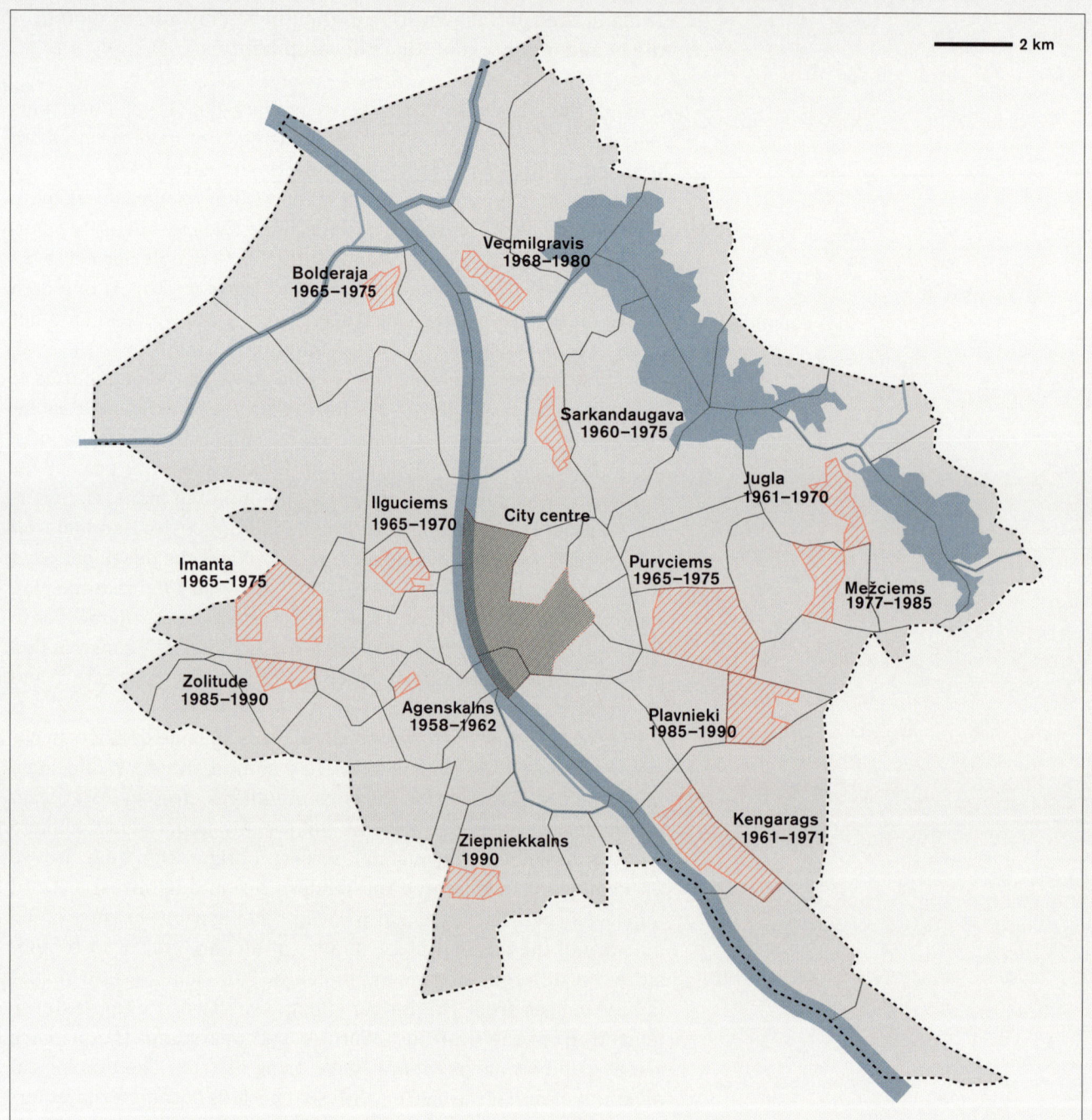

Figure 1:
Location of the Purvciems microrayon in Riga.
Source: Ekaterina Gladkova, 2023, based on Treija, Sandra, and Bratuškins, Uģis, 'Socialist Ideals and Physical Reality: Large Housing Estates in Riga, Latvia', *Housing Estates in the Baltic Countries*, 2019

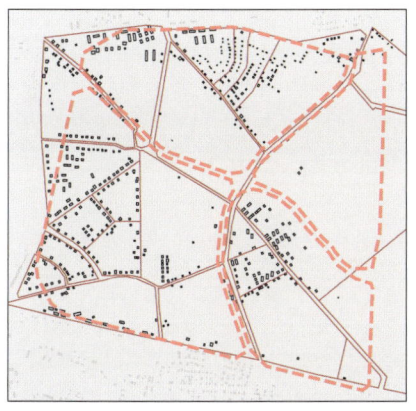
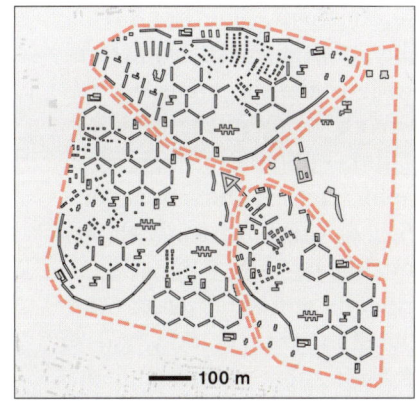

1955   **1964**   **2023**

Figure 2:
A comparison of red lines (boundaries between public spaces and street blocks), as planned in 1955, realised in 1964, and existing in 2023.

——— Boundaries of street blocks
- - - - Projected red lines

Ekaterina Gladkova, 2023, based on Latvijas Arhitektūras muzeja fondos, red-line plan map, Purvciems planning project, 1955, p. 2, and Latvijas Arhitektūras muzeja fondos, Poyasnitel'naya zapiska k proyektu detal'noy planirovki 'Purvciems' [Explanatory note to detailed planning project], 1964, vol. 1–2, 1964.

7   Latvijas Arhitektūras muzeja fondos, Red lines plan map, Purvciems planning project, 1955, p. 2.

centuries, when the area was largely uninhabitable due to its boggy terrain and soil structure. Over time the swamp gradually became less dangerous as the peat layers at the bottom dried up. As the edges of the swamp became more habitable, the settlement of Purvciems was established. Part of Purvciems was incorporated into Riga in 1828, while the remainder was not included in the city's administrative boundaries until 1924. The development of this neighbourhood was outlined in the Riga master plan, drawn up in 1923 under the leadership of the architect Arnolds Lamze. The main principles of the plan stipulated that only extensive low-rise buildings were permitted on the city's periphery.

Additionally, the soil quality here restricted the construction of anything other than low-rise structures. On the master plan the area of Purvciems was considerably larger and included the current districts of Plavnieki, Dārzciems, and Dreiliņi. The existing housing was concentrated on streets with water and sewerage connections, such as A. Deglava, Purvciema, Stirnu, and Vestienas streets. Some streets, such as Ieriku, Madones, Strautu, Vaidavas, and others, existed only on plans or were only realised in small segments due to the complicated soil conditions. Looking at the detailed planning project (*proyekt detalnoy planirovki, PDP*) of 1955, which shows the basic layout and the layout of red lines,[7] it is evident that the entire development of this area consists of single- and multi-family low-rise houses made from wood or masonry and standing on individual plots of land.

The post-war period of the 1950s was marked by a shift from construction of small buildings to mass housing projects driven by demographic growth and industrial development. The first Soviet master plan for Riga in 1955, led by the architect Vasilyev, prioritised the establishment of self-contained residential areas on the city's outskirts, especially on the left bank, to meet the growing housing demands.[8] From 1945 to 1959 Latvia's population increased 2.5 times, driven by natural demographic factors and migration. Housing issues and their resolution were political priorities, with the state fully subsidising housing and municipal services.[9] In newspaper articles accompanying the publication of the master plan in the 1950s and later, the deterioration of the old masonry and wooden housing stock is mentioned as an issue and a substantial argument for transitioning to mass standardised construction methods.[10,11]

Subsequent Soviet master plans for Riga in 1969 and 1984 focused primarily on extensive development of areas for housing and industrial purposes, based on projected growth of the urban population.[12] The plans encompassed development of not only Riga itself but also areas within a radius of 50–70 kilometres. Furthermore, expansion also targeted already developed low-rise areas, which were to be partially or entirely demolished and replaced with standardised multi-storey residential buildings. Valiulyte has noted that approximately half (eight of 14) of the microrayons examined in the study were built on the site of existing developments.[13] The aim was to provide housing and living space for the growing urban population. Given the land nationalisation that accompanied the Soviet regime, the planners largely proceeded on the premise that transforming, significantly densifying, or completely reconstructing already developed areas was in line with political decisions regarding industrialisation of housing construction.

Continuing the ideas of developing mass residential areas in Riga, the new street grid for Purvciems was presented as a part of the planning project in 1955, while the housing plan was ready in 1964, with construction commencing in the 1970s and extending through to the early 1980s. As emphasised by Neighborhood+, a local Riga media outlet,[14] 'the long and disjointed planning and construction process meant that microrayons were rarely realised by the same teams that developed the master plan, thus losing the clarity and strength of the original idea. Purvciems was one of those districts in Riga that underwent multiple, separate stages of development.' On the one hand, the initial idea underwent significant transformation, for example, with regard to the spatial organisation of residential sections. On the other hand, Purvciems may serve as an example of

8   Hess, Daniel Baldwin and Tammaru, Tiit, 'Modernist Housing Estates in the Baltic Countries: Formation, Current Challenges and Future Prospects', in Hess, Daniel Baldwin and Tammaru, Tiit (eds.), *Housing Estates in the Baltic Countries: The Legacy of Central Planning in Estonia, Latvia and Lithuania* (Cham: Springer, 2019), pp. 3–27.

9   Tsenkova, Sasha, *Housing Change in East and Central Europe: Integration or Fragmentation?* (Abingdon UK: Routledge, 2017).

10 Asaris, Gunārs, 'Rīgas ģenerālais attīstības plāns' [Riga general development plan] in *Māksla №2*, 1 April 1969.

11 Asaris, Gunārs, 'Uzmanību: rekonstrukcija!', [Attention: reconstruction!], in *Māksla №2*, 1 April 1968.

12 Treija, Sandra and Bratuškins, Uģis, 'Socialist Ideals and Physical Reality: Large Housing Estates in Riga, Latvia' in Hess, Daniel Baldwin and Tammaru, Tiit (eds.), *Housing Estates in the Baltic Countries: The Legacy of Central Planning in Estonia, Latvia and Lithuania* (Cham: Springer, 2019), pp. 161–180.

13 Valiulyte, Jomante, *Urban Transformation of Riga's Microrayons – From Sustainable Urban Design Perspective. Case Study: Mežciems* (master's thesis, Karlskrona, Sweden: Blekinge Institute of Technology / TU Braunschweig: Institute for Sustainable Urbanism, 2013).

14 'Loved, Hated, Misunderstood: Microrayons of Riga', *Neighborhood +*, 19 August 2023, <https://neighborhood.lv/en/real-estate/loved-hated-misunderstood-microrayons-riga/>, accessed 19 December 2023.

Figure 3:
Purvciems: a modernist residential microrayon on previously developed territory.
Photo: V. Lisitsyna (Latinform), from the newspaper *Rigas Balss*, 12 October 1978.

a more 'continuative' and less normative approach to the genesis of a new modernist residential area on previously developed territory (Fig. 3), even taking into account the nationalisation of land by the Soviet regime.

In particular, while the modernist project of mass housing construction significantly transformed the low-rise suburbs of major cities and the countryside itself as part of Soviet industrial policy, the case of Purvciems allows for a different perspective. The book *The Ideal Communist City*, originally published in English in 1968 and now reissued, frames the question of the future city around the idea of evolutionary or organic development: 'Today the city does not fulfil its essential purpose, which is to be an organic community ... We must find a structure that responds organically to the social and economic functions of the new urban life.'[15] Discussion of the future of socialist living spaces in the 1950s was built on ideas and questions about how to respond to rapid urbanisation using socialist ideals and collective spaces; the everyday life of the working person; the functional division of space for work, public life, and home; and future challenges to be faced by growing cities.

Looking at these questions from today's perspective, they remain just as relevant, and as a society or as planners, we continue to seek spatial answers to them. Finding ways to improve the quality of a space remains a planning task to be tackled by a collective effort.[16] The story of the Purvciems district reveals the opportunities for and consequences of spatial adaptability in a mass housing project, even if this was not the initial goal of the planning project. The result reveals how different layers and types of housing can coexist within the boundaries of a single district, and what values or challenges this can offer for its transformation or renewal.

15 Gutnov, Alexei, Baburov, Andrei, Djumenton, Georgi, Kharitonova, Zoya, Lezava, Ilya, and Sadovskij, Stanislav, *The Ideal Communist City*, eds. Bauer, Ute Meta, Oen, Karin G., and Tan, Pelin (Berlin: Weiss Publications, 2022).

16 Healey, Patsy, *Making Better Places: The Planning Project in the Twenty-First Century*, (London: Bloomsbury, 2017).

Planning, adapting, constructing, and transforming Purvciems, 1955 to 2023

Purvciems before and after the project of 1964

Until 1964 the residential development of the Purvciems district primarily consisted of single-family housing, which constituted 87 per cent of the residential area and was characterised by single-storey private houses standing on individual plots of land. Part of the district's land was also utilised for vegetable gardens and orchards. The average block size varied from four to eight hectares, with individual plot sizes ranging from 600 to 1400 square metres. The housing density ranged from 510 to 645 square metres of living space per hectare of developed land (see the detailed planning project for the Purvciems district). In other words, this was a low-density suburb with numerous private owners engaging in subsistence farming on the accessible part of the territory, while the other part was marshy. The question of densification and standardisation in housing construction emerged in the early post-war years, although a strong trend initially supported construction of one-family houses. In September 1945 the first plots of land for construction of one-family houses were allocated and transferred to the jurisdiction of the district executive committees.[17] Initially, preference was given to demobilised Red Army personnel, senior officers, and generals. The master plan of 1955 later amended the rules, making construction of one-family houses more accessible to workers, engineers, and civil servants. The country provided loans and materials to developers interested in such projects under the condition that they used a standard project, held a land lease for a specified number of years, and maintained the land and the building in a good condition. Notably, the plots and buildings were not private property; they belonged to the state. In 1959 the construction of one-family houses was criticised for perceived inefficiency compared to mass housing, yet such houses continued to be built.

In several parts of the Purvciems district low-rise, multi-apartment housing was constructed, most notably two- to three-storey post-war Series-M3 buildings with four to 12 apartments. The M3 (along with M1 and M2) series belongs to Riga's first generation of standardised housing construction and was introduced immediately after World War II. The series was developed by the architects A. Reinfelds, L. Ose, and L. Plakane. While the primary construction material for

17 'Reshenie № 650 Rizhskogo gorodskogo ispolnitel'nogo komiteta o vydelenii zemel'nykh uchastkov dlya individual'nogo stroitel'stva g. Rigi' [Decision no. 650 of the Riga City Executive Committee on allocation of land plots for individual construction in the city of Riga], in *LPSP Ziņotājs*, No.195, 20 September 1945.

M1, M2, and M3 buildings is brick, there are substantial wooden elements, such as floors, partitions, stairs, and ceilings. In M2 and M3 buildings ceilings could be of either wood or concrete. The eight-square-metre kitchen might have a wood-burning stove, depending on the version. The M2 and M3 series were designed for construction by various ministries or enterprises. Industrial developments in nearby areas, such as the State Electrotechnical Factory and the Riga Dairy Plant, required housing for their workers. However, housing policy soon shifted from one-family and low-rise buildings to denser, faster-built mass housing projects in order to accommodate the needs of the growing population.

In 1955 the planning project already showed red lines indicating road construction and the formation of large plots for future microrayon-based development (Fig. 2).[18] The Detailed Planning Project for the Purvciems district, established in 1964 by the Riga City General Planning Institute (Byuro Generalnogo plana goroda Rigi) to accommodate 60,000 residents, underscored the importance of the Housing Placement Report, 1966–1970 in justifying housing construction in this area. Approved by a resolution of the Riga City Committee of the Communist Party of Latvia and the Executive Committee of the City Council on 14 December 1963, this report highlighted factors such as proximity to the city centre and a potential development area of 1500 hectares, with an initial phase covering only half this area.

As Sandra Treija and Uģis Bratuškins have noted,[19] the decade of housing construction in Riga from 1965 to 1975 emphasised an urban planning approach that integrated green spaces, interweaving residential structures, public centres, and boulevard corridors. This concept, influenced by international modernism, was easily conceivable in open areas unrestricted by existing development but posed challenges when applied to already built-up areas. Nonetheless, the Purvciems project envisioned the transformation and demolition of existing structures by proposing a unified green zone, a transport infrastructure, and non-residential facilities, aiming for significant changes to the existing layout.

In terms of type of construction, in 1964 78 per cent of houses were listed as masonry and 22 per cent as wooden. Approximately 70 per cent of the houses were reported to be in good condition and had a connection to the public water supply. The majority (81 per cent) were single-storey, 18 per cent were two-storey, and one per cent were three-storey. The project involved demolishing 22,100 square metres or 22 per cent of all existing residential buildings.

---

18 See Grava, Sigurd, 'The Urban Heritage of the Soviet Regime'. *Journal of the American Planning Association*, vol. 59, No. 1, 1993, pp. 9–30; Drėmaitė, Marija, 'The Exceptional Design of Large Housing Estates in the Baltic Countries', in Hess, Daniel Baldwin and Tammaru, Tiit (eds.), *Housing Estates in the Baltic Countries: The Legacy of Central Planning in Estonia, Latvia and Lithuania* (Cham: Springer, 2019), pp. 71–93.

19 Treija, Sandra and Bratuškins, Uģis, 'Socialist Ideals and Physical Reality: Large Housing Estates in Riga, Latvia' in Hess, Daniel Baldwin, and Tammaru, Tiit (eds.), *Housing Estates in the Baltic Countries: The Legacy of Central Planning in Estonia, Latvia and Lithuania* (Cham: Springer, 2019), pp. 161–180.

Compensation for demolition included being given an apartment in a new residential building. This was calculated per square metre of living space, leading to a 15 per cent increase in construction costs per square metre. The first stage of demolition created space for the construction of new residential buildings, cultural and utility services, roadways, and transport structures. Further demolition was foreseen for the creation of communal green spaces, protective strips alongside motorways, etc. The preserved buildings consisted mainly of one- and two-storey masonry structures with a maximum of 30 per cent wear.

The planning documentation outlined specific principles only for Purvciems I, with a projected density of 2370 square metres per hectare and a mix of five-, nine-, and 16-storey buildings, as depicted on the plan of 1964. The planned residential area covered 690,000 square metres, with a gross density of 3270 square metres per hectare and a building coverage of 15 per cent.

Local development of standard house sections (section: in Soviet mass house-building a part or a whole of a building comprising a staircase – or staircase with elevator – and the apartments connected to this staircase on each floor from the bottom to the top of the building) was undertaken by Latgiprogorstroi. The urban planning principles included a hexagonal grid with five-storey buildings forming 50 per cent of the planned housing areas, ensuring views of greenery and good insolation. To break the monotony, nine-storey, wall-like buildings and 16-storey towers (29 per cent and 17 per cent, respectively) were strategically placed amongst the remaining buildings, 51 per cent of which had five storeys. Connectivity was emphasised through a new road system and a green pedestrian link from Biķernieku Forest to the city centre through Purvciems. New expressways on Braslas and A. Deglava streets were planned to enhance connectivity, with Braslas Street dividing the industrial complex and serving as a north–south connection.

Changes of 1969 and implementation of the plan

In 1969 a new master plan for Riga was published, and Purvciems became part of the new development plan for the city's eastern districts. To accommodate the changes introduced by the new general plan, Purvciems I had to be redesigned. One of the key issues was preservation of the existing low-rise housing, which was initially slated for demolition to make way for new residential areas, open spaces, and transport networks. The planning team at Pilsētprojekts, under the supervision of the architects Ē. Fogelis, M. Medinskis, I. Millers, and R. Dzene, modified the existing concept and preserved the existing street network. The housing stock of the new Purvciems I was planned to have a floor area of 730,000 square metres. Despite a reduction in the building area due to preservation of existing housing, the architects managed to plan the new district with a slightly larger amount of housing. Construction of Purvciems I got udnerway in 1969/1970 and was expected to be completed by the end of 1971. The new planning took into account the urban design principles of the 1964 project: where possible, a hexagonal grid of five-storey buildings was implemented, the centre and the entrance to Purvciems I were emphasised with a high-rise building, and a green city link was landscaped, all while retaining the existing structures. A second district (Purvciems II) was planned for construction in 1975, and a third district (Purvciems III) in the 1980s. After 1980 Purvciems II became Dārzciems and Purvciems III became Pļāvnieki.

Four types of series were used for the five-storey prefabricated buildings: Series 103, *Series 316/318*, the Lithuanian project (Series 464), and housing for small families.[20] The khrushchevka series, constructed of silicate brick, was the earliest and continued to be built until 1969. The type of house for small families, offering 20 one-room units on each floor, and the Lithuanian project were also utilised in almost every prefabricated district of Riga. The 103 series was special, as it was developed in the Latvian SSR in 1966 and implemented from 1971 onwards. Buildings in this series are constructed using a combination of bricks and prefabricated panels, offering advantages such as improved thermal insulation, flexibility for remodelling of apartments, relatively good construction quality, and practical, comfortable layouts with spacious rooms. This series remains popular due to its exterior load-bearing walls and ease of conversion.

Series 602 and Series 467 were used for the nine-storey buildings. The first Series-602 building in Riga was erected in 1967 on the corner of Dzelzavas and Vaidava streets. Series 467 is similar to Series 602 in layout and design but has a different façade. Unlike other panel houses, the outer walls of the nine-storey large-panel buildings in the 467 series can be decorated with coloured tiles or plastered with stone chips. Unlike the 602 series, these buildings have loggias. The 12-storey buildings were Series-104 prefabricated buildings of reinforced-concrete construction with two lifts.

Following implementation of the modified project, the district ended up with a mix of different building types: single-storey private houses

20 For the series, see Krišjāne, Zaiga, Bērziņš, Māris, Sechi, Guido, and Krūmiņš, Jānis, 'Residential Change and Socio-Demographic Challenges for Large Housing Estates in Riga, Latvia', in Hess, Daniel Baldwin and Tammaru, Tiit (eds.), *Housing Estates in the Baltic Countries: The Legacy of Central Planning in Estonia, Latvia and Lithuania* (Cham: Springer, 2019), pp. 225–245.

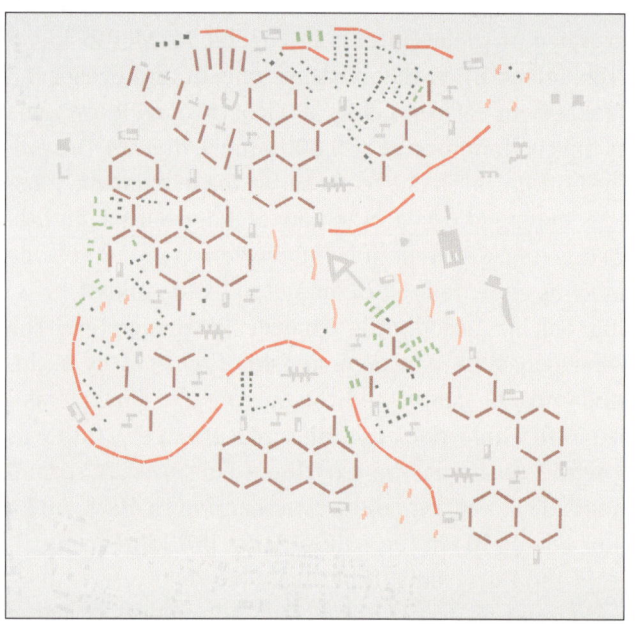 

with individual plots; two- and three-storey buildings with four to 12 apartments, and five-, nine-, and 12-storey standardised residential buildings with integrated, attached, or separate cultural and utility infrastructure (Fig. 4). Thus two types of spatial arrangement, oriented towards individual ownership (although a declaration of land nationalisation had been formally adopted in 1940) and communal use, are found within the boundaries of one district. This was largely an inherently contradictory coexistence in which, as Sigurd Grava has noted, from the outset in multi-storey buildings 'residents generally felt no responsibility for the spaces outside their own apartment.'[21] Standardised construction faced criticism early on for its monotony, uniformity, and aesthetics.[22] It was, in general, a fundamentally different way of organising space to maximise communal areas. However, this experience was to be explored in the years that followed.

Spatial transformation after 1990

Communal areas in microrayons came under significant pressure in Latvia and beyond immediately after the transition from state-regulated to free-market economies in the 1990s. They include open green or undeveloped areas as well as facilities for communal

Figure 4:
Mixture of housing types in Purvciems (left: the initial mix, based on detailed planning for Purvciems, 1964; right: the current state in 2023).

- ■ Single-family
- ■ 2-3-storey
- ■ 5-storey pre-fabricated
- ■ 9-storey pre-fabricated
- ■ 12, 16-storey pre-fabricated
- ■ post-Soviet

Source: Ekaterina Gladkova, 2023, based on Latvijas Arhitektūras muzeja fondos, *Poyasnitel'naya zapiska k proyektu detal'noy planirovki 'Purvciems'* [Explanatory note to the detailed planning project], 1964, vols. 1–2, 1964

21 Grava, Sigurd, 'The Urban Heritage of the Soviet Regime', *Journal of the American Planning Association*, vol. 59, No. 1, 1993, pp. 9–30.

22 Hess, Daniel Baldwin and Tammaru, Tiit, 'Modernist Housing Estates in the Baltic Countries: Formation, Current Challenges and Future Prospects' in Hess, Daniel Baldwin, and Tammaru, Tiit (eds.), *Housing Estates in the Baltic Countries: The Legacy of Central Planning in Estonia, Latvia and Lithuania* (Cham: Springer, 2019), pp. 3–27.

services and shared spaces within multi-apartment buildings. Originally conceived as a benefit, common space and the experience of shared space have faced, and continue to face, significant tensions. By the end of the Soviet regime communal space had come to mean 'unclaimed' as opposed to 'collectively managed' space.[23] Land reform, privatisation, and other market reforms further intensified this sense of being unclaimed, highlighting the issue of efficiency in the use of urban land resources. This was particularly pronounced closer to the city centre, particularly in the Purvciems area.

Categorising land as used and unused, depending upon whether it has been developed or is undeveloped, allows a different perspective on the microrayon, one that questions how much genuinely undeveloped land the municipal budget can sustain. A resource of unused land, viewed as potential for private development and as an object of municipal expenditure on maintenance and improvement, inevitably prompts inquiries into municipal land policy. Microrayons constructed with excess open space, specifically communal areas, represent both potential for income from development (including taxes for the city budget) and potential for high costs (if a significant part of the land remains on the city's balance sheet).

A third dimension is undeniably present: these areas can still influence the quality of the urban environment as public spaces bestowed by modernist development. However, the concern is that this often remains an ideal of socialism rather than a reality. A survey conducted in 1967 and 1968 revealed that 'the inhabitants of the new microrayon did not fully utilise the green areas because they were not satisfied with the available facilities. It was concluded that large urban spaces requiring considerable investment were not being used fully.'[24]

With the reduction of green and undeveloped areas available for densification, attitudes towards these areas have changed over time. Specifically, in Purvciems, compared to other mass housing districts in Riga, at least ten new developments were built by 2021,[25] influenced by the district's proximity to the city centre and relatively low population density with a mix of types of building. The new development has brought both positive trends, such as new infrastructure and landscaping, and negative aspects: the landscaping often caters to a limited audience, ignoring the fact that in Purvciems up to 23 per cent of residents are over 65 years old.[26] Moreover, part of the new development is enclosed, creating closed and isolated areas rather than integrating spatially with existing structures.[27]

---

23 Ibid.

24 Treija, Sandra, Bratuškins, Uģis and Koroļova, Alisa, 'Urban Densification of Large Housing Estates in the Context of Privatisation of Public Open Space: The Case of Imanta, Riga', *Architecture and Urban Planning*, vol. 14, No. 1, 2018, pp. 105–110.

25 Koroļova, Alisa, Open Space *Transformations in Large-Scale Housing Estates of Riga in The Post-Socialist Period* (Riga: RTU Press, 2021).

26 Ibid.

27 Treija, Sandra, Bratuškins, Uģis, and Koroļova, Alisa, 'Urban Densification of Large Housing Estates in the Context of Privatisation of Public Open Space: The Case of Imanta, Riga', *Architecture and Urban Planning*, vol. 14, No. 1, 2018, pp. 105–110.

At the same time, the most significant changes since the 1990s relate to land issues. The two processes of land restitution and housing privatisation that took place in Latvia in the 1990s have effectively created two parallel worlds – landowners and homeowners (more than 80 per cent of the housing stock is privately owned) – that do not align with each other. This is particularly evident in Purvciems on the cadastral map (Fig. 5), where many boundaries overlap buildings constructed in the 1950s to the 1980s, legally segmenting them into numerous fragments. The political decision regarding the return of confiscated land plots has yet to be implemented in terms of compensation and demarcation, resulting in the incomplete establishment of fully fledged ownership and management for both returned plots and multi-apartment buildings.

This, combined with the issue of multiple owners in multi-apartment buildings, effectively hinders properly systematic territory management. The history of the area's evolution and complex transformations present an intriguing case for studying the governance of such districts. The possibilities and limitations of managing genuinely mixed-use territories at all levels are further complicated by the property restitution process, which plays a significant political role but has created numerous legal issues between property owners and tenants. Although the issue remains unresolved after 40 years, in practice it currently favours tenants as users but restricts their use of land and territory. The management of multi-apartment buildings

Figure 5:
The northern part of Purvciems microrayon, where two land plot structures are clearly visible, in 1955 (left) and 2023 (right).
Source: Ekaterina Gladkova, 2023, based on Latvijas Arhitektūras muzeja fondos, Red line plan map, Purvciems planning project, 1955, p. 2, and the public cadastral map of Riga in 2023

requires specific skills, as does managing the territory of the microrayon itself, which involves various types of land ownership.

Conclusion and discussion

The Purvciems case demonstrates that inherited complexity, multilayered ownership, past decisions, and political transformations present unresolved challenges. It raises questions about compromise and its costs, not only for owners of land or apartments, the municipality, or developers, but for society as a whole, in terms of willingness to compensate for the outcomes of past policy decisions and the values of modernist planning in the face of rising energy, climate, and equity challenges.

In many cases criticism of the construction of this period, shortly after its inception in the 1960s, is rooted in the monotony, uniformity, and aesthetics of standardised housing. The example of Purvciems, however, demonstrates that it is primarily unresolved legal and financial issues that constrain the management tools available for renovation and transformation of the development. Where continuity is maintained, individual homeowners or tenants continue their lives, benefit from the amenities of dense construction, and bring additional infrastructure to the area. The complexity of multiple unit ownership simultaneously puts pressure on multi-apartment housing, the supply of common land, and the boundaries of old plots. Despite the coexistence of the two systems, the one in which people live effectively operates because they care about the space by inertia. The cumulative political benefits and costs, economic and social, determine dominant factors in decision-making. Purvciems remains an evolving environment, close to the city centre, and in demand. Each new house contributes to increased density.

In the absence of a viable political solution, local initiatives have emerged, such as the proposal put forth by Liva Kreislere, Olya Trebuhina, and Tamara Kalantajevska, that in the absence of a resolution of the issue of land ownership, the communal space for a multi-apartment building is to be considered the roof, which apartment owners can use as public space.[28] In terms of preventing vandalism, this provides a more secure option as public space for the community of residents of a building. The transition from the physical dimension of space to the social dimension represents an overall attempt at, and approach to, rethinking heritage and the active appropriation of space.

28 Kreislere, Liva, Trebuhina, Olya, and Kalantajevska, Tamara, 'Roof Escape: Unlocking the Unused Potential of Riga's Post-Soviet Microrayons', *Future Architecture*, Call for Ideas 2019 <https://futurearchitectureplatform.org/projects/35dc5f91-0aba-4a6b-beff-e5b6572ff4be/>, accessed 3 January 2024.

Acknowledgement

The authors express their gratitude to Sofia Bakanova for her invaluable assistance and the sacrifice of her time in collecting archival materials for this paper.

References

Asaris, Gunārs, 'Rīgas ģenerālais attīstības plāns' [Riga general development plan], *Māksla №2*, 1 April 1969.

Asaris, Gunārs, 'Uzmanību: rekonstrukcija!' [Attention: reconstruction!], *Māksla №2*, 1 April 1968.

City Population, s.v. 'Purvciems – Quarter in Riga City', 1 January 2021, <https://citypopulation.de/en/latvia/rigacity/LV113992__purvciems/>, accessed 15 December 2023.

Crawford, Christina E., Spatial Revolution: *Architecture and Planning in the Early Soviet Union* (Ithaca, NY: Cornell University Press, 2022).

Drėmaitė, Marija, 'The Exceptional Design of Large Housing Estates in the Baltic Countries' in Hess, Daniel Baldwin, and Tammaru, Tiit (eds.), *Housing Estates in the Baltic Countries: The Legacy of Central Planning in Estonia, Latvia and Lithuania* (Cham: Springer, 2019), pp. 71–93.

Drėmaitė, Marija, Baltic *Modernism: Architecture and Housing in Soviet Lithuania* (Berlin: DOM publishers, 2017).

Freimane, Santa, 'Visual Identity of Riga 21st Century Multi-Apartment Developments', *Architecture and Urban Planning*, vol. 17, no. 1, 2021, pp. 46–54.

Garkāje, Līva, 'Soviet Serial Apartment Buildings in Riga Historical Centre Streetscape: 1945–1990', *Rigas Tehniskas Universitates Zinatniskie Raksti*, vol. 15, no. 1, 2019, pp. 122–130.

Grava, Sigurd, 'The Urban Heritage of the Soviet Regime', *Journal of the American Planning Association*, vol. 59, no. 1, 1993, pp. 9–30.

Gutnov, Alexei, Baburov, Andrei, Djumenton, Georgi, Kharitonova, Zoya, Lezava, Ilya, and Sadovskij, Stanislav, *The Ideal Communist City*, eds. Bauer, Ute Meta, Oen, Karin G., and Tan, Pelin (Berlin: Weiss Publications, 2022), annotated facsimile of 1968 edn. (i Press Series on the Human Environment), trans. Renee Neu Watkins.

Healey, Patsy, *Making Better Places: The Planning Project in the Twenty-First Century* (London: Bloomsbury, 2017).

Hess, Daniel Baldwin, and Tammaru, Tiit, 'Modernist Housing Estates in the Baltic Countries: Formation, Current Challenges and Future Prospects' in Hess, Daniel Baldwin, and Tammaru, Tiit (eds.), *Housing Estates in the Baltic Countries: The Legacy of Central Planning in Estonia, Latvia and Lithuania* (Cham: Springer, 2019), pp. 3–27.

Koroļova, Alisa, *Open Space Transformations in Large-Scale Housing Estates of Riga in the Post-Socialist Period* (Riga: RTU Press, 2021).

Kreislere, Liva, Trebuhina, Olya, and Kalantajevska, Tamara, 'Roof Escape: Unlocking the Unused Potential of Riga's Post-Soviet Microrayons', *Future Architecture*, Call for Ideas 2019, <https://futurearchitectureplatform.org/projects/35dc5f91-0aba-4a6b-beff-e5b6572ff4be/>, accessed 3 January 2024.

Krisjane, Zaiga, Berzins, Maris, Ivlevs, Artjoms, and Bauls, Andris, 'Who Are the Typical Commuters in the Post-Socialist Metropolis? The Case of Riga, Latvia', *Cities*, vol. 29, no. 5, 2012, pp. 334–340.

Krišjāne, Zaiga, Bērziņš, Māris, Sechi, Guido, and Krūmiņš, Jānis, 'Residential Change and Socio-Demographic Challenges for Large Housing Estates in Riga, Latvia' in Hess, Daniel Baldwin, and Tammaru, Tiit (eds.), *Housing Estates in the Baltic Countries: The Legacy of Central Planning in Estonia, Latvia and Lithuania* (Cham: Springer, 2019), pp. 225–245.

Latvijas Arhitektūras muzeja fondos, Red lines plan map, Purvciems planning project, 1955, p. 2.

Latvijas Arhitektūras muzeja fondos, Poyasnitel'naya zapiska k proyektu detal'noy planirovki 'Purvciems' [Explanatory note to the detailed planning project for Purvciems], vols. 1–2, 1964.

'Loved, Hated, Misunderstood: Microrayons of Riga', *Neighborhood +*, 19 August 2023, <https://neighborhood.lv/en/real-estate/loved-hated-misunderstood-microrayons-riga/, accessed 19 December 2023.

Plaut, Steven, and Uzulena, Egita, 'Architectural Design and the Value of Housing in Riga, Latvia', *International Real Estate Review*, vol. 9, no. 1, 2006, pp. 112–131.

'Reshenie № 650 Rizhskogo gorodskogo ispolnitel'nogo komiteta o vydelenii zemel'nykh uchastkov dlya individual'nogo stroitel'stva g. Rigi' [Decision No. 650 of Riga City Executive Committee on allocation of land plots for individual construction in the city of Riga], *LPSP Ziņotājs*, No. 195, 20 September 1945.

Treija, Sandra, and Bratuškins, Uģis, 'Socialist Ideals and Physical Reality: Large Housing Estates in Riga, Latvia' in Hess, Daniel Baldwin, and Tammaru, Tiit (eds.), *Housing Estates in the Baltic Countries: The Legacy of Central Planning in Estonia, Latvia and Lithuania* (Cham: Springer, 2019), pp. 161–180.

Treija, Sandra, Bratuškins, Uģis, and Koroļova, Alisa, 'Urban Densification of Large Housing Estates in the Context of Privatisation of Public Open Space: The Case of Imanta, Riga', *Architecture and Urban Planning*, vol. 14, No. 1, 2018, pp. 105–110.

Tsenkova, Sasha, *Housing Change in East and Central Europe: Integration or Fragmentation?* (Abingdon UK: Routledge, 2017).

Tsenkova, Sasha, 'Managing Change: The Comeback of Post-Socialist Cities', *Urban Research & Practice*, vol. 1, No. 3, 2008, pp. 291–310.

Tsenkova, Sasha, 'Perspective Chapter: Reimaging Affordable Housing through Adaptive Reuse of Built Heritage' in Battisti, Alessandra (ed.), *Future Housing* [working title] (London: IntechOpen, 2023), <doi:10.5772/intechopen.110072>, accessed 3 January 2024.

Valiulyte, Jomante, *Urban Transformation of Riga's Microrayons – From Sustainable Urban Design Perspective. Case Study: Mežciems* (master's thesis, Karlskrona, Sweden: Blekinge Institute of Technology / TU Braunschweig: Institute for Sustainable Urbanism, 2013).

09

North Saltivka in Kharkiv, Ukraine.
Spatial neighbourhood development: from socialist city plans to post-war reconstruction

Hlib Antypenko

Introduction: North Saltivka as one of Kharkiv's large housing estates

With a population of more than 1.4 million people (as of 2020), Kharkiv is the second largest city in Ukraine and an important cultural and educational centre in the eastern part of the country. Before the Russo-Ukrainian war, Kharkiv's housing stock comprised 603,974 apartments with an average of 21 square metres of residential space per person.[1] Most of this residential space was created during the period of socialist mass housing construction in the twentieth century.[2] The first large housing estates (LHEs) in Kharkiv appeared before World War II in the form of *sotsmista* (socialist cities) adjacent to the growing industry.[3] However, most LHEs were built in the period after the World War II (1956 – 1991) using prefabricated technology in accordance with the city's new master plan, approved in 1967. The new plan provided for a clear functional division of the city into eight production and residential planning areas, interconnected with the city centre, places of employment, and urban and suburban recreation areas.[4] The main goals laid down in the master plan were implemented for 20 years until the end of the 1980s and the collapse of the Soviet Union and resulted in 13 large residential areas appearing on the map of Kharkiv.[5] These were designed to meet the housing shortage in the growing city and to implement socialist ideology in everyday life. By the 1990s around 21 per cent or 7.36 million square metres of the total area of the city was occupied by LHEs from the post–World-War-II period.[6]

North Saltivka (Fig. 1) is one of the city's latest large housing developments built under socialism. Today it is also one of the most damaged residential areas in Kharkiv, having suffered during the Russian invasion of Ukraine in 2022 (Fig. 2). In the more than 40 years of its existence, North Saltivka has undergone a construction period, with the implementation of socialist urban architecture and principles, then post-socialist development, and, finally, mass destruction and social upheaval associated with the war. After many problems and neglect towards post-socialist housing estates such as North Saltivka before the war, these housing estates are now receiving abundant media attention, igniting public discussion about their post-war reconstruction. Nevertheless, some recent actions by the municipality, residents, and public organisations show a lack of strategic vision for the sustainable future of estates such as this: long-term challenges are being tackled with short-term solutions. What

1 'Residential fund of Kharkiv', *Derzhavna Sluzhba Statystyky Ukrainy*, 1 February 2020, <http://www.ukrstat.gov.ua/>, accessed 10 November 2023.

2 Antypenko, Hlib, 'Kharkiv Mass Housing Estates: Socialist Past and Post-Socialist Present', *Facing Post-Socialist Urban Heritage: DOCONF19 Proceedings*, 2019, pp. 18–21.

3 Didenko, Catherine, Bouryak, Oleksandr, and Antonenko, Nadia, 'Residential Housing in Kharkiv (Ukraine), 1920–1935', *ZARCH: Journal of Interdisciplinary Studies in Architecture and Urbanism*, 2016, pp. 68–85.

4 Bouryak, Oleksandr, Vihdorovich, Olha, Gayevyi, Yuriy, and Golovchenko, Andriy, 'Innovative Approaches in the Period of Mass Industrial Development (on the Example of Residential Areas of Kharkiv)', *IOP Conf. Series: Materials Science and Engineering, Innovative Technology in Architecture and Design*, 2020, pp. 1–11.

5 Bouryak, Oleksandr, Antonenko, Nadia, and Lavrentiev, Ilia, 'Leonid Tyulpa – The Architect of the Period of Mass Industrial Development', *ZARCH Journal of Interdisciplinary Studies in Architecture and Urbanism*, vol. 8, 2017, pp. 154–169.

6 Hrynevych, Olena, Haievoi, Yurij, Viatkin, Valerj, and Karzhinerova, Tetyana, 'Problemy rekonstruktsii zhytlovykh budynkiv, scho pobudovani u 60–70 rr. khh stolittia u misti Kharkovi', *Naukovyi visnyk budivnytstva*, vol. 104(2), 2021, pp. 140–146 (in Ukrainian).

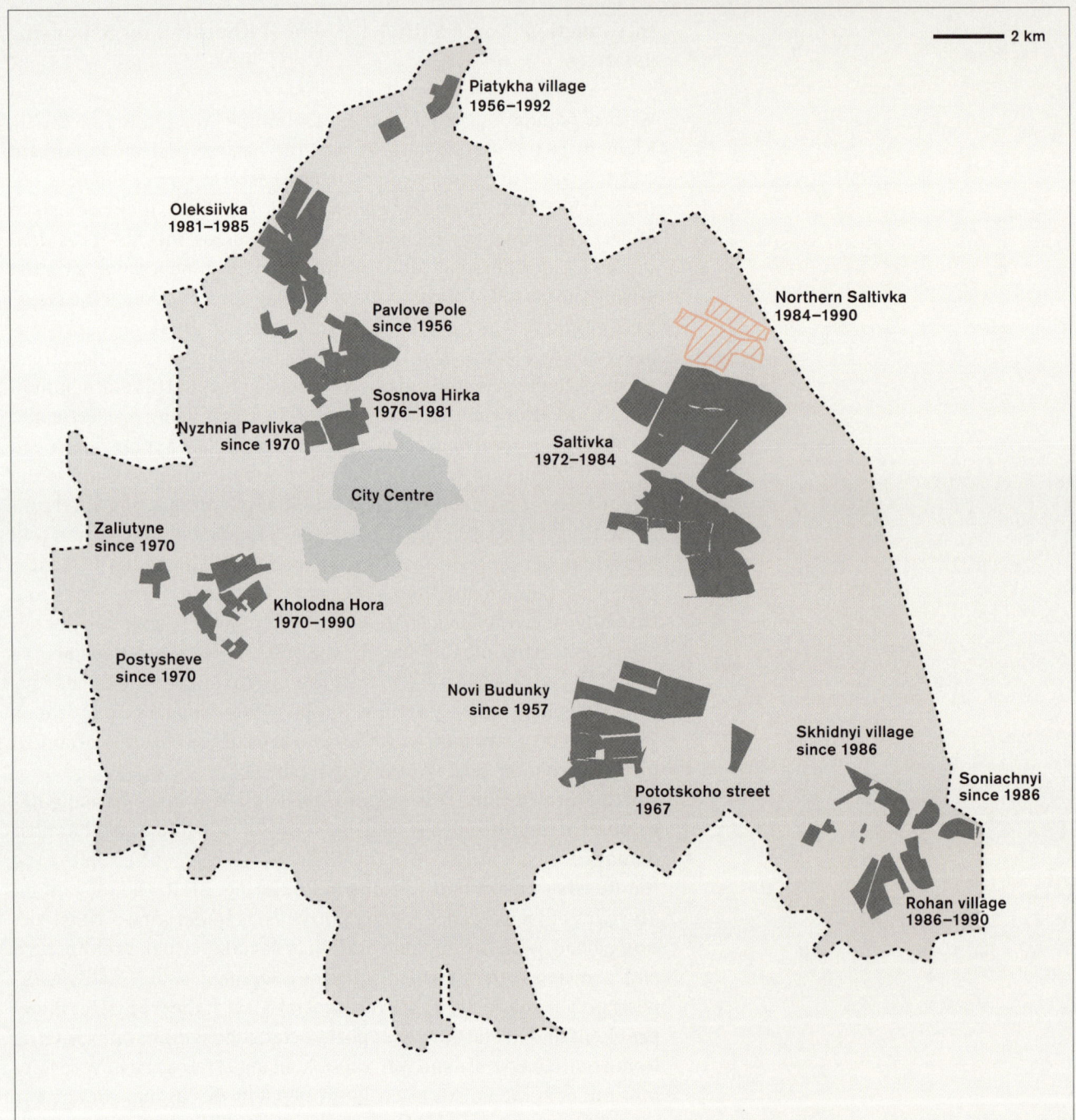

Figure 1:
North Saltivka and 12 other large post–World-War-II housing estates in Kharkiv, Ukraine.
Graphic: Author, 2023

Figure 2:
Damaged panel building in North Saltivka after Russian shelling.
Photo: Artur Kozhevnik, reproduced with permission of its author, 2022

7   Ignatov, Oleg and Petrenko, Viktoria, 'Layout of Residential Areas of Kharkov', *Stroitel'stvo i arkhitektura*, vol. 6, 1967, pp. 15–19.

was the original architectural and urban planning concept for North Saltivka? How has it changed in post-socialist times, and how much has it been affected by the war? What actions are the residents, private investors, and city municipality taking to rebuild the estate's destroyed functions? What impact can these actions have on its future spatial development?

North Saltivka: original planning concept

North Saltivka is one of the youngest large housing estates in Kharkiv. It was built between 1984 and 1993, marking the final period of the city's development under socialism. It is located on the city's north edge, adjacent to another large housing development, Saltivka, which is claimed to be the largest housing estate in Ukraine. Both Saltivka and North Saltivka were built using Soviet prefabricated panel structures produced by Kharkiv-based factories (DSK-1 and DSK-2). This allowed the construction of 320,000–480,000 square metres of housing annually; some nine-storey houses were erected in the space of one month. As a result, North Saltivka is composed of 9–16 storey buildings architecturally associated with the Brezhnev era of mass housing construction (Fig. 3), characterised by a combination of linear, curved, and tower-like residential buildings.[7] Due to the fact that they are taller than houses on earlier housing estates, the panel buildings were arranged at a distance of up to 100 metres from each other for better solar insolation. This 'loose' planning structure allowed for large open courtyard spaces, which were envisioned as a green park for everyone. Public functions in the estate were laid out according to the 'focusing' method as a general principle of spatial development. The method was developed by the architects of the estate, led by Leonid Tyulpa. The method can be considered innovative, as it was first used at the Saltivka LHE and later applied to LHEs all over Soviet Ukraine. The idea was to place major social and infrastructure facilities around public transport stops within an accessibility radius of 400–450 metres, making these areas the main public foci on a housing estate. The number and type of public functions in each focus area were also carefully calculated. Focus areas were typically located on the peripheries of micro-districts, leaving the remaining parts of each micro-district as quieter and greener residential areas. According to the stepped system of public function distribution, primary educational facilities (schools and kindergartens) were placed in the centre of micro-districts. They were the only fenced areas on

Figure 3:
Standard-design residential panel buildings on the North Saltivka large housing estate.
Photo: Author, 2019

Figure 4:
Spatial layout of North Saltivka. Buildings damaged in the Russo-Ukrainian war are shown in red.

▬ Buildings on the LHE
▬ Damaged buildings on the LHE
— Main transport axis

Graphic: author, 2023

the estate and employed standard designs for both built and open spaces. The architects of North Saltivka wanted to create large, open green courtyards with all the facilities needed for recreation and to protect residential houses from noise and create privacy.

As a result, North Saltivka consists of five micro-districts and an unclassified area containing the tram depot. The micro-districts are divided by Les Serdyuk, Gvardeytsev Shironintsev, Natalia Uzhviy, Metrostroiteley, Druzhby Narodov, and Rodnikovaya streets. Les

Serdyuk Street is a continuation of one of the main thoroughfares of Saltivka and of Kharkiv as a whole – Academika Pavlova Street. It also connects Kharkiv with the neighbouring small town of Tsirkuny. The LHE was originally planned with five schools, eight kindergartens, and a district hospital operating in each of its micro-districts. Between the upper two micro-districts and the lower three there is a large green recreational area – Manzhosiv Yar – with several small lakes created by Manzhosiv Stream (Fig. 4).

Post-socialist spatial development

The post-socialist period of urban housing development in Kharkiv began when Ukraine gained its independence in 1991. This political change initiated the country's immediate transition from a planned to a market economy. Privatisation was one of the key economic and social consequences, first and foremost in the field of housing.[8] North Saltivka LHE is one of many examples of these developments. Although troubled by some technical and aesthetic problems, the original panel buildings on the estate still functioned well and were not demolished; their physical renovation was mostly carried out by residents. The ground floors of the original residential buildings originally contained apartments but, following privatisation, were often converted for use by small businesses and services. Self-organised renovations resulted in numerous extensions, steps, and canopies erected on the residential buildings (Fig. 5). During more than 30 years of post-socialist development in Ukraine there was no organised, state-funded programme for comprehensive renovation of panel buildings. The state only provided for limited maintenance of public spaces and technical work needed to support the city's communal property and engineering systems.

Some areas of the North Saltivka LHE began to be densified with separate multi-storey residential buildings, retail facilities, and shopping centres.[9] At the time of construction, the architects reserved free space for additional public functions such as schools and kindergartens. Much of this has remained empty, if it has not been used by developers for new commercial and multi-storey residential buildings. In the new market-based economic situation and without any real municipal control, developers have tried to fit as many housing units as possible on a plot in order to maximise their profits. In this context the construction of more extensive public

[8] Antypenko, Hlib, Antonenko Nadia, and Didenko, Kateryna, 'Urban Transformations of Kharkiv's Large Housing Estates: Novi Budynky and Pavlovo Pole After 1991', *Építés – Építészettudomány journal*, 2021, DOI: 10.1556/096.2021.00017.

[9] Yablonskaya, Anna, 'Организация высокоплотной городской среды. Регенерация микросайтов сложившейся жилой застройки на принципах самоорганизации и аутентичности' [Organisation of a high-density urban environment: regeneration of microsites in existing residential development based on the principles of self-organisation and authenticity], *Mistobuduvannya ta terytorial'ne planuvannya*, vol. 42, 2011, pp. 456–465.

Figure 5:
Panel building in North Saltivka: the balcony has been enclosed and the ground floor converted for use by a post office.
Photo: author, 2019

Figure 6:
One of the 'focus' areas in North Saltivka during the post-socialist period of spatial development.
Photo: author, 2019

10 Bachynska, Lyudmila, 'Evoliutsiia arkhitektury i mistobuduvannia Ukrainy z kintsia XIX do pochatku XX stolit', *International Scientific and Practical Conference 'WORLD SCIENCE'*, vol. 1, No. 10(26), 2017, pp. 43–48.

facilities was considered unprofitable, which is why such construction has not taken place on the estate.[10] New housing developments try to take advantage of the existing urban infrastructure provided by the LHE. The new buildings are of approximately the same height as the original panel buildings (12–20 storeys), with minimal integration of public functions and usually without underground parking; this means that parking areas take up much of their plots. Built on privatised land, the new buildings are often fenced in, becoming gated communities. New supermarkets, commercial centres, and residential buildings have mainly been built on the periphery of the estate, close to the legacy 'focus' areas. Although these new residential and public additions add functions to the 'focus' areas, the latter remain relatively underdeveloped and somewhat deserted (Fig. 6). The original public buildings, mainly basic educational and service facilities, have been slightly renovated but retain their original 'prefab' appearance and functions.

North Saltivka's low density has caused many problems for the design of its open spaces and functional quality. School stadiums and playgrounds were often used as places for recreation and walking (Fig. 7). The abandonment of the courtyard areas, with their poorly maintained greenery, creates an environment that is less safe and less pleasant. The courtyard spaces are not fully equipped with sports and

Figure 7:
Functional composition and landscaping of a schoolyard in residential North Saltivka.
Photo: author, 2019

play facilities, or these are often insufficient for the number of residents. As a result, families with children often spend time on better-equipped playgrounds in schoolyards or go to Manzhosiv Yar. The lack of landscaping when the buildings were erected has been compensated for by the efforts of new residents, who in the early years organised volunteer clean-ups and planted trees in their yards. Areas adjacent to the original residential buildings are often used by residents as self-planted gardens (Fig. 8) since the city does not offer an alternative programme for community and private gardening. Manzhosiv Yar remains the largest green space in the LHE, making it de facto the district park. It has been renovated by the municipality in recent years and may be considered a strong recreational asset for the estate.

The planned metro station in North Saltivka has yet to be built, leaving this housing area poorly connected to the rest of the city. This has resulted in less active new commercial development compared to the neighbouring Saltivka LHE, where 'focus' areas around metro stops are now very busy public hotspots. While plans for a new metro stop in the vicinity of North Saltivka remain on the agenda, there are five buses and five trolleybuses to provide public transport for residents of the estate. The closest metro station, Heroiv Truda, is 2.3 kilometres from the centre of the estate and is in one of Kharkiv's busiest commercial areas. The pedestrian network is poorly developed, with many pavements in need of renovation and improved water drainage. Infrastructure for alternative means of transport has not been added to the estate. Besides public transport,

Figure 8:
Self-planted garden adjacent to a residential panel building in North Saltivka.
Photo: author, 2019

many residents have therefore had to rely on private transport, resulting in a high level of car dependency. On its north and east sides, the estate is bordered by lines of private garages. A typical phenomenon on large housing estates in Ukraine, such lines of garages first emerged in the Soviet era but became truly prevalent in the post-socialist period. For some residents, private garages became an alternative place where they could make themselves busy, but the lack of planning and scale of these improvised structures creates safety problems and visual clutter. Inside the estate the parking problem is also typical of these residential areas. Cars are often parked in the green areas of residential courtyards because the original parking areas are insufficient and were designed for fewer cars.

Overall, even after 30 years of post-socialist development, the original functions of the built and open spaces still prevail on the estate, while new residential and commercial buildings have taken advantage of the original planning structure and transport infrastructure. Unlike many other large housing estates in Kharkiv, North Saltivka has remained peripheral: the city has not expanded beyond its border. North Saltivka has all the basic public infrastructure needed by its residents, although the inner city and even neighbouring sub-centres remain more attractive destinations for work and entertainment, which encourages residents to use public and private transport to go there daily.

The effect of the war and wartime reconstruction plans

The Russian invasion of Ukraine in February 2022 had a serious impact on the spatial development of North Saltivka. Before the war, this was one of the most populated residential areas in the city, with more than 200,000 inhabitants. During the most active periods of the war in 2022, most of North Saltivka's population left it; only a few thousand residents remained. In 2023, when the attacks on the city decreased, some of the population returned to the housing estate. There is no data on the estate's actual current population; the situation is constantly changing. The war has also killed 35 and wounded 61 residents of North Saltivka.[11] Around 30% of the housing (mainly socialist panel buildings) and public buildings (Fig. 4) have been partially or fully damaged by the war. This has much to do with the geography and morphology of the estate: located on Kharkiv's northern border, this residential area is one of the closest in the city to the Russian border (40 kilometres away). In the first

11   'Since the beginning of the war…', *Kharkiv Today*, 16 June 2022 (in Ukrainian), <https://2day.kh.ua/ua/kharkow/iz-pochatku-viyny-na-pivnichni-saltivtsi-zahynuly-ne-menshe-35-zhyteliv>, accessed 10 November 2023.

weeks of the war, the Russian army was stationed just one kilometre from the estate.¹² Another factor is that the estate consists of 9–16 storey slab buildings and towers, which are more vulnerable to missile attacks. Consequently, it is mainly residential multi-storey buildings that have been heavily damaged, while smaller public buildings have been less affected (Fig. 9). To date, there is no publicly available data on the character of damage to each building, although the municipal institution responsible, Zhylkomservis, claims to assess the extent of damage, ranging from broken windows and façade details to a need for full renovation or even demolition of a building.¹³ Nevertheless, representatives of the construction sector offer an optimistic prognosis, saying that only a few buildings in North Saltivka will need to be demolished, while 99 per cent of the estate can be rebuilt. They also claim that rebuilding damaged buildings is 15 times less expensive than new construction.¹⁴ In fact, panel buildings that were initially designed as a temporary solution to the post–World-War-II housing shortage have proved quite resilient, even in the war. Development of the new Kharkiv master plan, led by architect Norman Foster and his foundation,¹⁵ was announced by Kharkiv City Council in April 2022. The new master plan has not yet been revealed, but some strategies have already been announced. For example, the new plan will focus on five core projects: industry, heritage, housing, rivers, and the science district. The housing project will retrofit existing panel-housing blocks to provide safe, modern, and energy-efficient housing across the city. However, there is currently no comprehensive concept or strategy for post-war reconstruction of large housing estates such as North Saltivka.

The municipality, together with residents, is doing its best to take immediate action to repair the estate and restore its functionality. This involves clearing open spaces of rubble, DIY restoration of broken façade elements (windows, loggias), repairs to roofs and engineering communications, etc. Many residents do not want to wait for the promised reconstruction by the government and are trying to repair their homes with their own hands and finances (Fig. 10). Meanwhile, several private initiatives and organisations are presenting their ideas for the future reconstruction of North Saltivka. In 2023 'Rebuild Ukraine', the Canadian Embassy in Ukraine, and WZMH Architects in Canada jointly initiated an architectural competition to design the reconstruction of one of the most damaged panel buildings in North Saltivka. They also conducted a survey of 243 residents from the Saltivka large housing area (including North

Figure 9:
Damaged upper floors of a residential panel building after shelling.
Photo: Artur Kozhevnik, reproduced with permission of its author, 2022

12   Kuzubov, Dmytro, 'Post-apocalypse in North Saltivka…' *Ukrajinska Pravda*, 30 May 2022 (in Ukrainian), <https://www.pravda.com.ua/articles/2022/05/30/7349457/>, accessed 4 November 2023.

13   Chagovets, Olesya, Bozhenko, Anastasiia, 'From Workers' Settlements to Mass Housing Estates: Evolution of Post-socialist City (Kharkiv case)', *Facing Post-Socialist Urban Heritage: DOCONF2023* Proceedings, 2023, pp. 116–130.

14   Merkulova, Natalia, 'Houses destroyed by war…', *Vremya*, 29 August 2022 (in Ukrainian), <https://timeua.info/aktualnoe-segodnya/zrujnovani-vijnoyu-budinki-znesti-ne-mozhna-vidnoviti-alternativa-bez-rozdilovih-znakiv/>, accessed 1 November 2023.

15   'Kharkiv Masterplan', Norman Foster Foundation, <https://normanfosterfoundation.org/?project=kharkiv-masterplan>, accessed 5 November 2023.

Figure 10:
Self-initiated repairs to windows in a panel building after damage caused by an explosion.
Photo: Artur Kozhevnik, reproduced with permission of its author, 2022

16   Kolomiiets, Maryna and Holubova, Olha, et al.,'Saltivka 243', sociological survey, Kharkiv Academy of Design and Arts, 2022, online: *Rebuild Ukraine Hackathon.*,<https://www.rebuilduahackathon.com/_files/ugd/4c951b_33e275b0faca48c89a7b698c3e05bbcc.pdf>, accessed 6 November 2023.

17   'WZMH Architects' unique solution to restore Ukraine's war-torn housing', *WZMH*, 10 August 2022, <https://www.wzmh.com/news/featured-article-speedstac-rebuilding-ukraine>, accessed 5 November 2023.

Saltivka) to identify residents' actual needs with regard to their experience of living in panel buildings. According to the survey, 65 per cent of residents described their living in panel houses as a monotonous, box-like experience devoid of an aesthetic component. At the same time, the remaining 35 per cent related their experience to childhood nostalgia, stressing the familiar and typical environment. 39.5 per cent of respondents were in favour of demolition of panel buildings; 18.5 per cent were neutral; and more than 40 per cent were concerned and/or negative.[16]

The competition encouraged the use of new methods of prefabrication, including 'Speedstac' – a prefabricated, modular building block construction system made of ISPs (intelligent structural panels), devised by the Canadian firm WZMH Architects.[17] This technology makes it possible to create concrete modules that can be installed in the damaged parts of the panel buildings or used to erect new buildings up to 30 storeys high. The creators of this technology promote its cost-efficiency and flexibility. At the same time, disadvantages are its use of concrete as the main material, which is not a 'green' technology. However, the technology's developers promise to find a more sustainable solution in future versions. Another issue is logistics: like the concrete panels made by the Soviet house-building factories (DSKs), the new prefabricated models will also require local production infrastructure. Most of the winning proposals in the competition propose partially or fully replacing old structures with Speedstac modules, therefore completely changing the interior and exterior of the old panel buildings (Fig. 11).

The Kharkiv-based architecture studio Egohouse also presented its plans for the spatial development of North Saltivka. Egohouse's concept replaces the estate's modernist free planning structure with a new high-density, neighbourhood-like urban form. The architects propose preserving some of the existing panel buildings that do not require reconstruction – but only a few. New neighbourhoods will consist of mixed-use housing with a maximum of six storeys; this would double the estate's original residential floor area. Existing public facilities, such as schools and kindergartens, are to be replaced with new ones according to their radiuses of accessibility. The architects do not, however, take into account the higher population density of the new development, meaning they will offer fewer primary facilities than the original urban plan of North Saltivka. The new plan also includes bomb shelters, ground-floor parking, and an organised system of waste collection. The new development will have three

Figure 11:
Second place in the competition: 'Leleka house' by Hleb Semyakin, Nataliya Kalinina, and Oleksandr Fil. This project proposes construction of a new multi-storey curving house with a stepped contour, using 'Speedstac' modules as the main construction element. The building will replace the damaged multi-storey original panel building in North Saltivka.
Visualisation by Hleb Semyakin, Nataliya Kalinina, and Oleksandr Fil, reproduced with permission of its authors, 2023

types of functional zone: residential, commercial, and educational.[18] Such an urban strategy aims to maximise densification and gives no consideration to the estate's inherited urban form. Despite the many benefits of such development, it remains unclear how effective this kind of high-density development can be in the post-war context of Kharkiv, with its smaller population and economic problems. Such a scenario also poses the question of how to house residents of the the old panel buildings in temporary homes during the demolition and new construction.

Scenarios for the post-war spatial development of North Saltivka

Taking into account the current developments in North Saltivka and available projects for its reconstruction, we can identify three major pathways for its future spatial development.
The first scenario sticks close to current spatial and social developments in the estate. Those residents whose homes have been spared or have been only slightly damaged by the bombing will return and commence self-organised renovation of the interior spaces of the panel buildings and exterior patchwork renovation of the adjacent façades. In the future the city may provide funding to homeowners affected by the war, so that self-organised renovation can continue as it did before the war. Some highly damaged residential and public buildings will probably be demolished by the city, but, given that the population is likely to return only slowly, the district will not be densified with many new built functions, so the overall density of North Saltivka will decrease. As before the war, the city will provide general

18 'North Saltivka', *Egohouse Architects*, <https://egohouse.ua/project/pivnichna-saltivka/>, accessed 7 November 2023.

maintenance of open spaces by clearing rubble, repairing pavements, and sustaining greenery, but the district will remain functionally monotonous, lacking privacy and security. North Saltivka will thus resume its pre-war, post-socialist spatial development, carried out without any strategic vision but based on current social and market-driven factors. Most of the estate's pre-war architecture and urban character will accordingly be preserved, but this will be a stagnating residential area with a traumatic past, a reduced population and functions, and a slowly regenerating built environment.

The second scenario, and the least likely one, involve's radical transformation of the estate's architecture and urban form. As Kharkiv's most damaged housing area, it can, in the case of positive economic and demographic post-war growth, become a testing ground for a radical approach to post-war reconstruction of the inherited open space and built environment. Former socialist panel settlements such as North Saltivka are criticised for being monotonous, low-density, and unattractive, so in the eyes of many do not possess any heritage value at all. Politicians may accordingly decide to create an appealing image of post-war reconstruction by demolishing most of North Saltivka's original built environment and replacing it with contemporary, neighbourhood-like, mixed-use housing blocks. Such a scenario requires considerable investment of financial and human resources as well as plans to temporarily rehouse current residents of the estate.

The third scenario is an intermediate approach between preserving the inherited built and open space structure and modernising it radically. This will require thorough analysis of the current condition of the damaged built structures and long-term strategic planning that takes into account the future social and economic situation in Ukraine. Most of the existing panel buildings can continue to function after undergoing technical modernisation. According to the municipality, renovation will cost 15 times less than new construction; in the first post-war years many of the panel buildings can continue to function. The main question for the new strategy is how to organise renovation of panel buildings where all apartments have been privatised. Nonetheless, since pre-war self-organised renovation of these buildings proved inefficient, greater involvement by the municipality is needed, taking into consideration residents' actual needs. Highly damaged or destroyed buildings can be replaced with contemporary ones. New prefabrication technologies, such as Speedstac, can be used for faster and more efficient construction, but it is important to hold open competitions and involve residents and citizens in designing the estate's new buildings and functions. Another important issue is the functions, design, and maintenance of the open spaces. Since they are owned by the city, open spaces on estates such as North Saltivka are largely dependent on top-down actions initiated by the municipality. Greater involvement of residents in the design and programming of the open-space functions will create a more liveable and inclusive environment on the estate. It is also a major responsibility of the municipality to improve public transport on the estate in order to better connect it to the entire city, reduce parking areas, and establish an alternative 'green' transport infrastructure.

Conclusion

During its more than 40 years of spatial development, North Saltivka has undergone several testing periods, from rapid construction, through post-socialist stagnation, to the recent massive destruction and population loss. The case of North Saltivka is not unique in Ukraine: many large housing estates have suffered similar or worse damage from the war. The question of post-war urban and architecture regeneration of inherited LHEs is crucial for many Ukrainian cities. Unfortunately, the original planning concepts of LHEs such as North Saltivka have yet to be properly studied and are rarely taken into account when making decisions about their reconstruction and modernisation. The original panel buildings that were criticised before the war for their inferior aesthetic, technical, and functional qualities have largely withstood the war damage and continue to function, providing homes for many residents. At the same time, the war has made more relevant many of the post-socialist spatial development problems of estates such as North Saltivka. A lack of official data about the exact extent and type of damage to buildings on the estate makes it difficult to create sustainable plans for reconstruction. However, it is already clear that a comprehensive strategic master plan for reconstruction of North Saltivka should take into account the original planning concepts, residents' current needs, and long-term sustainability. It should also be aligned with the city's overall development goals and be seamlessly integrated with neighbouring areas. New social, economic, and technological models are needed to ensure the spatial development of North Saltivka as a vibrant, sustainable, and resilient neighbourhood in the future.

References:

Antypenko, Hlib., Antonenko Nadia, Didenko, Kateryna, 'Urban Transformations of Kharkiv's Large Housing Estates – Novi Budynky and Pavlovo Pole After 1991', *Építés – Építészettudomány journal*, 2021, DOI: 10.1556/096.2021.00017.

Antypenko, Hlib, 'Kharkiv Mass Housing Estates: Socialist Past and Post-Socialist Present', *Doconf19 conference proceedings*, 2019, pp. 18–21.

Bachynska, Lyudmila, 'Evoliutsiia arkhitektury i mistobuduvannia Ukrainy z kintsia XIX do pochatku XX stolit', *International Scientific and Practical Conference "WORLD SCIENCE"*, vol.1, No. 10(26), 2017, pp. 43–48.

Bouryak, Oleksandr, Vihdorovich, Olha, Gayevyi, Yuriy, Golovchenko, Andriy, 'Innovative Approaches in the Period of Mass Industrial Development (on the Example of Residential Areas of Kharkiv)', *IOP Conf. Series: Materials Science and Engineering, Innovative Technology in Architecture and Design*, 2020, pp. 1–11.

Bouryak, Oleksandr, Antonenko, Nadia, Lavrentiev, Ilia, 'Leonid Tyulpa – The Architect of the Period of Mass Industrial Development', *ZARCH Journal of Interdisciplinary Studies in Architecture and Urbanism*, vol. 8, 2017, pp. 154–169.

Chagovets, Olesya, Bozhenko, Anastasiia, 'From workers' settlements to mass housing estates: evolution of post-socialist city (Kharkiv case)', *Doconf2023 – Facing Post-Socialist Urban Heritage conference proceedings*, 2023, pp. 116–130.

Didenko, Catherine, Bouryak, Oleksandr, Antonenko, Nadia, 'Residential Housing in Kharkiv (Ukraine), 1920-1935', *ZARCH: Journal of interdisciplinary studies in Architecture and Urbanism*, 2016, pp. 68–85.

Hrynevych, Olena, Haievoi, Yurij, Viatkin, Valerj, Karzhinerova, Tetyana, 'Problemy rekonstruktsii zhytlovykh budynkiv, scho pobudovani u 60-70 rr. khh stolittia u misti Kharkovi', *Naukovyi visnyk budivnytstva*, vol. 104(2), 2021, pp. 140–146, (in [Ukrainian])

Ignatov, Oleg, Petrenko, Viktoria, 'Layout of Residential Areas of Kharkov', *Stroitel'stvo i arkhitektura*, vol. 6, 1967, pp. 15–19.

'Kharkiv Masterplan', *Norman Foster Foundation*, https://normanfosterfoundation.org/?project=kharkiv-masterplan, accessed 5 November 2023.

Kuzubov, Dmytro, 'Post-apocalypse in North Saltivka...' *Ukrajinska Pravda*, 30 May 2022, https://www.pravda.com.ua/articles/2022/05/30/7349457/, accessed 4 November 2023.

Merkulova, Natalia, 'Houses destroyed by war...', *Vremya*, 29 August 2022, https://timeua.info/aktualnoe-segodnya/zrujnovani-vijnoyu-budinki-znesti-ne-mozhna-vidnoviti-alternativa-bez-rozdilovih-znakiv, accessed 1 November 2023.

'North Saltivka', *Egohouse architects*. https://egohouse.ua/project/pivnichna-saltivka/, accessed 7 November 2023.

'Residential fund of Kharkiv', *Derzhavna Sluzhba Statystyky Ukrainy*, 1 February 2020, http://www.ukrstat.gov.ua/, accessed 10 November 2023.

'Saltivka 243', *Rebuild Ua Hackathon*. https://www.rebuilduahackathon.com/library, accessed 6 November 2023.

'Since the beginning of the war...', *Kharkiv Today*, 16 June 2022, https://2day.kh.ua/ua/kharkow/iz-pochatku-viyny-na-pivnichni-saltivtsi-zahynuly-ne-menshe-35-zhyteliv, accessed 10 November 2023

'WZMH Architects unique solution to restore Ukraine's war-torn housing', *WZMH*, 10 August 2022, https://www.wzmh.com/news/featured-article-speedstac-rebuilding-ukraine, accessed 5 November 2023.

Yablonskaya, Anna, 'Organization of a High-Density Urban Environment. Regeneration of Microsites of the Existing Residential Development Based on the Principles of Self-Organization and Authenticity', *Mistobuduvannya ta terytorial'ne planuvannya*, vol. 42, 2011, pp. 456–465.

10

Solnechny in Samara, Russia.
A microrayon's urban renewal prospects through the eyes of planners and residents

Vitaly Stadnikov

In the 2010s there was a period of rapid development of Russian urban planning practices. Cities grew rapidly and extensively but in outdated forms with all the disadvantages of microrayons – in the form of mono-type, mono-functional, multi-storey development without a clear vision of how these residential areas could be maintained in the future. The federal government began to actively participate in the process of regulating the real estate market through the 'Housing' state programme, which was aimed at supporting construction of affordable housing. Regional authorities were assigned the responsibility of reporting on yearly target indicators for housing construction.[1] Consequently, the quantity of housing built became the primary objective, resulting in the expansion of large-scale residential development and revitalisation of outdated house-building factories.

However, the introduction of market mechanisms has not diversified the range of building types on the market. On the contrary, the combination of outdated technologies with an unregulated market has led to increased density and a higher number of floors in buildings, thereby diminishing the social benefits that were characteristic of Soviet microrayon development, such as schools, kindergartens, healthcare facilities, and extensive landscaping. As a result of this housing policy, over 90 per cent of new residential districts in Russia are built using a single type of building. Moreover, the volume of post-Soviet mass construction has already reached almost three-quarters of the volume of mass housing built during the Soviet period after the transition to mass housing development in 1955. Seventy-seven per cent of the housing stock consists of standard series of houses from the Soviet period and modern mass housing development.[2]

In the current market reality, with the emergence of land ownership, the responsibility for maintaining micro-districts is no longer solely in the hands of the factories and institutions that built them. This has led to the challenge of managing these territories and dividing their spaces into zones of responsibility of different entities. The problem of maintenance has been aggravated by free privatisation of housing, which has resulted in the emergence of a large class of homeowners who are unable to maintain the buildings in which they live. Currently, more than 83 per cent of residential premises are privately owned.[3] Furthermore, new developments continue to be built as if the land is still publicly owned, without the creation of condominium courtyard spaces. Management of the newly constructed housing is typically entrusted to state and other large management

[1] Government of Russian Federation, 'Federal'naya Tselevaya Programma "Zhilische"' [Federal target programme 'Housing'], 5 November 2011, <https://rg.ru/documents/2011/02/01/jilische-site-dok.html>, accessed 10 November 2023.

[2] Dom RF, 'Svod principov kompleksnogo razvitiya gorodskih territorij. Kniga 1' [Set of principles for the integrated development of urban areas. Vol. 1] (Moscow: Strelka KB, 2019), p. 16.

[3] Institut Economiki Goroda, 'Rossiyane privatizirovali pochti 700 tys. pomesheniy za pyat' let bessrochnoy privatizatsii. Ekspertnaya otsenka IEG' [Russians have privatized almost 700 thousand premises over five years of open-ended privatisation. Expert assessment by IEG], 24 February 2022, <https://www.urbaneconomics.ru/centr-obshchestvennyh-svyazey/news/rossiyane-privatizirovali-pochti-700-tys-pomeshcheniy-za-pyat-let>, accessed 10 November 2023.

Figure 1:
Panorama of Solnechny microrayon, 2012. In the 2000s new brick houses were inserted into gaps between panel high-rise buildings built in the 1980s.
Photo: M. Malakhov

companies, rather than homeowners' associations (HOA). Overall, more than 80 per cent of the housing stock is managed by such companies rather than HOAs.[4]

The microrayon as a battleground for new development

The concept of the microrayon, which originated during the Soviet era and viewed land as a collective asset, has experienced a decline due to the pressures of new development. In the 2000s developers and authorities began to see the excessive openness of these areas as an opportunity for new construction. Kindergartens, previously maintained by factories and institutions, were sold off for commercial purposes and for use as offices. The Russian Orthodox Church also became a significant player in territorial development. The Land Code allows for allocation of land for religious facilities without competition or fees. Consequently, chapels have been built on sites where kindergartens and schools were intended and have then rapidly transformed into proper churches with expanding grounds. In Samara this hunting for land reached its peak with the introduction of modular churches.

Microrayons have become battlegrounds for acquisition of new land resources. The only solution to this problem lies in land surveying, proper structuring of land use, and consolidation of rights and responsible ownership. Updating planning techniques and adapting them to the conditions of the free market and private property has accordingly become a pressing issue. A change in design ideology and the establishment of a regulatory framework for new forms of urban planning are imperative.

Federal legislation has undergone significant transformation, embracing liberal values in order to establish a competitive real estate market and reduce dependency on the state. During this period there has been a shift from the principles of the Modernist City towards the concepts of the Compact City and New Urbanism.

Implementation of the Compact City approach can be seen in the master plan for Perm, which was drawn up by an international team in 2009.[5] This master plan influenced Perm's General Plan and Land Use Regulations and is a prominent example of a new urban planning approach in post-Soviet Russia. One of the key aspects of this plan is the 'block strategy', which aims to increase the density of dispersed microrayons through construction of mid-rise buildings. This approach optimises land usage, establishes clear responsibilities,

[4] Malakhov, Matvei, 'Analiz vozdejstviya pravovyh faktorov na morfologicheskie kharakteristiki i osobennosti razvitiya gorodskih obrazovaniy' [Impact of legal factors on urban morphology and development] (master's dissertation, Moscow: HSE University, 2016), p. 38, <https://www.hse.ru/edu/vkr/175666626>, accessed 10 November 2023.

[5] KCAP Architects & Planners, 'Strategicheskiy masterplan Permi. Prilozhenie S: Pravila zastroyki kvartalov' [Strategic master plan for Perm. Appendix C: Rules for the development of street blocks] (Perm, 2010), p. 60.

enhances functional diversity and mixed-use, and reduces commuting. Analytical diagrams in the Perm master plan revealed micro-districts' inefficient utilisation of space, large distances between buildings, lack of well-defined public spaces, sparse road network, and inconvenient service locations.

To address these issues, it was proposed to fill the 'inefficiently used' gaps with construction that would create cohesive city streets, condominium courtyards, and public recreational areas within the residential clusters. It seemed obvious that, given the opportunity to register land ownership and a clear structure of land use, residents would gain protection from random insertions of new buildings and encroachments on public areas for commercial development. The desire to test this concept in practice led to a subsequent project in another Russian city, Samara, where this article's author worked as a city architect.

Solnechny as a test platform

The Solnechny-4 micro-district, once green and spacious, has been subjected to continuous development pressure – attempts to fill it with new residential complexes. The large volume of 'unregistered' territory is fertile ground for all sorts of abuses, such as allocation of land plots and issuing of permits for construction. In infill development pure market mechanisms come into play as the developer tries to squeeze the maximum volume of development out of a piece of land. It is quite obvious that this reduces the level of comfort of the conditions in which local residents live. Schools as well as kindergartens became overcrowded, and recreational areas have disappeared under pressure from active development. There have been many complaints from residents about lack of social services and opportunities. The Office of the Chief Architect has proposed a master plan aimed at preserving the environmental and social qualities of this area.

Solnechny microrayon is a district situated on the outskirts of Samara, a large industrial city in the Volga region with a population of 1.2 million people. Spanning 180 hectares, Solnechny comprises six parts that were constructed in the late 1980s. During the final years of the Soviet period, it was the municipality rather than state enterprises that undertook the construction of micro-districts. As a result, the district consists of a mixed population. It provided housing for the Soviet middle class, including specialists from various

Figure 2:
Solnechny microrayon, with panel blocks from Series 90-K.
Source: https://www.zdanija.ru/forum/topic-1482.html

factories, the military, and individuals relocated from dilapidated buildings in the historical centre. Consequently, Solnechny contains both marginalised and prosperous buildings, reflecting a sense of ownership and responsibility.

The district's layout is based on the concept of 'group development', which was widely implemented in the 1980s and 1990s. This approach aimed to introduce diversity by incorporating buildings of different configurations and heights. Each superblock in the microrayon contained multiple such groups, although the divisions between them were not always clear. The Solnechny micro-district is as an example of such development, comprising six superblocks ranging in size from 20 to 40 hectares. Each superblock consists of two to four groups of buildings. The last 'Soviet' microrayons, including Solnechny, were constructed using Series 90-K, which was specifically developed for Samara in 1987 and offered enhanced comfort. Buildings from the 90-K series can be recognised by their distinctive curved loggias (Fig. 2).

Solnechny is well connected to the central and industrial districts of the city. It boasts a favourable ecological position, situated on the slope of the Volga River and surrounded by pristine forest oak groves and dachas. As for the microrayon, however, the picturesque landscape has been built up with standardised panel buildings. The planning concept drawn up in the 1980s aimed to preserve the groves, ravines, and ponds. Unfortunately, the constraints of being a 'closed city' (a city closed to the public because it contained secret plants belonging to the defence industry) hindered the implementation of customised design projects. Consequently, the valuable natural landscape was largely destroyed by ill-suited standard buildings that had not been adapted to the terrain. In the final years of the Soviet era insufficient funds were allocated for both landscaping and construction of essential amenities such as shops and children's facilities. Shops were established directly in apartments. No allowance was made for the delicate work required to harmonise architecture and topography. Public spaces, areas for organised socialisation, and forums were not given due consideration. Nevertheless, in Solnechny-1 and Solnechny-4 fragments of natural areas have managed to survive. These territories are still regarded by residents as the most treasured elements in their locality.

Solnechny-4 occupies a 27.5-hectare plot. Until the mid-1980s this area housed a sanatorium nestled amidst a grove, dachas, and apple orchards. The neighbourhood is divided into two parts by a natural gap with an oak grove, a pond, and a large square with greenery. The residential buildings are from the 90-K panel series and have nine to 12 storeys. In the 2000s several additional multi-storey residential buildings were erected in Solnechny-4, resulting in a population density increase of approximately 35 per cent. Regrettably, no corresponding social facilities were added, and part of the grove was lost in the process.

With the increase in motorisation, there has been a significant rise in the occupation of space by spontaneous parking. However, the most crucial issue has been the emergence of garages – impromptu structures built for cars on unregistered land. The garages serve not only as storage spaces for vehicles but also as utility sheds and traditional meeting places for men, who gather under plausible pretexts while actually spending their time drinking. As is widely known, microrayons were constructed as cohesive complexes without any borders between house land plots. Land in Solnechny-4 was registered only for the sanatorium and housing built in the 2000s. All Soviet-era houses, which account for more than two-thirds of the block's total area, lacked formalised plots or clear courtyard boundaries. In preserving this large proportion of unregistered territory, the city administration was clearly motivated by economic considerations. The administration would establish and register land plots in the cadastral system, which were then provided to developers on a reimbursable basis. Land plots

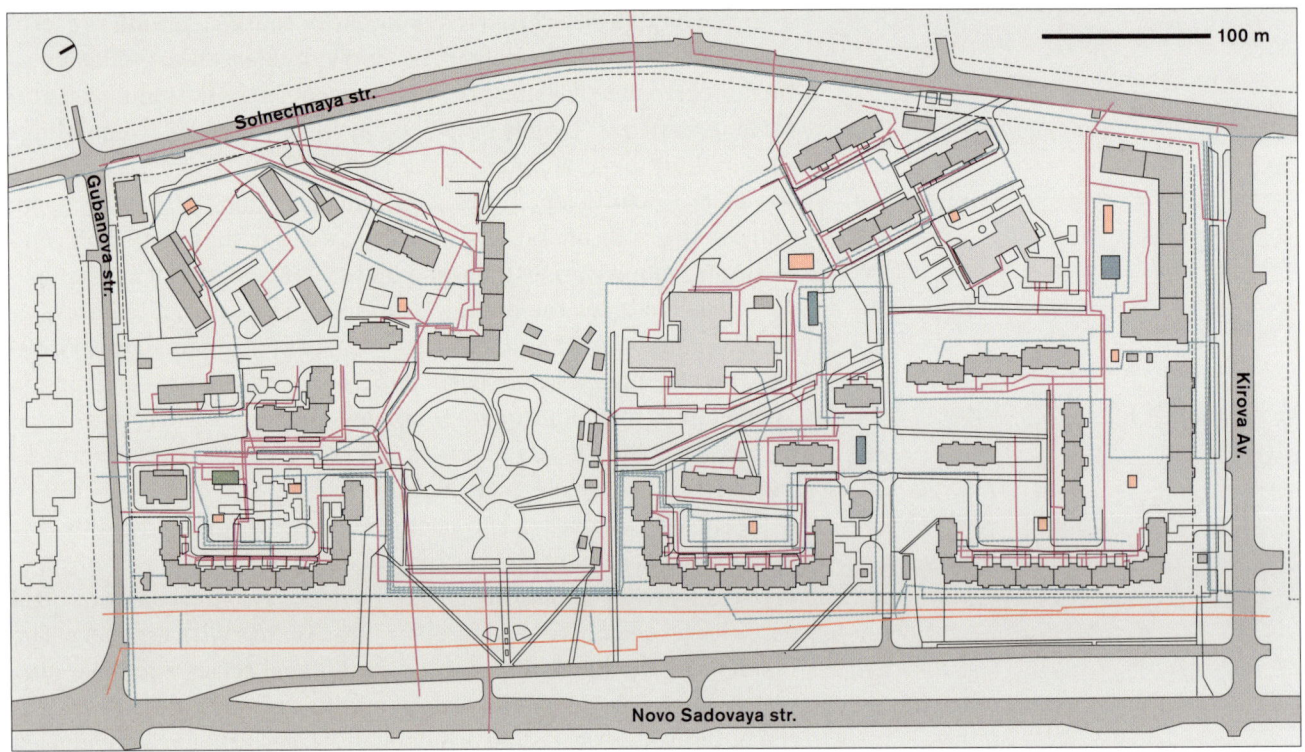

Figure 3:
Analysis of use of the site. Networks were haphazardly laid. Intra-block networks intersect the courtyards of neighbouring houses.

— Sewerage
— Water supply
— Electricity supply
▪ Heating station
▪ Pumping station
▪ Supply substation

Source: Master plan of Solnechny microrayon, 2013. RBTS planners: V. Stadnikov, K. Afrikantov, O. Fedorov, and M. Malakhov

were allocated for all kindergartens, schools, hospitals, and other non-residential buildings, along with the accompanying territory. Additionally, numerous small land plots were registered for cadastral purposes, including some private garages, engineering infrastructure, and container sites. Along the perimeter of the block, in the space between building lines and red lines (i.e. borders dividing roads and thoroughfares from the territory of a block), there was a scattering of land plots designated for temporary shopping pavilions and parking lots. There was no street network serving as a system of public spaces; instead, fire lanes were used as passages and transport corridors.

Due to the absence of differentiation between public areas and courtyard areas inside the block, utilities networks were haphazardly laid out without considering ease of maintenance. Intra-block networks intersected the courtyards of neighbouring houses, completely disregarding the concept of independent and autonomous maintenance. In order to minimise distances, utility networks were even routed through the basements of buildings. The same applied to the system of intra-block passages. Any disruption to the water supply or heating pipes or a fire incident would result in the blockage of all adjacent courtyard areas. Initially, it was challenging to reconcile all the requirements for improvement and utility networks into a cohesive and harmonious framework. As the density of construction increased, this task became nearly impossible. Underground networks formed their own distinct pattern, rendering any attempts at rational courtyard improvement futile (Fig. 3).

However, there was a large area of unstructured territory without clear conditions governing responsibility and maintenance. More than one fourth of the site was occupied by disorganised parking lots, garages, landfills, garbage dumps, and untamed vegetation. The internal paths, which were not designated as streets, posed a safety hazard (Fig. 4).

Intentions of the master plan

The revitalisation project aimed to enhance the microrayon by implementing parcelling strategies to create blocks with car-free courtyards. The main objective was to allocate plots for each existing multi-apartment block, clearly defining the responsibilities of residents, the municipality, and commercial establishments. Furthermore, the plan aimed to establish well-designed city streets and public spaces.

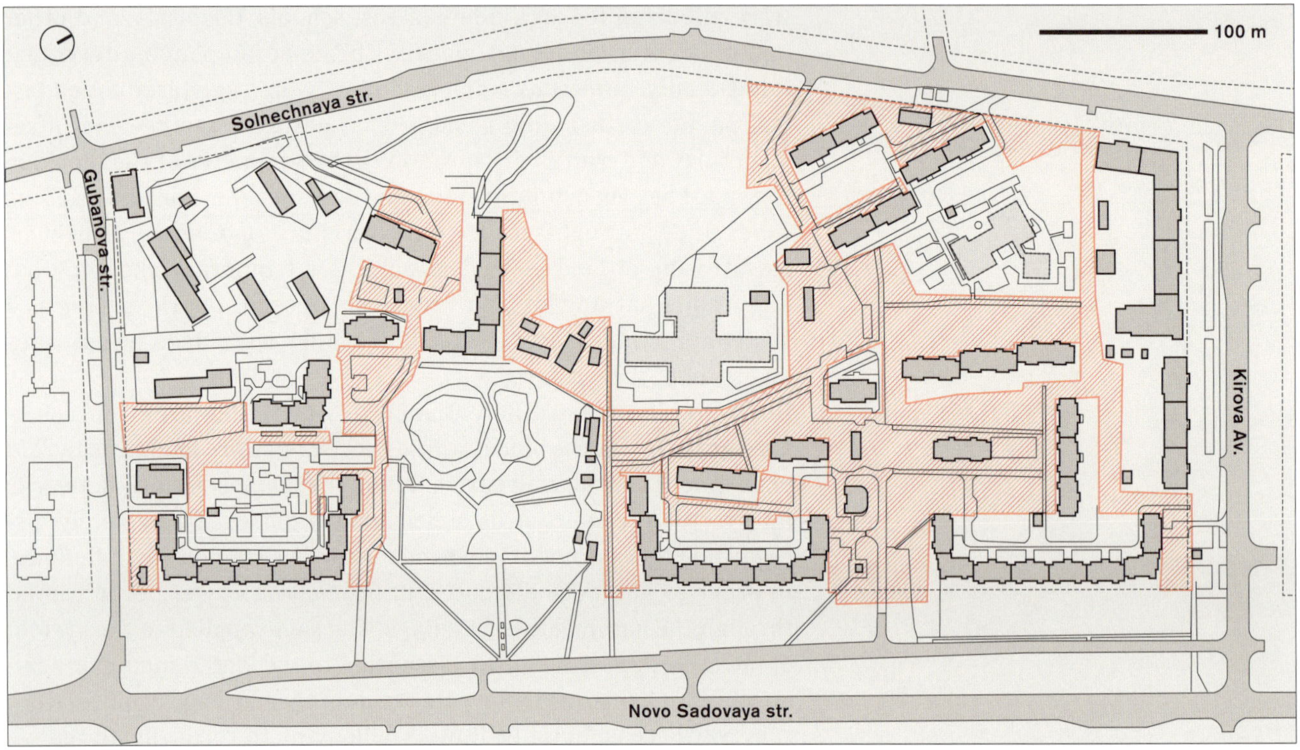
100 m
Solnechnaya str.
Gubanova str.
Kirova Av.
Novo Sadovaya str.

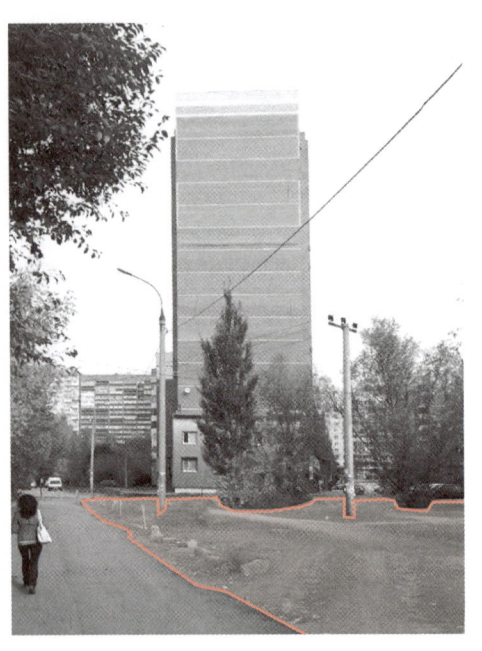

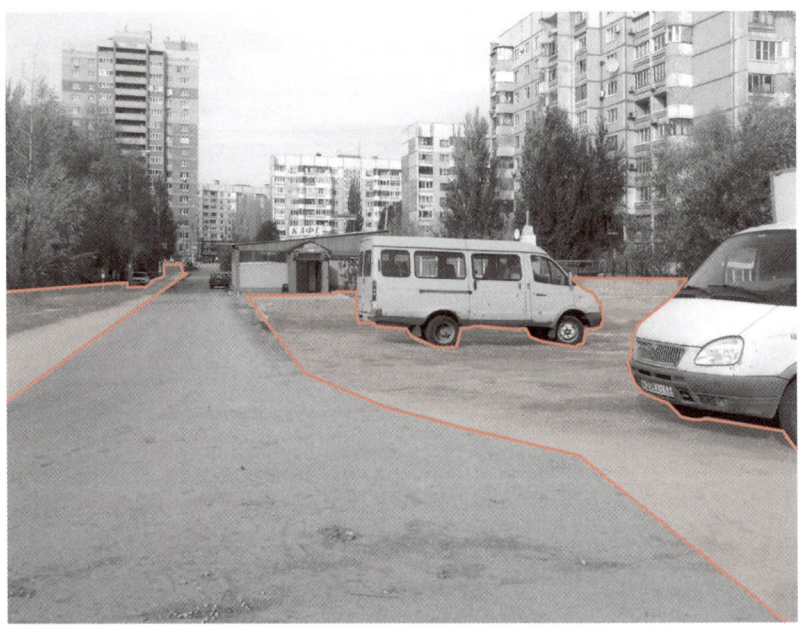

Figure 4 (left page):
Analysis of use of the site shows that 26 per cent of Solnechny-4's territory either remained unused or was illegally occupied by environmentally detrimental objects such as landfills and improvised parking lots, accounting for a total of seven hectares.

Source: Master plan of Solnechny microrayon, 2013. RBTS planners: V. Stadnikov, K. Afrikantov, O. Fedorov, and M. Malakhov.

Additionally, the plan sought to unlock the area's potential by incorporating low-rise commercial establishments such as shops, cafés, and children's facilities. Ultimately, the benefits derived from these improvement measures would outweigh the associated costs.

The master plan (Fig. 5) aimed to achieve the following objectives:

1. Preserve natural areas by designating them as recreational zones.
2. Establish clear boundaries for blocks with courtyards by emphasising the borders of groups of houses.
3. Create plots for multi-apartment buildings, including surrounding areas for use by the buildings.
4. Designate district streets with borders defining public areas.
5. Develop public spaces with commercial and service functions along the streets.
6. Allocate organised parking zones along the streets, thereby freeing intra-block areas from parking and enabling reservation of underground parking spaces.
7. Streamline utility corridors for improved efficiency of land use.
8. Implement landscaping measures to create a safe and accessible environment for pedestrians and individuals with limited mobility.

Upon the recommendation of the city's member of parliament and with the endorsement of the mayor, a proposal was put forth to establish a city children's dance theatre on land occupied by landfill and improvised parking lots. The proposition garnered support from the local community of mothers and proactive community leaders. The area is conspicuously lacking in opportunities for the development and recreation of children and youth, and the theatre had the potential to serve as a cultural hub and club for the area's youngsters, lifting a 1980s disadvantaged neighbourhood to meet the standard of social welfare commonly associated with neighbourhoods constructed in the 1940s and 1950s.

Residents' objections

Once the development plan had been presented at the municipality and disseminated to all area residents through the media, it became apparent that a significant majority were against implementation of

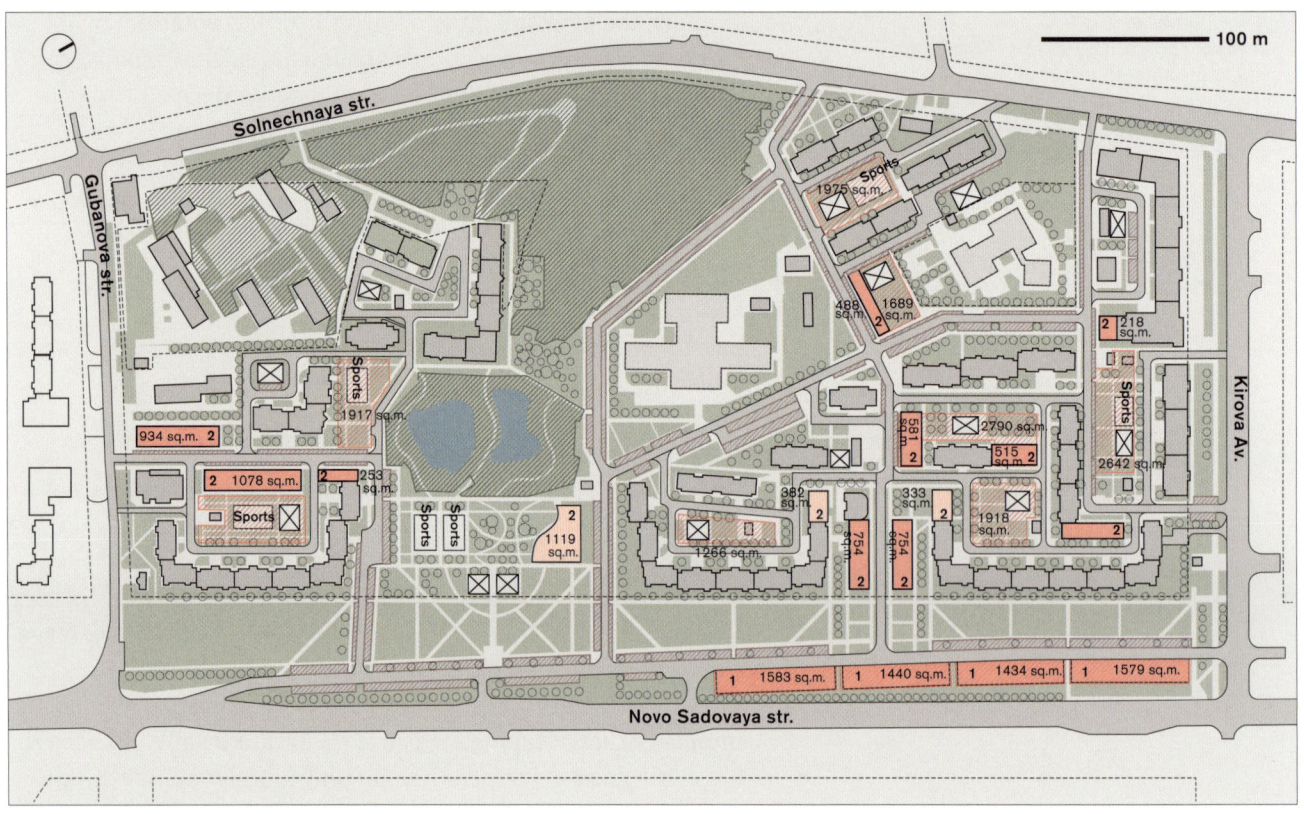

Figure 5:
Master plan of Solnechny microrayon.

- Possible sites for public / commercial buildings
- Childcare facilities
- Underground parking
- Street parking
- Green areas
- Landscaping measures

Source: Master plan of Solnechny microrayon, 2013.
RBTS planners: V. Stadnikov, K. Afrikantov, O. Fedorov, and M. Malakhov

the master plan. In response, residents began to write complaints. We held multiple meetings to elucidate the concepts behind the master plan. However, it was too late: people perceived the development plan as an imposition from higher authorities with no input from themselves. Moreover, they doubted that the objectives adopted for the master plan would improve their own quality of life. The plan was seen as a ploy to enable new construction, camouflaged in the attractive guise of good intentions.

The following arguments were put forth by residents:

1. The inclusion of a theatre is merely a pretext to encroach upon another part of the recreational area. There is no guarantee that the theatre will be constructed, but the likelihood of the site being developed for other purposes is high.
2. Demarcating sports grounds within a park exposes them to the risk of becoming construction sites.
3. There is no necessity to delimit the territory surrounding houses with adjacent land, as this would entail the payment of land taxes.
4. The marking and identification of parking areas is superfluous as the number of spaces available is already insufficient.
5. Residents were particularly agitated by the attempt to designate areas for service and commercial amenities along emerging streets. This was seen as a direct infringement upon personal space.
6. The argument about the need to define courtyard boundaries was met with incomprehension; people failed to grasp this necessity.
7. Lastly, the most pressing objections revolved around the potential demolition of garages.

None of the arguments put forth about the need for land surveying to safeguard against development risks were accepted. The master plan itself served as confirmation of the potential risks for the residents. It can be stated that the concerns stemmed from a deep-seated distrust of the authorities, rooted in the lack of positive experiences with outcomes that benefitted residents. However, it is crucial to note that the social groups advocating for the construction of a children's theatre and the establishment of sports playground areas differed from those opposing the project.

The former consisted of individuals residing in the very same new buildings constructed during the post-Soviet era, which significantly diminished the quality of life for residents of panel houses from the 1980s. Women were predominantly represented within this group. On the other hand, those living in housing built during the Soviet era were generally opposed to land surveying and transformations. There were some men among this group – an unusual development since men often refrain from involvement in public affairs.

Spatial monotony but social diversity

This disparity in the perception of space highlighted a distinction between those who purchased apartments independently and those who received them from the government. The residents of post-Soviet buildings viewed property as a right and as a safeguard, drawing from their own positive experiences and actions. Possessing a strong potential for civic consciousness, they later participated in protests against the construction permit for a new building (Solnechnaya 51A) in this microrayon, successfully achieving their objective in 2015. In our case their goal was positive, albeit non-essential.

Our opponents constituted a passive yet notable social group. For them, the redevelopment of the neighbourhood posed a threat to their established way of life. Primarily, it entailed the risk of losing their garages and sheds. While their garages were situated on public land, the users regarded them as their rightful possessions. The allocation of land occupied by garages for construction of the theatre was the main reason why the theatre was not built. Another perceived threat concerned car parking, specifically the challenge of identifying parking spaces and the loss of the ability to utilise any unoccupied area. The most realistic risk was associated with demarcation of areas for shops and small businesses along new streets. People doubted that multi-storey buildings would not be constructed in the next phase. This outcome was entirely possible. However, the most crucial aspect was that this part of the population had no wish to accept that different parts of the territory would gain owners. This community found it unacceptable to pay property taxes on their residential plots. They believed that the project would lead to excessive commercial development and uncontrolled construction in areas they considered to be their own. They were sceptical that parcelling and land ownership for a specific part of the territory would give them improved quality of life. They were not prepared to accept defined boundaries after being accustomed to an undefined whole. Since the construction of Solnechny, the entire area of the housing estate had been open for public use, and any form of fencing was seen as an encroachment upon communal property. Originally, the residential area was designed as a collective space, which is why adapting it to the conditions of private property is so challenging.

It is important to acknowledge our oversight as planners. Underestimating the value of tools of social interaction, we architects imposed our own vision. Despite its physical homogeneity and uniformity, the neighbourhood environment is socially diverse and complex. This case demonstrates that the stage of a project involving development of a planning brief should be based on collective development of a vision involving residents of the area. Social moderation should take precedence and be an integral part of project initiatives. The outcome of this experiment is the conclusion that residents need to be involved in developing a renewal programme from the outset. It is also clear that the proposed system for transforming a city of microrayons into a 'compact city' cannot be taken literally. The aim can hardly be to densify the population but rather to create functional diversity – through the addition of missing services. In any case, residents can only cease to be an impediment if clear benefits for them are identified. Thus, despite the apparent spatial monotony, the microrayon presents a complex and diverse picture of social relationships.

References

Dom RF, 'Svod printsipov kompleksnogo razvitiya gorodskikh territorij. Kniga 1' [Set of principles for the integrated development of urban areas. Vol. 1] (Moscow: Strelka KB, 2019), p. 16

Government of Russian Federation, 'Federal'naya Tselevaya Programma "Zhilische"' [Federal target programme 'Housing'], 5 November 2011, <https://rg.ru/documents/2011/02/01/jilische-site-dok.html>, accessed 10 November 2023.

Institut Economiki Goroda, 'Rossiyane privatizirovali pochti 700 tys. pomesheniy za pyat' let bessrochnoy privatizatsii. Ekspertnaya otsenka IEG' [Russians have privatised almost 700 thousand premises over five years of open-ended privatisation. Expert assessment by IEG], 24 February 2022, <https://www.urbaneconomics.ru/centr-obshchestvennyh-svyazey/news/rossiyane-privatizirovali-pochti-700-tys-pomeshcheniy-za-pyat-let>, accessed 10 November 2023.

KCAP Architects & Planners, 'Strategicheskiy masterplan Permi. Prilozhenie S: Pravila zastroyki kvartalov' [Strategic master plan for Perm. Appendix C: Rules for the development of street blocks], Perm, 2010, p. 60.

Malakhov, Matvei, 'Analiz vozdeystviya pravovykh faktorov na morfologicheskie kharakteristiki i osobennosti razvitiya gorodskikh obrazovaniy' [Impact of legal factors on urban morphology and development] (master's dissertation, Moscow: HSE University, 2016), p. 38, <https://www.hse.ru/edu/vkr/175666626>, accessed 10 November 2023.

11

Universitetsky in Irkutsk, Russia.
Identifying the value of functional balance

Anastasia Malko and Lyudmila Kozlova

Mass housing estates represent a significant resource of housing stock all over the world. In Russia alone about 8.6 million Russians live in them.[1] But the quality of the urban environment and infrastructure, as well as the size of the living spaces in them, make the question of how to utilise this potential for future generations highly controversial. Discussions about whether buildings from the Khrushchev and Brezhnev eras have urban planning, ideological, or cultural value are increasingly attracting the attention of both the expert community and the authorities involved in urban planning, as well as of the residents of micro-districts themselves.

Micro-districts of panel construction are built heritage that represent a huge resource primarily due to the functionality of the space used. In most cases, micro-districts were originally designed in accordance with a unified urban planning concept with a clear urban structure, which includes a balance of space distribution and a hierarchy of functions. When designing residential micro-districts, architects created a special environment – compact housing modules integrated into a system of public spaces, connected by pedestrian paths on the basis of a unified urban planning concept and characterised by an integral urban structure within walking distance from socio-cultural facilities.[2] Urban planning parameters such as cohesion, measured density, functionality, and walkability are evident, underlining the potential of these housing developments as valuable resources for diverse populations. There is growing recognition among residents and urban planners alike of the value of the micro-district as a process.[3]

This article will analyse the transformation of micro-district functionality through three stages of evolution: micro-districts originally designed and implemented in the 1960s–1980s; changes in socio-economic conditions in the 1990s–2000s; and the development of the market economy in the 2000s–2020s. This will entail examining micro-districts of mass urban development from their original planning and design to the present day.

Methodology and focus of the research

The Siberian city of Irkutsk, located 5000 kilometres from Moscow, is an interesting example of the functional transformation of residential areas under the influence of mass housing construction. In 1963 a long-term plan and maps of functional zoning of the city were developed. This served as a framework for development of a strategy

1   Bulin, Dmitry, 'Skol'ko eshche prostoyat "khrushchevki" v Rossii', *BBC News Russian Service*, 4 October 2013.

2   Benkő, Melinda, 'Budapest's Large Prefab Housing Estates: Urban Values of Yesterday, Today and Tomorrow', *Journal of Hungarian Studies*, vol. 29, nNos. 1–2 (2015), pp. 21–36; Kazakova, Olga, 'Intangible Heritage' in *Perspectives for the 'Socialist City'*, conference proceedings, 7–8 September 2018 (Irkutsk, 2018).

3   Snopek, Kuba, *Belyaevo Forever: A Soviet Microrayon on its Way to UNESCO* (Berlin, DOM publishers, 2015); Yerofeyev, Nikolay, 'Estetika sovetskoy zhiloy arkhitektury' [Aesthetics of Soviet residential architecture], Archi.ru, 10 August 2015; Malko, Anastasia, and Kozlova, Lyudmila 'Revealing the "Hidden" Values of Panel Housing in Microdistricts: Their Identity and Future', *Projekt Baikal*, vol. 59, 2019, pp. 56–61.

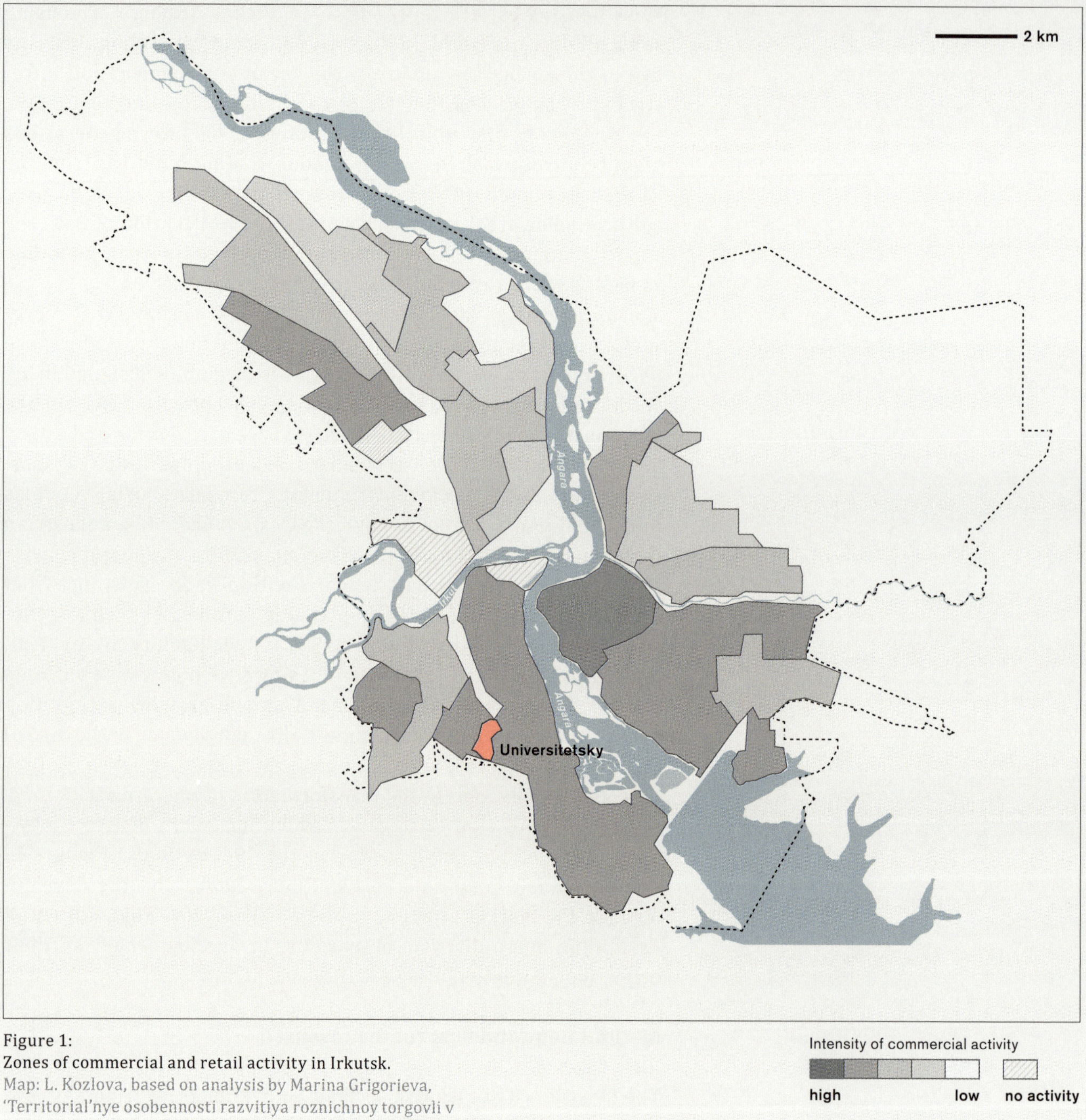

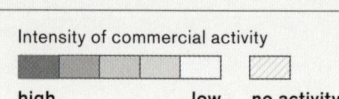

Figure 1:
Zones of commercial and retail activity in Irkutsk.
Map: L. Kozlova, based on analysis by Marina Grigorieva, 'Territorial'nye osobennosti razvitiya roznichnoy torgovli v usloviyakh ekonomicheskikh reform (na primere irkutska)' [Territorial features of the development of retail trade under conditions of economic reforms (using the example of Irkutsk)], dissertation, Irkutsk: Institute of Geography, Siberian Branch of the Russian Academy of Sciences, 2004

that objectively revealed the advantage of developing the left-bank districts as a means of maintaining of a compact city. The urban planning strategy was based on expansion of city-forming functions and creation of new residential areas in response to the constant growth of Irkutsk's population (from 505,000 inhabitants in 1950 to 640,000 inhabitants in 1964).[4] This strategy soon required adjustment of the general plan and concurrent development of plans for construction of large residential areas on vacant land close to industrial zones. The development of micro-districts here can be traced through three specific historical stages. The first stage, from the 1960s to the 1980s, involved the design and construction of these districts. The second stage, from the 1990s to the 2000s, saw significant transformation due to changes in socio-economic conditions, resulting in changes to the functional structure. In the third stage, from the 2000s to the 2020s, ongoing development of the market economy influenced Irkutsk's mass housing estates, manifesting different models of functional transformation of territories, ranging from zones of above-average activity to zones of low activity (Fig. 1).[5] The above-average activity zone is one of the most important in the city due to its proximity to the historical centre and high potential for territorial development. Universitetsky micro-district is located in the city's Sverdlovsk administrative district in a zone of above-average trading and commercial activity. The Sverdlovsk district is characterised by considerable functional and territorial differentiation with high population saturation and a location on major city roads, which predetermines the possibility of the most complete identification of the features of functional transformation under the influence of trade development. Universitetsky micro-district has been undergoing active functional transformations over the last 15 years. The cardinal change in distribution of functions initially established by the project has led to a functional imbalance in the district; a rethinking of the distribution of functions under the new conditions is now required, taking into account analysis of international experience.

Universitetsky was built between 1987 and 1992 on a previously vacant site that was occupied by a forest. This micro-district covers approximately 44.7 hectares, including a green zone and a creek. The area has a complex topography with a natural slope of up to 28 per cent, which required terraces, retaining walls, stairs, and other such devices. Additionally, to avoid building on the banks of the creek, the architects had to concentrate all the planned construction in a 32-hectare area. This increased the density of development;

[4] Kozlov, Valeriy, *Gradostroitel'naya istoriya Irkutska* (Irkutsk: Izdatel'stvo IRNITU, 2019), p. 180.

[5] Grigor'yeva Marina, 'Territorial'nyye osobennosti razvitiya roznichnoy torgovli v usloviyakh ekonomicheskikh reform (na primere Irkutska)', dissertation (Irkutsk: Institute of Geography, Siberian Branch of the Russian Academy of Sciences, 2004).

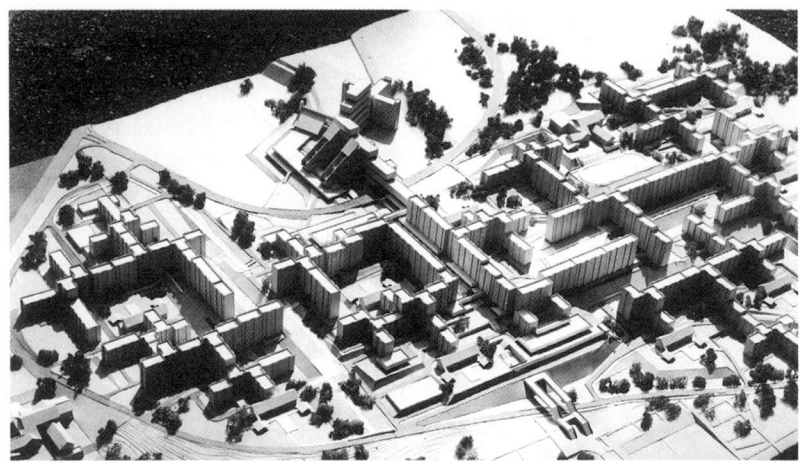

Figure 2:
Model (1: 2000), Irkutskgrazhdanproyekt, from the personal archive of Nikolay Zhukovsky

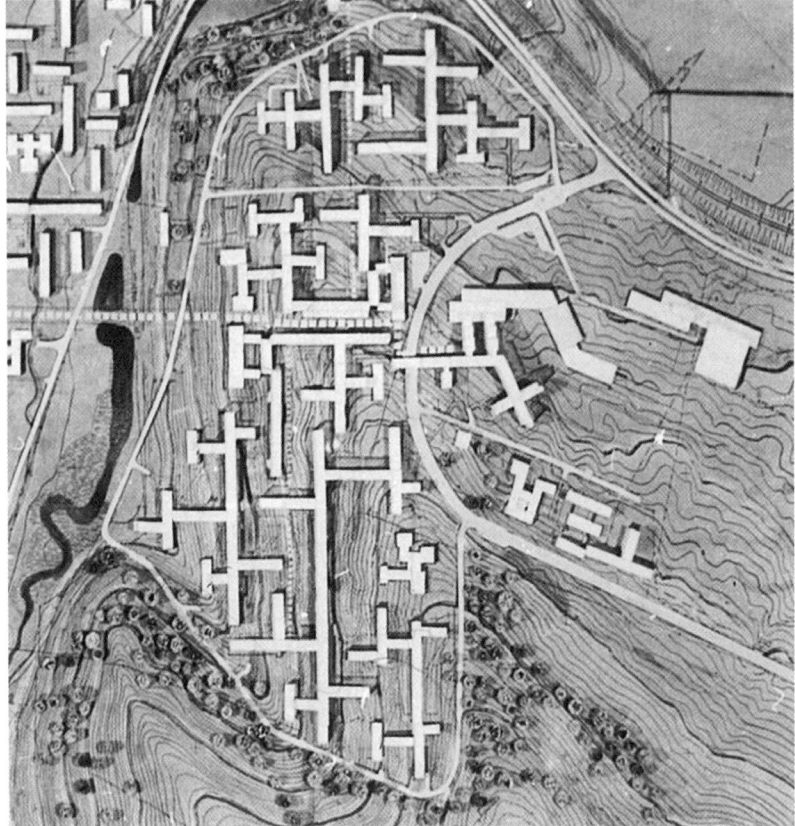

Figure 3:
Model, (1:500), Irkutskgrazhdanproyekt, from the personal archive of Nikolay Zhukovsky

[6] Zhukovsky, Nikolay, Interview by Malko, A. (20 August 2018).

the main pedestrian routes and functional nodes were still clearly distributed, however.[6]

Universitetsky has undergone significant changes since its creation. Its population increased from 22,000 to 25,000 between 1990 and 2018. From 2000 to 2023, new residential complexes were built in adjacent micro-district areas, including the Novo-Irkutsky village of single-family dwellings, which has been under construction in the forest since 2000. This has noticeably altered the structure of development and the presence of recreational buffer zones in Universitetsky micro-district. Another new residential complex, Soyuz, was built in 2015. In addition, the micro-district was densified through the construction of residential complexes in 2010, 2011, and 2013. These changes have had a significant impact on the micro-district's original functional structure.

The purpose of this study is to determine the dynamics of change in functional saturation and its impact on the spatial structure of the micro-district. What distribution and balance of functions is necessary for a viable micro-district and a high-quality residential environment? How should function inside a micro-district differ from function on a major transportation axis or a major boulevard? How can function drive the development of intra-micro-district spaces and invigorate the intra-micro-district life of a 'dormitory-town' community? Social activity is directly related to functional saturation. Functions in turn are concentrated in nodes of social activity, and functional saturation, for its part, contributes to intensity of space utilisation.

Evolution of concentration patterns of functional activity nodes

A comparison of the original project proposal with the realised development reveals significant discrepancies as a result of changes in economic structure after 1990. In most cases the planned improvement of residential yards and pedestrian zones has not been implemented. Many functionally important facilities, such as kindergartens, schools, and bus stops, are not provided with proper shortest routes, which complicates the movement of residents and forces them to seek shortcuts, crossing green spaces uphill. The proposed internal pedestrian axis that was intended to connect the entire micro-district could not be fully implemented due to the location of pre-existing utilities. Since it was initially designed to serve as

a connecting axis with Pervomaysky micro-district, the fact that it has not been implemented has had a significant impact on the micro-district's functional structure. One of the main functional elements was the department store, which was originally positioned at the micro-district compositional centre and at the end of the main pedestrian axis, adjacent to the traffic artery, thus allowing it to function simultaneously as a social hub and a vibrant centre of the micro-district, together with the proposed secondary functional nodes on the pedestrian axis. Although built in the mid-1990s, this large utilitarian department store was designed specifically to sell fast-moving consumer goods. But due to the lack of additional functions on the main pedestrian axis, the load on this facility increased rapidly immediately after its construction: pavilions were added on, together with an upper-storey extension, to sell products that are occasional buys. This has led to a functional imbalance.

By the late 1990s Universitetsky was the second zone of above-average functional activity after the historical centre – an indication of the need for intensive functional development following the change of economic conditions in the country. Prior to the emergence of a free-market, in the Soviet era, residential areas in the zone of above-average commercial activity mainly had grocery shops, hardware shops, and pharmacies, i.e. retailers oriented towards fast-moving consumer goods. However, by 1998, according to Grigoryeva's research in the Universitetsky micro-district, the first node of functional activity, including the aforementioned department store as a key element adjacent to the traffic artery, had been significantly augmented by as many as 50 kiosks and street vendors (Fig. 4).[7]

Figure 4:
Left: the department store, designed in Soviet times, photo by Nikolay Zhukovsky (1998) from his archive.
Right: here the Soviet-era department store has been augmented by new shopping centres, a fitness centre, and an extension.
Photo: Roman Malinovich, 2021

[7] Zhukovsky, Nikolay L., Interview by Gladkova, E. (20 June 2020).
Grigor'yeva, Marina, 'Territorial'nye osobennosti razvitiya roznichnoy torgovli v usloviyakh ekonomicheskikh reform (na primere Irkutska)', dissertation (Irkutsk: Institute of Geography, Siberian Branch of the Russian Academy of Sciences, 2004).

In the 2000s the number and size of commercial facilities began to increase due to the fact that they were now located not only in purpose-built premises but also in premises adapted for this purpose – in apartments on the ground floors of buildings, in basements, and in other empty premises. Figure 4 shows how nodes of functional concentration have evolved in size and composition. In the period 2000–2015 street trading was partly replaced with pavilions and medium-sized shopping centres. In 2015–2023 large shopping centres with up to 100 retail units were added to the existing functional node (a mixture of small pavilions, the existing shopping centre, and kiosks on the same site). All the active public functions are located along a traffic artery, while internal pedestrian links and their infrastructure remain undeveloped.

The two main functional nodes have become busier, resulting in increased traffic and lower quality of public spaces (Fig. 5). Public transport stops located along the same thoroughfare also lack landscaping to make people comfortable as they wait for transport and lack a comfort zone for space utilisation.

Functional facilities located on the main pedestrian axis do not attract the attention of residents and are unprofitable. As a consequence, ownership of these facilities is constantly changing, and many facilities remain closed. In addition, this space is used for parking. As a result, the micro-district's most important central space, which could have improved the quality of the environment and been the possible centre of social activity, has been lost.

One of the most significant features of this micro-district is the presence of a large number of open spaces, which are of undeniable value as a functional and recreational resource. Nevertheless, these spaces' potential is currently partially or completely wasted due to 'clogging' by unauthorised buildings or car parking. The original concept of pedestrian connections through the micro-district does not work, and no new such connections have been created, leading to chaotic appropriation of undeveloped areas for commercial use and parking; spaces inside the micro-district remain unadapted to the new economic conditions.

One of the main problems is the lack of functions such as entertainment, sports, and culture for all age groups; this forces residents to travel to the city centre. This factor only intensifies the micro-district's status as a 'dormitory-town' community. The lack of recreational functions such as cafés is acutely felt. Despite the fact that new cafés and restaurants have been built from 2010 to 2020, their

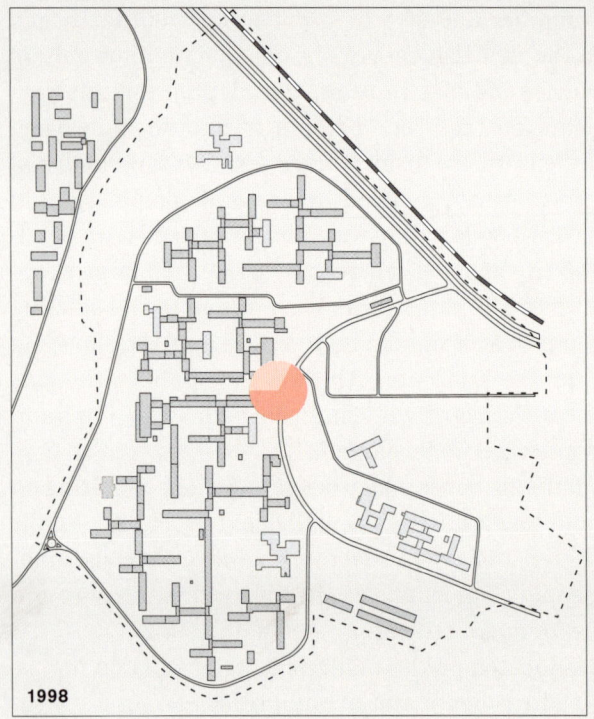
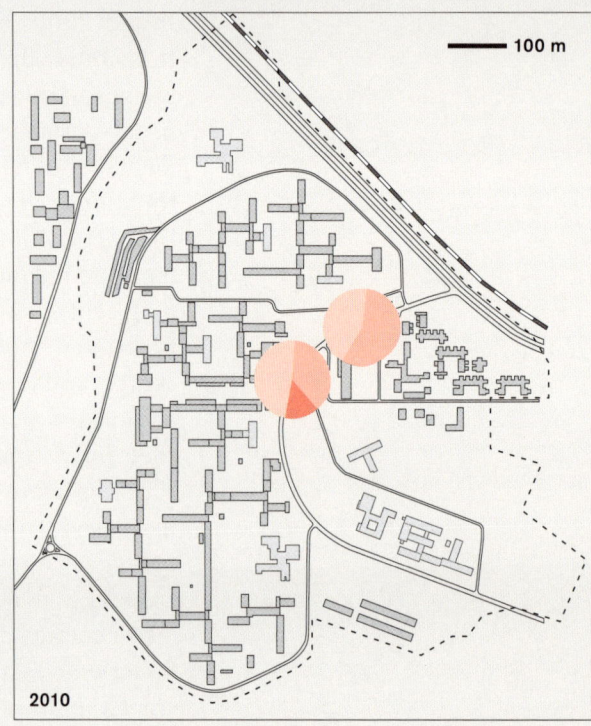
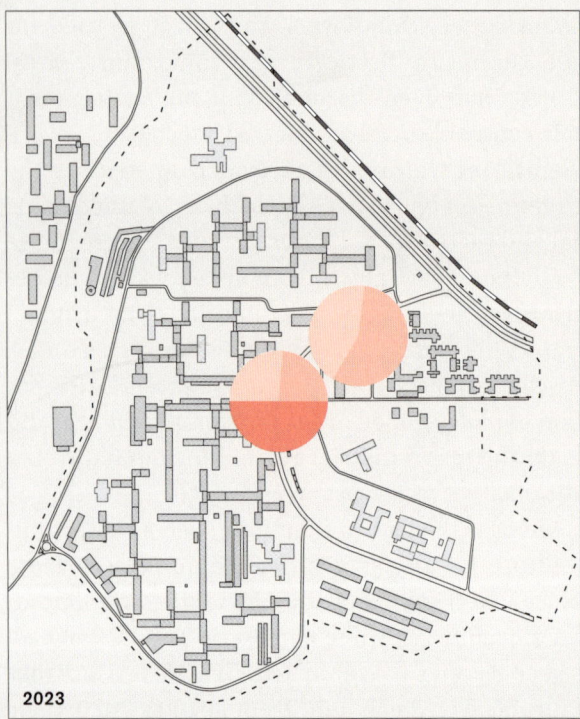

Figure 5:
Territorial peculiarities of retail trade development under conditions of economic reform (based on the example of Irkutsk); dynamic functional oversaturation of main roads in Universitetsky micro-district at different stages in 1998, 2010, 2023.

Kiosk
Pavilion
Street trading
Shopping mall

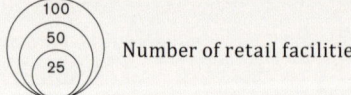

Number of retail facilities

Maps: Lyudmila Kozlova, based on archival information supplied by Nikolay Zhukovsky, 1990s–2020s, interviews conducted by Anastasia Malko in 2020, research by Marina Grigoryeva, 2004

locations inside the original department store on the main traffic route are unfavourable: in most cases there is no adjacent greenery and thus no space for socialising. Sports and children's playgrounds have outdated and partially broken equipment or an unfriendly environment in which exercise equipment is enclosed by an iron fence, which creates a danger for young users. The aggressive environment caused by the increased concentration of functions gives the place a transitory character.

Since the 2020s Universitetsky micro-district has seen the emergence of delivery points for goods ordered online, which has significantly changed and weakened the importance of the retail function. The retail market is the most susceptible to digitalisation: as the previous model of commerce (sustainable logistics, offline shops, outdated lead generation methods) no longer functions, technological change in this sphere is inevitable. This only, however, emphasises the need for a comfortable environment that facilitates communication, especially for recreational functions and public spaces. The small changes planned for the district within the framework of the 'Comfortable Urban Environment' federal programme, which is being implemented throughout Russia over the period 2018 to 2024, are sporadic; the absence of an overall concept for this micro-district is hindering its development and may lead to its functional collapse.[8]

In interviews with the inhabitants of the micro-district the following main drawbacks were identified: overly dense development, the monotony and impersonality of the buildings, residents' lack of identification with their micro-district, and an acute lack of recreational areas for different age groups, along with gradual loss of the micro-district's buffer zone due to construction of a village of single-family dwellings.[9]

The functional analysis we conducted (Fig. 6) shows the transformation of functions from the initial project to the present. The salient features are as follows: inefficient use of territories, lack of an interconnected network of spaces, insufficient functional content and inefficient distribution of services, and the urban environment's lack of formed visual characteristics that could be a source of identification for residents of the area.

In the initial project for Universitetsky micro-district, specific spatial principles of functional object distribution were established, but these have been significantly altered in response to changing market conditions:

[8] Project Directorate of the Ministry of Construction of Russia, Proektnaya deyatel'nost'Federal'nyy proekt «Formirovaniye komfortnoy gorodskoy sredy», 2023.

[9] Potapov, Vasiliy, Interview by Malko A. (20 August 2023).

The first principle is accessibility – the equidistance of objects of the same type of demand frequency from dwellings, which was established in the 1980s, has changed since the 2000s under the influence of ongoing processes. The key factor for functional location is now maximum proximity to a guaranteed flow of consumers; equidistance from dwellings is only partially preserved. Figure 6 shows use of the originally planned pedestrian axis connecting with Pervomaysky district; this axis now functions as an improvised car park. The increasing number of large and small shopping centres aggravate the traffic load, causing traffic congestion in the micro-district and blocking its internal development. Paths to kindergartens and schools have not been laid out for convenient use, preventing them from functioning as fully fledged social objects. New sports facilities are likewise not served by convenient pathways and do not function as potential social centres (Fig. 6).

The second principle of the initial design was functional hierarchy, i.e. the hierarchy of distances from houses to the main public services with different frequencies of demand accompanied by a favourable urban environment. Since the 2000s a spatially divided model has emerged within sectors of intermittent and occasional demand; only large hub formats and local 'street formats' have survived.[10] Based on the example of Universitetsky micro-district, it is clear that functional hierarchy is one of the key principles for development of a viable micro-district; if not respected, an acute imbalance will occur, blocking development of the area.

The third principle is discreteness. The prevailing absence of spatial clusters of individual objects, established in the 1980s, has been transformed into a concentration of objects. The original project provided for a permeable space without the accumulation of functions in any one place. Permeability was accordingly a key attribute of the urban environment: functions were distributed so as to be not only accessible but also convenient.

The above analysis of functional transformation that has occurred in the area allows us to conclude that the shopping centres close to the arterial road have erased the area's functional diversity and de-energised the main pedestrian axis, turning it into a car park for the shopping centre. The continuous expansion of the shopping centre has taken over open spaces that could have been developed earlier and connected to the pedestrian boulevard originally foreseen by the project. In order to improve the situation, it is worth analysing the German experience, where micro-districts similar in scale and type of development have been positively redeveloped.

---

10 Aksenov, Konstantin, 'Transformatsiya gorodskikh prostranstvenno-vremennýkh sistem (na primere vliyaniya riteyla na rayony massovoy zhiloy zastroyki v Leningrade–Sankt-Peterburge 1989–2016' *Izvestiya Russkogo geograficheskogo obshchestva*, vol. 151, No. 1, 2019, pp. 29–44.

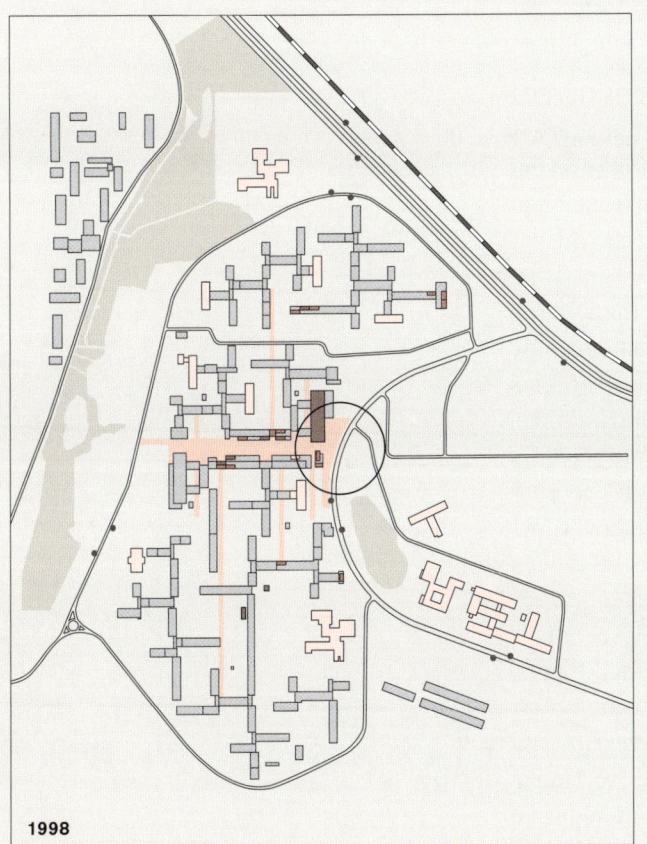 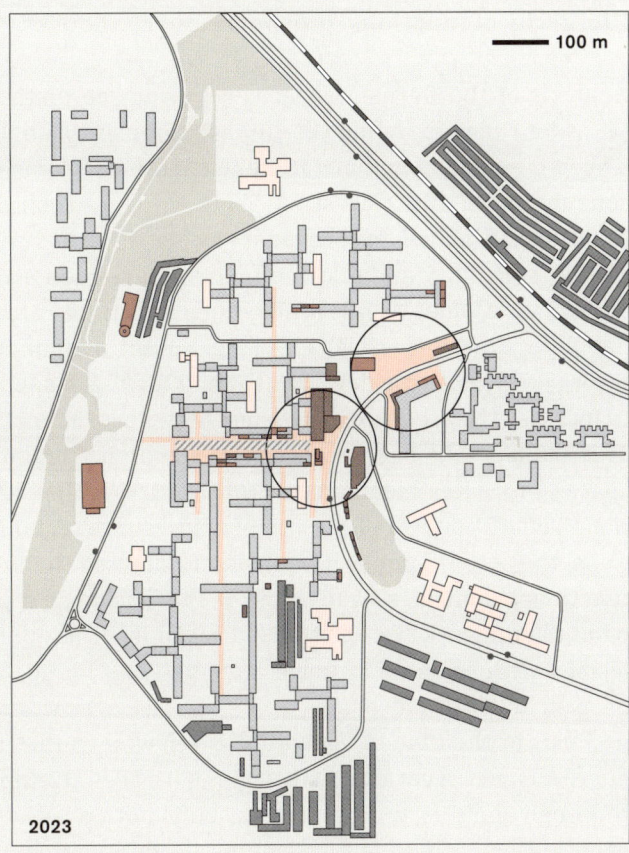

Figure 6:
Detailed analysis of functions, their distribution, transformation, and impact on the revitalisation of space (left: 1998, right: 2023), with a scheme showing development of the system of intra-block connections.

- Trade buildings
- Service
- Education
- Garages
- Street parking
- Pedestrian areas
- Bus stops
- Active public nodes

Graphic: Lyudmila Kozlova, 2023

Hierarchy of functions: prospects and challenges

Analysis of the German experience, using the districts of Gorbitz (Dresden) and Fennpfuhl (Berlin) as examples,[11] shows that there is a need for a functional hierarchy to ensure development of internal connections in a micro-district. When there is a clear distribution of functions, principal and secondary nodes form, ensuring the micro-district's viability and taking into account residents' different ages. For example, older people need quieter functional areas than young people. In the micro-district of Fennpfuhl dynamic demographic waves have led to the development and testing of specific strategies to increase the area's attractiveness and create a functional balance. This balance has been achieved by combining high-quality public spaces with a flexible functional infrastructure that includes recreational, educational, and essential facilities. By combining such functions, the activity nodes have firmly reinforced the micro-district's functional connectivity. In addition, this has made it possible to expand the network of decentralised social facilities, to link school offerings with socio-educational offerings, and for social facilities to be used on an all-day basis.

Analysis of the case of Fennpfuhl is relevant to the Universitetsky micro-district. A variety of strategies have been attempted, so a more thorough analysis, with consideration of both positive and negative experiences, is possible. For example, in addition to improving public spaces, vacant tenancies at a large shopping centre in Fennpfuhl led to its conversion to luxury apartments. However, according to long-term residents, the former shopping centre is currently functionally deficient despite the presence of a network of functional spaces; this demonstrates the importance of having a large functional node as a dominant centre. In the Universitetsky micro-district, on the other hand, there are no recreational spaces allowing comfortable use of the shopping centre's functions in the presence of this node. This gives the function a transient character, exacerbating the functional load on transport and increasing imbalance.

The example of Gorbitz also highlights the importance of having a main public centre with smaller functional nodes arranged in a spatial hierarchy. With its comfortable public spaces, Gorbitz is a kind of promenade along the central east–west axis, accompanied by a tram route and intersected by a green north–south axis. At the intersection of the axes is the micro-district's centre with public facilities and a variety of shopping opportunities.[12] One of the key focuses of the

11 Stahl, Anka, 'Stadtumbaugebiet Fennpfuhl, Bezirk Lichtenberg' (Berlin: SenStadt, 2023); Breuste, Jürgen, and Wiesinger, Frank, 'Qualität von Grünzuwachs durch Stadtschrumpfung – Analyse von Vegetationsstruktur, Nutzung und Management von durch Rückbau entstandenen neuen Grünflächen in der Großwohnsiedlung Halle-Silberhöhe', *Hallisches Jahrbuch für Geowissenschaften*, vol. 35, 2013, pp. 1–26; Landeshauptstadt Dresden, 'Integriertes Handlungskonzept "Soziale Stadt Gorbitz 2" für den Zeitraum 2016–2025 mit den Handlungsfeldern und Projekten des "Europäischen Sozialfonds"', 5 April 2016.

12 Landeshauptstadt Dresden, 'Integriertes Handlungskonzept "Soziale Stadt Gorbitz 2" für den Zeitraum 2016–2025 mit den Handlungsfeldern und Projekten des "Europäischen Sozialfonds"', 5 April 2016.

German examples is the integration of all population groups and the creation of a specialised and flexible functional infrastructure for this purpose. Despite the presence of major thoroughfares in both micro-districts, the principle that social infrastructure facilities and micro-district centres should be accessible without the need to cross a main road is supported by promenades; independent of the road and adjacent to it are pedestrian and bicycle paths that are also adjacent to public open spaces (including playgrounds) and residential areas. These promenades are also oriented towards a park, thus preserving the original structure with a clear internal orientation and features of the structured and open city model. At the same time, the internal functions are divided into subgroups: cafés, shopping centres, recreation – the variety of spaces ensures there is no drab monotony; and despite the presence of shopping centres on the main traffic artery, functions located inside the micro-district are active due to the quality of the public space connections (Fennpfuhl, Berlin).[13] These changes were carried out as part of a specialised reconstruction programme, Stadtumbau Ost (Urban Redevelopment East).[14] The renovation and adaptation of the social infrastructure is of great importance because it improves inhabitants' quality of life and creates vitality in the micro-district. Reconstruction, remodelling, demolition, and the reuse of properties were employed to respond to the new tenant mix and residents' changing needs. The main objective of the urban redevelopment of these areas was to transform them into attractive residential micro-districts. Analysis of the German experience shows that modernisation of public space, which was the focus of these projects until 2010, has made it possible to achieve a comfortable urban environment, which has led to a growing population and the need for adaptation of social infrastructure as a second step, commenced in 2011. The latter includes upgrading of public walkways and parks, including surrounding residential courtyards; reconstruction and strengthening of the district centre; transformation of derelict land into a play and sports area; reorganisation and renovation of apartments; and creation of alley crossing points. In general, these urban renewal measures have greatly strengthened these micro-districts.

In Universitetsky micro-district, in comparison to the German examples above, the district's internal axis, which could also have connected with recreational areas and facilitated the formation of a functional framework for the territory, has never been developed. It is of crucial importance to create and identify nodes of functional activity in a micro-district, including recreational, educational, and

---

[13] Stahl, Anka and Senatsverwaltung für Stadtentwicklung, Bauen und Wohnen (SenStadt) Berlin, 'Aufwertung des Anton-Saefkow-Platzes' (Berlin: SenStadt, 2023).

[14] The federal-state programme Urban Redevelopment East was started in 2002 in the five eastern federal states and Berlin and merged in 2017 with the federal-state programme Urban Redevelopment West to form the Urban Redevelopment programme; Bundesinstitut für Bau- Stadt- und Raumforschung (BBSR) (ed.), *Anreizinstrumente für Investitionen im Stadtumbau Ost* (Bonn: BBSR, 2014); Nelle, Anja, '25 Jahre Neubauerneuerung in Ostdeutschland', in: Altrock, Uve, Kurth, Detlef, Kunze, Ronald, Schmitt, Gisela, and Schmidt, Holger (eds.), *Stadterneuerung im vereinten Deutschland – Rück- und Ausblicke. Jahrbuch Stadterneuerung* (Wiesbaden: Springer VS, 2018).

everyday amenities, which, in the case of Universitetsky, have undergone a change of transitional character.

Analysis of the German experience reveals principles that can be used in post-Soviet micro-districts to regulate activity nodes with regard to intensity of use of functions in accordance with spatial position. These include: accessibility, functional hierarchy, and discreteness.

These principles have led to an increase in the efficiency of the use of the micro-districts' land to improve competitiveness in the urban economy and quality of life. The increase in the proportion of service functions and jobs in these micro-districts serves to promote an equal opportunity policy. There has been adaptation to the socio-economic context of collective mobility systems: densification of functional links and an increase in the sites' permeability. Systems of public spaces have been created that function as a continuous, clearly articulated linking element. There has been an increase in the intensity and compactness of development, as well as reconfiguration to facilitate efficient management and maintenance of the community – buildings or groups of houses. In addition, the urban ecosystem has been transformed, and a new, continuous green network has been created based on revision of existing green spaces.

Universitetsky micro-district has great potential for further development, given a competent distribution of functions and the creation of a flexible system of comfortable public spaces with shortest paths between functional points. The planned improvement of the embankment between Universitetsky and Pervomaysky micro-districts, as well as the cessation of development of the forest area adjacent to the site will provide a quality living environment.

In Universitetsky micro-district a phased transformation of the environment is necessary: (1) modernisation of public space; (2) adaptation of the social infrastructure. This will make it possible to develop a system of internal functional connections.

Based on study of the German experience, the following steps for Universitetsky may be identified:

- Provision of a structure of centrality for residential areas and micro-districts though creation of areas of mixed functional use, abandoning the principles of rigid functional zoning and including in the planning structure objects with various purposes: cultural, recreational, educational, etc.
- Development of a system of pedestrian communication: a hierarchy of streets with increased importance given to pedestrian

links that permeate the district where the main service facilities and places of work are located. This will involve creation of a system of landscaped, green intra-block connections.
- Distribution of principal and secondary public functions through functional and structural differentiation of open intra-block spaces by means of architectural and planning allocation of their constituent units: groups of buildings with landscaped yards, internal passages, public pedestrian spaces (demarcation of land with the introduction of a spatial hierarchy – public / semi-public / semi-private / private).
- Functional features of courtyard spaces should be designed taking into account the desires of local residents (participatory design).

The main strategy for developing the value of the prefabricated housing estates can be formulated as creation of a positive identity through intelligent distribution of existing functions and introduction of new ones. The goal is to make each residential block unique within the framework of the general concept through inclusion of original spatial elements (art, landscape design, etc.).
Analysis of the German experience in development of districts of mass housing shows that it is possible to improve their quality while preserving their historically embedded spatial and ideological meanings. Prefabricated housing estates have a characteristic value which allows us to see possible strategies for their development in modern conditions. The original concept of universal compact residential units in a structure of spacious public spaces, embodying the idea of cohesion of residents, can become attractive again if we propose a modern development scenario that takes into account these districts' historically established structure and their residents' current needs.
Universitetsky micro-district needs an overall development strategy, the objective of which should be to create a balance in distribution of functions in order to make the micro-district viable and improve the quality of the residential environment. This requires variety of functions, not only on the main thoroughfares but also inside the district, starting with development of a centre of social activity on the main pedestrian axis. The development of recreational functions for different population groups can become an impetus for improvement of intra-block spaces, activating the intra-block life of this 'dormitory-town community'.

References

Aksenov, Konstantin, 'Transformatsiya gorodskikh prostranstvenno-vremennyykh sistem (na primere vliyaniya riteyla na rayony massovoy zhiloy zastroyki v leningrade–Sankt-Peterburge 1989–2016' [Transformation of urban space-time systems (based on the example of the influence of retail on areas of mass residential development in Leningrad-St Petersburg, 1989–2016], *Izvestiya Russkogo geograficheskogo obshchestva*, vol. 151, No. 1, 2019, pp. 29–44.

Benkő, Melinda, 'Budapest's Large Prefab Hosing Estates: Urban Values of Yesterday, Today and Tomorrow', *Journal of Hungarian Studies*, vol. 29, Nos. 1–2, 2015, pp. 21–36.

Bulin, Dmitri, 'Skolko esche prostojat "khruschovki" v Rossii' [How long will 'krushchevki' stay standing in Russia?], BBC News Russian Service, 4 October 2013, <http://www.bbc.com/russian/society/2013/10/131004_russia_slums_khruschev>, accessed 21 July 2016.

Breuste, Jürgen, and Wiesinger, Frank, 'Qualität von Grünzuwachs durch Stadtschrumpfung – Analyse von Vegetationsstruktur, Nutzung und Management von durch Rückbau entstandenen neuen Grünflächen in der Großwohnsiedlung Halle-Silberhöhe' [Quality of green growth due to urban shrinkage – analysis of vegetation structure, use and management of new green spaces created through dismantling in the large housing estate Halle-Silberhöhe], *Hallisches Jahrbuch für Geowissenschaften*, vol. 35, 2013, pp. 1–26.

Bundesinstitut für Bau-, Stadt- und Raumforschung (BBSR) (ed), *Anreizinstrumente für Investitionen im Stadtumbau Ost* [Incentive instruments for investments in urban redevelopment in the East] (Bonn: BBSR, 2014).

Dolgov, Aleksandr, Balukhina, Natal'ya, and Gibadulina, Al'fiya, 'Prostranstvennye operatsii po renovatsii zhiloy zastroyki v masshtabe mikrorayona' [Spatial operations in renovation of residential buildings on the scale of the micro-district], *Akademicheskiy vestnik URALNIIPROEKT RAASN*, No. 3 (46), 2020, pp. 46–52.

Grigor'yeva, Marina, 'Territorial'nye osobennosti razvitiya roznichnoy torgovli v usloviyakh ekonomicheskikh reform (na primere Irkutska)' [Territorial features of the development of retail trade in conditions of economic reform (using the example of Irkutsk)], (dissertation, Irkutsk: Institute of Geography, Siberian Branch of the Russian Academy of Sciences, 2004.

Irkutsk City Administration, Informatsiya o vyborakh deputatov na izbiratel'nyy okrug v mikrorayone Universitetsky [Information about the election of deputies to the electoral district in Universitetsky micro-district], 2018.

Kalabin, Aleksandr, and Kukovyakin, Aleksey, 'Massovaya zhilaya zastroyka: problemy i perspektivy', *Akademicheskiy vestnik uralniiproekt RAASN*, vol. 3, 2017.

Kazakova, Olga, 'Estetika ottepeli: novoe v arkhitekture, iskusstve i kul'ture' [Aesthetics of the 'Thaw': new developments in architecture, art, and culture], proceedings of the Nauchno-issledovatelskiy institut teorii i istorii arkhitektury i gradostroitel'stva (NIITAG) Conference, 20 September 2011 (Moscow: NIITAG 2011).

Kozlov Valeriy, *Gradostroitel'naya istoriya Irkutska* [Urban-planning history of Irkutsk] (Irkutsk: Izdatel'stvo IRNITU, 2019), p. 198.

Landeshauptstadt Dresden, Stadtplanungsamt, 'Integriertes Handlungskonzept "Soziale Stadt Gorbitz 2" für den Zeitraum 2016–2025 mit den Handlungsfeldern und Projekten des "Europäischen Sozialfonds"' [Integrated action plan 'Socially Integrative City Gorbitz 2' for the period 2016–2025 with the fields of action and projects of the 'European Social Fund'], draft resolution, 5 April 2016.

Lazarev, Maksim, 'Mikrorayonnaya zastroyka: pro et contra' [Micro-district development: pro et contra], in Mysenko, G. (ed.), *Aktual'nye problemy sotsial'no-gumanitarnykh znaniy: sbornik statey* (Moscow: Pero, 2015), p. 1821.

Malko, Anastasia, and Kozlova, Lyudmila, 'Revealing the "Hidden" Values of Panel Housing in Microdistricts: Their Identity and Future', *Projekt Baikal*, vol. 59, 2019, pp. 56–61.

Nelle, Anja, '25 Jahre Neubauerneuerung in Ostdeutschland' in Altrock, Uve, Kurth, Detlef, Kunze, Ronald, Schmitt, Gisela, and Schmidt, Holger (eds.), *Stadterneuerung im vereinten Deutschland – Rück- und Ausblicke. Jahrbuch Stadterneuerung* (Wiesbaden: Springer VS, 2018).

Ogorodnikova, Ol'ga, 'Mass Housing Construction in Soviet History of Routine', *Universum: Obshchestvennyye nauki*, vol. 3, No. 44, 2018.

Potapov, Vasiliy, Interview by Malko, A. (20 August 2023).

Project Directorate of the Ministry of Construction of Russia, 'Proektnaya deyatel'nost' Federal'nyy proekt «Formirovaniye komfortnoy gorodskoy sredy» (FKGS)' [Project activities: Federal project 'Formation of a comfortable urban environment' (FCGS)], Pdminstroy.ru, 2023,<https://pdminstroy.ru/federalniy-proekt-fkgs>, accessed 21 July 2023.

Sevast'yanova Anzhelika, Periferiya krupnogo goroda kak aktual'ny ob"ekt issledovaniya [The periphery of a large city as a relevant object of study], *Derzhavinskiy forum*, vol. 3, no. 9, 2019.

Stadt Halle (Saale), Der Oberbürgermeister, Kuhn, Ina, Weissflog, Romy, Elstermann, Franziska, Panian, Antti, and Ziegenbein, Brigitta, 'Integriertes Handlungskonzept "Soziale Stadt" Silberhöhe 2030 – 1. Fortschreibung 2018–2024' [Integrated action concept 'Social City' Silberhöhe 2030] (Halle a. d. Saale, 2017).

Stahl, Anka, and Senatsverwaltung für Stadtentwicklung, Bauen und Wohnen (SenStadt) Berlin, 'Stadtumbaugebiet Fennpfuhl, Bezirk Lichtenberg' [Fennpfuhl urban redevelopment area, Lichtenberg district] (Berlin: SenStadt, 2023).

Stahl, Anka, and Senatsverwaltung für Stadtentwicklung, Bauen und Wohnen (SenStadt) Berlin, 'Aufwertung des Anton-Saefkow-Platzes' [Upgrade of Anton-Saefkow-Platz, Fennpfuhl] (Berlin: SenStadt, 2023).

Yerofeyev, Nikolay, 'Estetika sovetskoy zhiloy arkhitektury' [Aesthetics of Soviet residential architecture], *Archi*, 10 August 2015, <https://archi.ru/russia/64030/estetika-sovetskoi-zhiloi-arkhitektury>, accessed 29 March 2023.

Zhukovsky, Nikolay, Interview by Malko, A. (20 August 2018).

Zhukovsky, Nikolay, Interview by Gladkova, E. (20 June 2020).

12

Vazha-Pshavela Block VI in Tbilisi, Georgia.
Community-driven spatial transformations

Barbara Engel

Since the dissolution of Soviet power, many cities in the countries of the former USSR are still in a phase of transition, as is Tbilisi. Its urban fabric and infrastructures have to be adapted to new social, functional, and technical demands and requirements. The microdistricts that were realised since the 1960s represent an enormous part of the residential structure in the Georgian capital. Many of the buildings are in bad condition and do not meet citizens' demands. Since responsibility for urban planning was handed over from the state to local authorities in 1991, and with the shift from state regulation to a market economy, municipal planning strategies have failed to successfully guide spatial transformation processes. In the Vazha-Pshavela district in Tbilisi, the inhabitants have transformed their living environment, the buildings themselves, and the open spaces according to their individual needs. This article reflects on how public and private spaces in the modernist neighbourhood have been reshaped by people's initiatives and how the Soviet heritage has been transformed in an individual, yet Georgian, way.

The historical development of the Soviet neighbourhood of Vazha-Pshavela

Tbilisi was rapidly transformed during the course of the Soviet regime. Peaking in terms of urban development in the 1960s and 1970s, it grew from an insignificant city of about 240,000 people at the beginning of the Soviet occupation in 1921 to a major metropolis of over 1.2 million people in 1991.[1] Tbilisi was an important political, social, and cultural centre in the USSR. Like other Soviet cities, it was developed within the framework of a single vast plan aimed at massive expansion by the communist leadership through normative acts and laws. The end of World War II launched a strong wave of industrialisation in the South Caucasus, followed by development of industrial areas. Industrialisation and new factory growth brought more people to Tbilisi, which increased demand for housing and prompted the construction of new housing estates. This trend was driven by continual migration from rural areas.[2]

The growing demand for housing was discussed at the congress of the Union of Georgian Architects in Tbilisi in 1955, where it was stated that urban development should shift to a new structure, exemplified by the creation of new residential areas – 'micro-districts'.[3] In the following years, building programmes and council agreements were approved, laying the ground for a massive expansion of the city.[4]

---

1 Tsitsagi, Mariam, Kharebava, Nino, Nikolaishvili, Dali, Kupatadze, Ia, Gadrani, Lela 'Tbilisi Through Time', Georgian Geographical Journal, vol. 2, No. 1, 2022, pp. 62–72, here: p. 64; Gogishvili, David, 'Gldani: From Ambitious Experimental Project to Half-Realised Soviet Mass-Housing District in Tbilisi, Georgia' in Mariotti, Jasna, and Leetma, Kadri (eds.), *Urban Planning During Socialism: Views from the Periphery* (London: Routledge, 2023), pp. 191–205, here p. 191.

2 Ibid., p. 70.

3 Asatiani, Nino, 'City Building Problems in 1960–70 Georgia (Based on the Example of Tbilisi)' *Ars Georgica*, 2015,m <https://www.academia.edu/35893557/Problems_of_Tbilisi_city_Planing_in_1960ies>, accessed 3 January 2024.

4 Ibid.

Figure 1:
Buildings in Saburtalo in 1964.
Source: Shota Kavlashvili Private Archive

From the 1960s forwards, many prefabricated mass housing estates took shape on the outskirts of Tbilisi, built according to Moscow's standardised urban planning principles. New centrally planned districts were realised on the periphery, such as Gldani, Varketili, Saburtalo, and Temka and Dighomi Massif. These are all typical new districts of the time with grid-based urban layouts and panel buildings. Khrushchevka and brezhnevka apartment blocks, the signature of Soviet urban planning, dominated Tbilisi's urban landscape.[5] First, the Saburtalo and Dighomi areas were developed as extensive mass housing estates, although they were not as fully established as were, later on, the Gldani and Temka areas.[6] Saburtalo, with its mass-produced architecture, helped to shift the residential centre of Tbilisi from its historical core to the city's new modern districts. It also ushered in demographic change: Saburtalo housed thousands of Georgians from across the republic who migrated to work in the capital's growing industries, transforming Tbilisi from a city with a cosmopolitan plurality to one with an ethnic Georgian majority for the first time in centuries.[7]

The Vazha-Pshavela district of Saburtalo is located to the northwest of the city centre. It was planned by the architects Sh. Kavlashvili, A. Bakradze, D. Grdzelidze, and I. Kavlashvili in 1956–1957 and built from 1958 to the 1960s. With its large blocks of panel buildings from the I-464 series, wide streets, and abundant greenery, it is important heritage that is a typical example of modernist housing from the Soviet period At the time when it was being built, Sarbutalo was the city's largest large housing estate, covering an area of almost 300 hectares and possessing a total population of approximately 45,000. Its density was around 150 people/hectare, with an average of 11.8 square metres of greenery per person. Saburtalo was planned as a complete neighbourhood with amenities, workplaces, and infrastructure, while other districts, such as Dighomi, Gldani, and Varketilli, were realised as simply produced, homogeneous dormitory communities'.[8]

Vazha-Pshavela Block No. VI, with an approximate area of 10–12 hectares, was organised strictly in accordance with the layout of a modernist urban structure. It was built up with four- to five-storey houses that are placed parallel to each other mainly along a northwest/southeast axis. The project implemented for Vazha-Pshavela differed in some ways from the original master plan drawn up by Soviet planners in 1955. Buildings that were to be placed along the framing streets in the northern and southern parts of the district were turned at angles of 90 and 45 degrees. The planned rooftop

[5] Kotzias, Nikos-Pavlos, 'Urban Renewal and Disconnect: Varying Perceptions on the Value of Urban Development in Tbilisi, Georgia' (master's thesis, Utrecht University, 2023), p. 21, <https://studenttheses.uu.nl/handle/20.500.12932/45389>, accessed 4 January 2023.

[6] Tsitsagi, Mariam, Kharebava, Nino, Nikolaishvili, Dali, Kupatadze, Ia, and Gadrani, Lela, 'Tbilisi Through Time', *Georgian Geographical Journal*, vol. 2 No. 1, 2022, pp. 62–72, here p. 69.

[7] Wheeler, Angela (ed.), *Tbilisi: Architectural Guide*, (Berlin: DOM publishers, 2023), p. 309.

[8] Asabashwili, Levan and Mirzikashvili, Rusudan, 'Housing the Masses: Soviet Housing in Tbilisi' in Wheeler, Angela (ed.), *Tbilisi: Architectural Guide*, (Berlin: DOM publishers, 2023), pp. 347–351, here: p. 350.

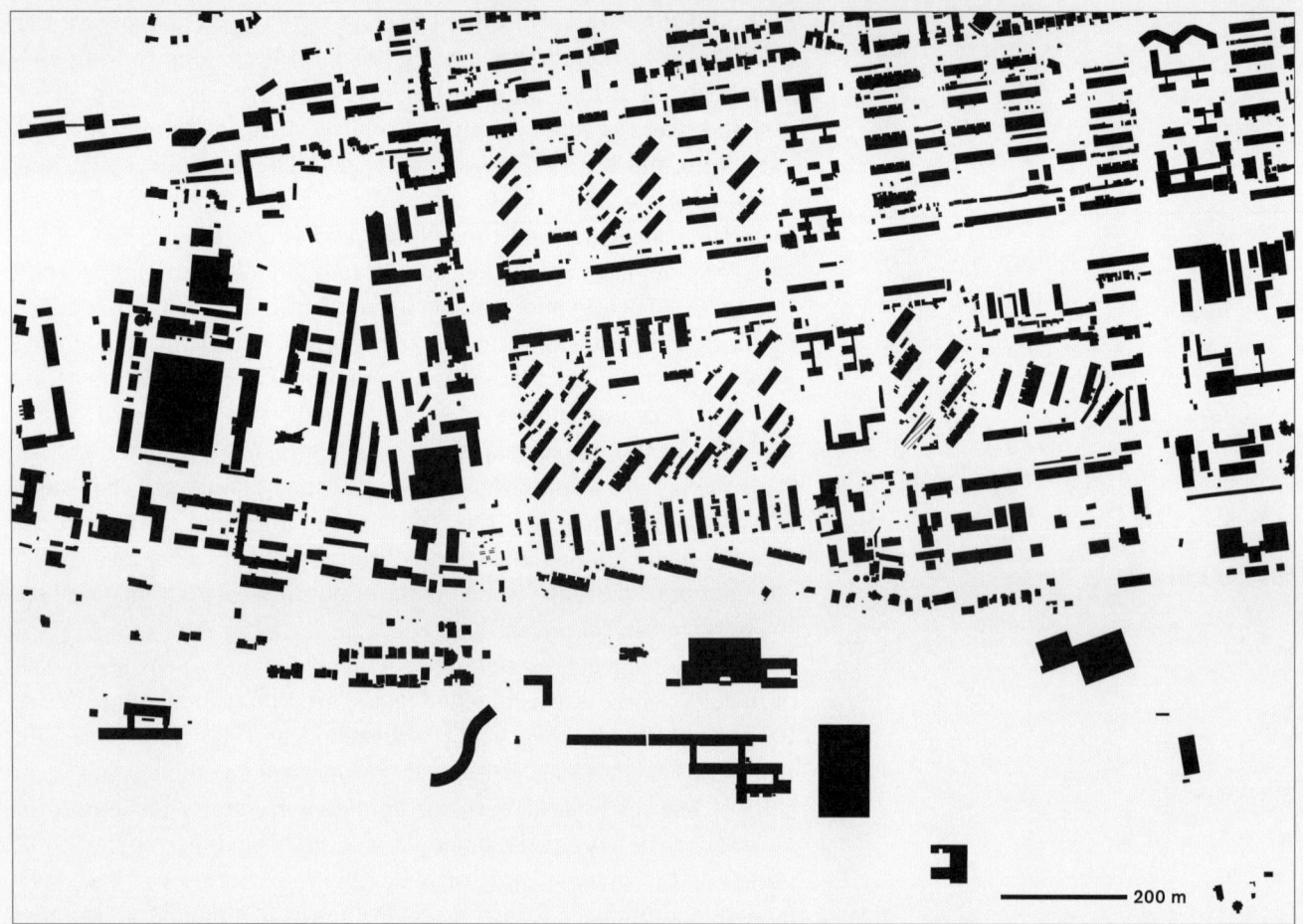

Figure 2:
Footprint of the Saburtalo area.
Source: Nora Staab, based on google maps and on maps from the National Agency of Public Registry (NAPR), Georgia (https://maps.gov.ge)

building additions and extensions of the living space along the complete façade were not realised. A swimming pool was also not built due to a lack of funds.

During the Soviet era it was mainly engineers and technical academics who lived here. To this day you will see many different nationalities among the residents and many children. Following the principles of modernism, functions were divided; public services such as schools, sports facilities, even a stadium, and functions serving daily needs were placed in separate buildings.

City in transition – district in transformation

The Republic of Georgia, as it is called today, was founded on 9 April 1991, shortly before the collapse of the Soviet Union. After independence, the city faced a turbulent period of political instability, economic decline, poor and corrupt governance, and a deficient institutional and legal framework. The dismantling of state socialism brought with it the abolition of communist restrictions on residential mobility and migration but also a dramatic decline in living standards. This was further exacerbated by the slow expansion of the housing market.

A key feature of the new political situation was privatisation, first of buildings and then of land. The new dominance of the private sector was accompanied by the almost complete withdrawal of the government from urban development. Planning policies and master plans were absent.[9] As in many other post-Soviet cities, the situation was characterised by a lack of housing and green and public spaces in general, homelessness, poor construction quality, chaotic development practices, and ignorance of regulatory norms.[10]

The privatisation of housing, which began in the early 1990s, has had an enduring and significant impact on the shape of the microdistricts. Initially, housing privatisation was carried out on request and for a certain fee, but this practise was soon replaced by the automatic privatisation of almost the entire housing stock in favour of the then tenants.[11] At the same time, the state handed over all responsibilities for building maintenance, utility payments, and insurance to municipalities and private owners. However, the inability and unwillingness of most residents to pay for repairs and maintenance resulted in a rapid deterioration of almost all Tblisi's apartment buildings, prompting the city to take back some of the powers and responsibilities it had earlier relinquished.[12] By 2004 almost 95 per cent of the housing stock had been privatised.[13]

---

9   See Salukvadze, Joseph and Javakhishvili, Ivane, 'Market Versus Planning? Mechanisms of Spatial Change in POST-SOVIET Tbilisi', in Van Assche, Kristof, Salukvadze, Joseph, and Shavishvili, Nick (eds.), *City Culture and City Planning in Tbilisi: Where Europe and Asia Meet* (Lewiston, NY: Edwin Mellen Press 2009), pp. 158–187, here: p. 169, <https://www.researchgate.net/publication/290008134_Market_versus_planning_Mechanisms_of_spatial_change_in_post-Soviet_Tbilisi/link/57f7ea9908ae91deaa60683d/download?_tp=eyJjb250ZXh0Ijp7ImZpcnN0UGFnZSI6ImB1YmxpY2F0aW9uIiwicGFnZSI6ImB1YmxpY2F0aW9uIn19>, accessed 3 January 2024.

10 Van Assche, Kristof and Salukvadze, Joseph, 'Urban Transformation and Role Transformation in the Post-Soviet Metropolis, in Lara, J. (ed.), *Remaking Metropolis: Global Challenges of the Urban Landscape* (London: Routledge, 2013), pp. 86–102, here: p. 88, <https://www.researchgate.net/publication/289986549_Urban_transformation_and_role_transformation_in_the_post-Soviet_metropolis>, accessed 4 January 2024.

11 Bouzarovski, Stefan, Salukvadze, Joseph, and Gentile, Michael, 'A Socially Resilient Urban Transition? The Contested Landscapes of Apartment Building Extensions in Two Postcommunist Cities', *Urban Studies*, vol. 48, No. 13, 2011, pp. 2689–2714, here: p. 2692.

12 Salukvadze, Joseph and Javakhishvili, Ivane, 'Market Versus Planning? Mechanisms of Spatial Change in Post-Soviet Tbilisi' in Van Assche, Kristof, Salukvadze, Joseph, and Shavishvili, Nick (eds.), *City Culture and City Planning in Tbilisi: Where Europe and Asia Meet* (Lewiston, NY: Edwin Mellen Press 2009), pp. 158–187, here: p. 179, <https://www.researchgate.net/publication/290008134_Market_versus_planning_Mechanisms_of_spatial_change_in_post-Soviet_Tbilisi/link/57f7ea9908ae91deaa60683d/download?_tp=eyJjb250ZXh0Ijp7ImZpcnN0UGFnZSI6ImB1YmxpY2F0aW9uIiwicGFnZSI6ImB1YmxpY2F0aW9uIn19>, accessed 3 January 2024.

13 Gogishvili, David, 'Competing for Space in Tbilisi: Transforming Residential Courtyards to Parking in an Increasingly Car-Dependent City', *Eurasian Geography and Economics*, 18 October 2021, pp. 1–27, here: p. 9, <https://doi.org/10.1080/15387216.2021.1993292>, accessed 4 January 2024.

Figure 3:
Distribution of ownership in Vazha-Pshavela, Block VI.

- ▢ Municipal
- ▢ Shared ownership
- ▢ Private investment properties

Source: Lara Marquardt, and Kevin Schulz, based on maps supplied by
National Agency of Public Registry (NAPR), Georgia (https://maps.gov.ge).

Due to the emerging forces of deregulated land and real estate markets, Tbilisi's built environment in general and the microrayons in particular underwent erratic change. Territorial and building safety deterioration and visual degradation also took place in Vazha-Pshavela. The neighbourhood's spatial form changed considerably, including as a result of extension of existing buildings and construction of new ones, unregulated parking of vehicles, and and the piecemeal, unplanned appropriation of open spaces.

Transformation of buildings

A key feature of the physical transformation of Vazha-Pshavela has been alterations to buildings in the form of façade extensions, superstructures, additional storeys, or lofts on top of existing buildings.[14] Buildings have been seemingly transformed with additional balconies, doors, and windows, reflecting a newfound sense of individuality and adaptability. Residents opt to either expand their living spaces or partition them into smaller units. With creativity and resourcefulness, they have taken liberties so as to enhance their living conditions. Apartments have even been marketed with the enticing tagline 'potential for expansion', encouraging residents to envision and implement personalised modifications. Some khrushchevka owners have taken even bolder steps, acquiring adjacent apartments and merging them with their own, resulting in more spacious and versatile living quarters.[15]

The building extensions, so-called 'ABEs' (apartment building extensions), are one way in which inhabitants have reacted to the state's inability to provide sufficient housing. They have increased the size of apartments by 25 per cent and even more, compared to previous dwelling sizes.[16] These adaptations are often improvised works based on the intuitions of the individual apartment owner and are carried out within the limits imposed by availability of materials, often resulting in both ingenuity and absurdity.[17] The immense variety of micro-scale appropriations causes buildings to mutate. The façades of modernist houses have been transformed with a range of different claddings in a variety of colours and textures.[18]

The extensions and additions are used for a variety of purposes: some serve as new bedrooms and living rooms; others provide auxiliary functions, such as kitchens, extended 'loggias', balconies, and storage rooms. New entrances to housing blocks have been built.[19] Use of added space for commercial purposes is rare and usually only

---

14 Bouzarovski, Stefan, Salukvadze, Joseph, and Gentile, Michael, 'A Socially Resilient Urban Transition? The Contested Landscapes of Apartment Building Extensions in Two Post-communist Cities', *Urban Studies*, vol. 48, No. 13, 2011, pp. 2689–2714, here: p. 2700.

15 Mumladze, Mayram, 'Finding Happiness in a Krushchevka', 28 March 2018, https://chaikhana.media/en/stories/651/finding-happiness-in-a-khrushchevka, accessed January 7th 2024

16 Bouzarovski, Stefan, Salukvadze, Joseph, and Gentile, Michael, 'A Socially Resilient Urban Transition? The Contested Landscapes of Apartment Building Extensions in Two Post-Communist Cities', *Urban Studies*, vol. 48, No. 13, 2011, pp. 2689–2714, here: p. 2690.

17 Ibrahim, Thomas, 'The House is Never Complete: A Cartography of Idiosyncrasy in Socio-Political Maelstrom' (master's thesis, TU Delft, 2022), p. 34, <https://repository.tudelft.nl/islandora/object/uuid:24e07142-b100-4291-9298-efc3aa490a4a/datastream/OBJ5/download>, accessed 10 January 2024.

18 Ibid., p. 18.

19 Ibid., p. 18.

Figures 4, 5:
Building extensions in Vazha-Pshavela, September 2023.
Sources: Marina Sapunova

occurs if the original apartment is located on the ground floor of a building – in which case mini-markets, fast-food kiosks, or beauty salons are most common.[20] Due to their volume and physical incongruity with the host buildings, these additions have brought dramatic changes to the neighbourhood's clear physical plan. They have had a major impact on the exterior appearance of apartment blocks.[21] They have also had a negative impact on building safety, green spaces, and lighting.

Initially, the building extensions were constructed by state-owned building companies, which had already started installing metal extension frames in 1987. Architectural co-operatives soon entered this business, however, and in the 1990s private enterprises and builders took over the sector completely. A significant number of these extensions were constructed by the residents themselves. In the early days of such modifications, the structures were viewed favourably by urban planners and the academic community, who hoped that they would bring colour and diversity to the grey, monofunctional Soviet housing estates while improving living standards for the population. Although the chaotic and haphazard nature of the building extensions was recognised, it was even sometimes suggested by local officials that finished extensions should be considered legal and be recorded in the property of real estate.[22] However,

[20] Bouzarovski, Stefan, Salukvadze, Joseph, and Gentile, Michael, 'A Socially Resilient Urban Transition? The Contested Landscapes of Apartment Building Extensions in Two Post-Communist Cities', *Urban Studies*, vol. 48, No. 13, 2011, pp. 2689–2714, here: p. 2705.

[21] Ibid., p. 2708.

[22] Ibid., p. 2701.

the discourse soon changed due to the rapid and unregulated expansion of this phenomenon and its negative impacts on the visual appearance and socio-economic functionality of urban space.[23]

It is difficult to assess the physical impact of building extensions on the old and weak building fabric and to what extent serious safety problems exist or are amplified by the additional structures. Reliable information on the quality of the buildings is hard to come by. The municipality and the district management pay little attention to renovation or technical improvement of buildings, nor do they maintain the existing infrastructure. They act only when a building or part of it collapses. So it remains unclear whether the assertion made by the head of Vazha-Pshavela district that all the buildings are in good condition is a reflection of the buildings' objective state or is simply an attempt to avoid administrative work.

Although the building extensions have clearly helped address the population's housing needs over the short term, they are realised to a low technical standard – especially in terms of energy efficiency and safety standards. While this has sporadically and temporarily improved the living conditions for some, it has also reduced the quality of courtyard space and led to deterioration of the residential buildings.

Transformation of open space

Open spaces played a major role in the planning of Soviet microdistricts. The green areas between the buildings of a residential complex were primarily intended as a means of improving the micro-climate and abating noise and as an important design element. Places for social life, sports, children's games, and the like were located at a distance from courtyards so that residents could spend time in the latter in peace and quiet.[24] The spaces between the buildings and the yards were designed as enclosed areas to prevent them becoming throughpaths and ensure that they remained calm, attractive spaces for rest and relaxation.[25]

Although the amount of green space has diminished from 45 per cent in the 1960s to 37 per cent today, the district is still very green, with large trees growing between the buildings and maintaining the quiet atmosphere in the neighbourhood. There is no noise coming from the major roads running around the block on its northern and western sides. However, the 'green jungle' and the fact that there is no hierarchy of streets and alleys make orientation inside this

23 Ibid., p. 2709.

24 Kiselevich, Lev N. and Rabinovich, Izidor L., *Kompozitsiya massovyh zhilyh domov i ansamblya zastroyki* (Moscow, 1973), p. 84.

25 Ibid., p. 89.

12 Vazha-Pshavela Block VI in Tbilisi, Georgia

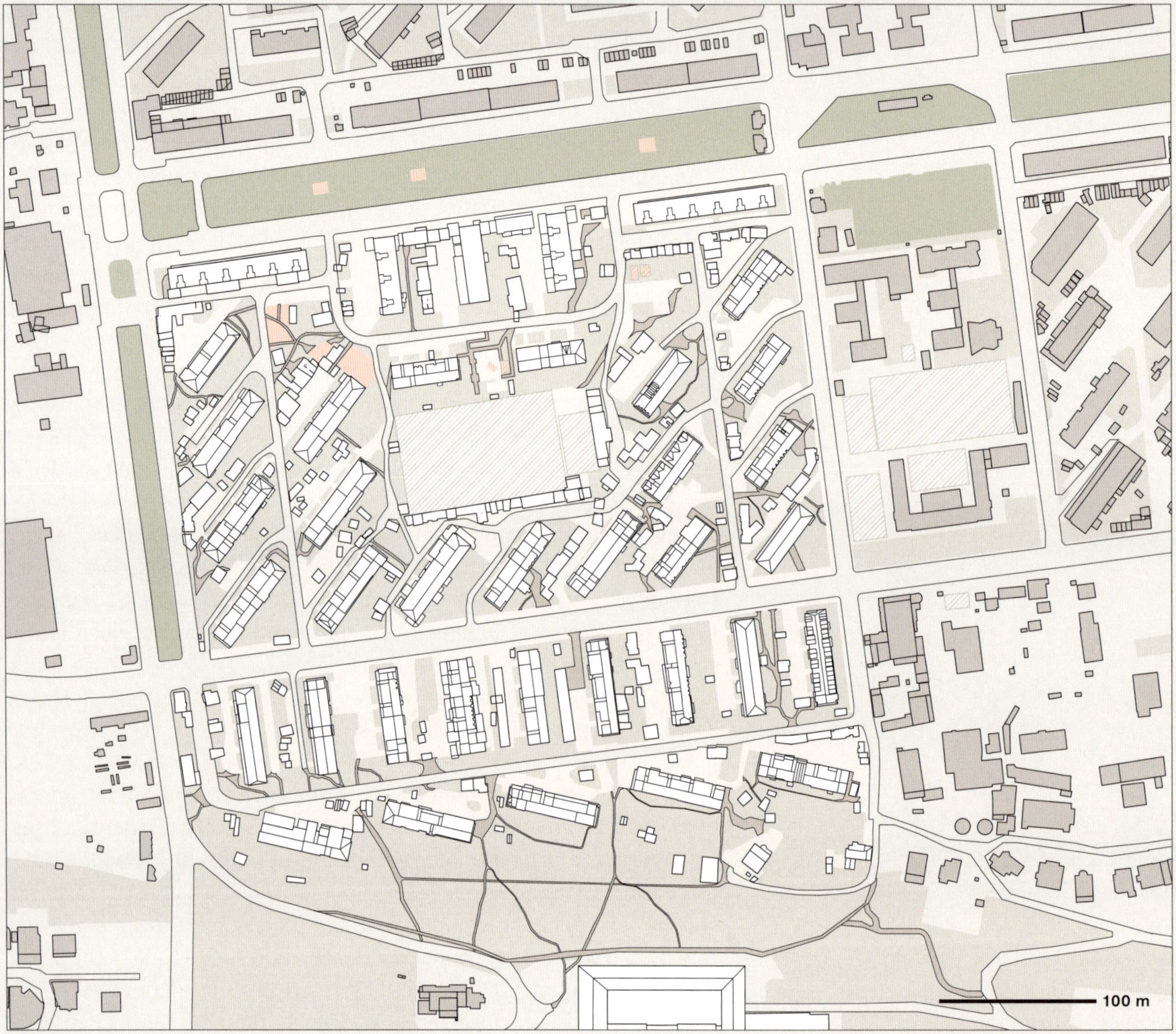

Figure 6:
Open and green spaces in Vazha-Pshavela, Block VI.

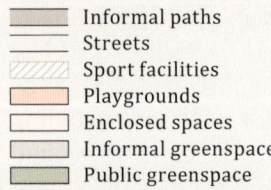

- Informal paths
- Streets
- Sport facilities
- Playgrounds
- Enclosed spaces
- Informal greenspace
- Public greenspace

Source: Cara Stiller, Loana Köhler, Sofia Vinnik, Jasmin Maichle, based on maps from the National Agency of Public Registry (NAPR), Georgia (https://maps.gov.ge).

megablock difficult. The green and open spaces are very important for ventilation of the district.

Since the early 1990s the lack of governmental control has also led to occupation of open spaces in micro-districts, including streets, pathways, and residential courtyards. When urban land was privatised, different interest groups started competing for desirable property, often using illicit practices, such as bribes and influence. Under this lack of regulation, commercial, financial, service, and other high-value land uses expanded into the residential districts.[26]

In addition, courtyards in Tbilisi have been deeply affected by mass privatisation and the dramatic increase in motorisation rates; this is manifested particularly clearly in the parking problem.[27] Courtyards between residential blocks are usually gathering places for inhabitants but are often far from comfortable.

Since the 1990s the increased dominance of the automobile in Tbilisi has led to rapid modification and deterioration of the communal areas of multi-storey apartment blocks. Courtyards have been transformed from leisure areas into parking spaces. These changes to Tbilisi's street-level fabric have produced greater flows of vehicles in areas planned as residential, leading to conflicts over parking.[28] The lack of parking for inhabitants of micro-districts was the result of a Soviet-wide foregrounding of public transport, a policy which was reflected in the widespread absence of private vehicles.[29] Saburtalo, along with Vake, is now among districts with a very high rate of motorisation and the highest rate of parking problems.[30] The space consumed by on-street parking is a major challenge for the city since it affects the quality of pedestrian paths, for example.[31]

Today one sees open spaces being invaded by a variety of alien elements as well as reconfiguration of the spaces themselves. Sheds, parking garages, private gardens, workshops, and small shops

26 Gogishvili, David, 'Competing for Space in Tbilisi: Transforming Residential Courtyards to Parking in an Increasingly Car-Dependent City', *Eurasian Geography and Economics*, 18 October 2021, pp. 1–27, here p. 11, <https://doi.org/10.1080/15387216.2021.1993292>, accessed 4 January 2024.

27 Ibid., p. 3.

28 Ibid., p.11.

29 Ibid., p. 3.

30 Municipal Development Fund of Georgia (MDF), 'Consulting Services for Organization of a Transportation Household Survey in Tbilisi Metropolitan Area. Final Report', 5 August 2016, pp. 20, 27, <https://tbilisi.gov.ge/img/original/2018/4/20/THS_Final_Report_Eng.pdf>, accessed 12 January 2024.

31 Ibid., p. 52.

Figures 7, 8:
Additional functions have been implemented in the neighbourhood in the form of new buildings.
Sources: Barbara Engel (7), Ekaterina Gladkova (8)

Figure 9:
Uses in the neighbourhood.

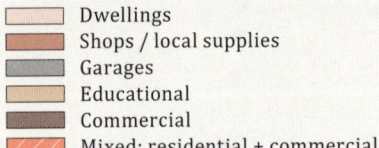

Dwellings
Shops / local supplies
Garages
Educational
Commercial
Mixed: residential + commercial

Source: Quendrese Bardiqi, Celine Martin, Sarah Schlindwein, based on maps from the National Agency of Public Registry (NAPR), Georgia (https://maps.gov.ge).

Figures 10, 11:
'Comparmentalisation' of open spaces in Vazha-Pshavela, individually organised by residents. September 2023.
Source: Barbara Engel (10), Ekaterina Gladkova (11)

regularly take up the space surrounding buildings, often extending into and occupying public streets. A total of 318 garages are visible, located along streets and in courtyards. Garages have been built between housing blocks. They are hardly ever used for parking, though; more often, they serve as storage spaces. Sometimes, in more populous districts with greater pedestrian traffic across avenues between housing blocks, they are used as commercial spaces, such as bakeries and outlets for vendors of comestibles.[32] On some avenues where commercial opportunities existed along streets, new sheds and single-storey buildings have been built.[33] In cases where the ground floors of modernist housing blocks offered commercial opportunities, new entrances have been created to enable new commercial functions.

Courtyards have been 'compartmentalised' using a bewildering variety of walls, fences, hedges, and markings.[34] People have appropriated green spaces for themselves, fencing off small plots for individual gardens or communal meeting spaces and playgrounds. Although these areas are primarily used by the inhabitants of the adjacent houses, they may be considered publicly accessible because they are not fully enclosed, except in rare cases where gates restrict entry. Through the installation of parking barriers, residential courtyards have been privatised and turned into essential components of the automobility system: car parks.[35]

Planning policies

Transformations take place in formal, legal, and illicit ways, mostly relying on concessions from other residents; this is a widespread practice that few would want to condemn.[36] In Vazha-Pshavela informality has played an important role, given that local government has decided to turn a blind eye to privatisation of courtyard spaces. Incapacity and/or disinterest has allowed these unique structural transformations and permutations to take place.[37] Certain rules have nevertheless been approved to give order to the process, but, it seems, more to apply a veneer of official legality to this DIY urbanism *post factum* rather than to guide consciousness of the planning process.

Georgia's socialist government passed a decree in 1987 allowing interventions in state-owned housing. Given that this decision was followed by uncontrolled intensification of building extension activities, the government adopted a more specific resolution in 1989, which permitted construction of attached structures and extensions to buildings up to nine storeys high. The resolution defined rules for projections, construction, and technical supervision while regulating the size and volume of extensions. Thanks to such policies, metal-framed building extensions were attached to the walls of many prefabricated buildings.

As the process of attaching extensions to buildings continued, additional rules were adopted, such as Rules for the Use and Development of Territories in the City of Tbilisi, adopted in accordance with Decision 4-13 of Tbilisi City Council in March 2009. The latter rules allowed the construction of extensions provided that they exhibited a uniform appearance and had the aim of improving living comfort. As problems with safety for residents and buildings increased, in 2016 a new law, Article 20 of the Regulations on Use and Development of Territories in the Tbilisi Municipality, was adopted under Resolution 14-39 of the City Council of Tbilisi Municipality, with the aim of restricting extensions. This law prohibits the construction, extension and/or building of a mansard on multi-apartment residential buildings, except in specific cases.

While some transformations have been carried out legally or have been legalised after their implementation, they do not follow a holistic strategy or master plan. The do-it-yourself implementations fulfil short-term and individual needs but not public or socially balanced interests.[38] There is a lack of effective measures to regulate the process of bottom-up interventions and private initiatives. Also lacking

[32] Ibrahim, Thomas, 'The House is never complete. A Cartography of Idiosyncrasy in Socio-political Maelstrom', 2022, https://repository.tudelft.nl/islandora/object/uuid:24e07142-b100-4291-9298-efc3aa490a4a/datastream/OBJ5/download, accessed, 10 January 2024.

[33] Ibid., p. 18.

[34] Salukvadze, Joseph, Javakhishvili, Ivane, 'Market Versus Planning? Mechanisms of Spatial Change in Post-Soviet Tbilisi' in Van Assche, Kristof, Salukvadze, Joseph, and Shavishvili, Nick (eds.), City Culture and City Planning in Tbilisi: Where Europe and Asia Meet (Lewiston, NY: Edwin Mellen Press 2009), pp. 158–187, here: p. 179, <https://www.researchgate.net/publication/290008134_Market_versus_planning_Mechanisms_of_spatial_change_in_post-Soviet_Tbilisi/link/57f7ea9908ae91deaa60683d/download?_tp=eyJjb250ZXh0Ijp7ImZpcnN0UGFnZSI6InB1Ymxp Y2F0aW9uIiwicGFnZSI6InB1YmxpY2F0aW9uIn19>.

[35] Gogishvili, David, 'Competing for Space in Tbilisi: Transforming Residential Courtyards to Parking in an Increasingly Car-Dependent City', *Eurasian Geography and Economics*, 18 October 2021, pp. 1–27, <https://doi.org/10.1080/15387216.2021.1993292>, accessed 4 January 2024.

[36] Kotzias, Nikos-Pavlos, 'Urban Renewal and Disconnect Varying Perceptions on the Value of Urban Development in Tbilisi, Georgia' (master's thesis, Utrecht University, 2023). here: p. 77, <https://studenttheses.uu.nl/handle/20.500.12932/45389>, accessed 4 January 2023.

[37] Gogishvili, David, 'Competing for Space in Tbilisi: Transforming Residential Courtyards to Parking in an Increasingly Car-Dependent City', *Eurasian Geography and Economics*, 18 October 2021, pp. 1–27, here p. 22, <https://doi.org/10.1080/15387216.2021.1993292>, accessed 4 January 2024.

[38] Salukvadze, Joseph and Van Assche, Kristof, 'Multiple Transformations, Coordination and Public Goods: Tbilisi and the Search for Planning as Collective Strategy', *European Planning Studies*, vol. 31, No. 3, May 2022, pp. 1–19, here: p. 4.

are public policies from municipal governments with regard to both public and private space.

The future of modernist housing

Discussion in Tbilisi today about the neighbourhoods of khrushchevkas is multifaceted. During his election campaign in 2019 the current mayor of Tbilisi, Kakha Kaladze, announced his intention to gradually demolish and replace the approximately 700 khrushchevka buildings that exist across Tbilisi as they are dangerous and ugly places in which to live.[39] As a statement of Soviet power, the micro-districts are perceived by many Georgians as unwanted heritage. Undoubtedly, there are disadvantages to the neighbourhoods with panel buildings in poor condition. In addition, the buildings have outdated floor plans, low ceilings, and small kitchens and bathrooms. With poor insulation, uneven floors, cracked walls, dilapidated staircases, and no lifts, the apartments do not meet today's standards of comfort. But there are positive aspects as well. The micro-district offers large, community-focused courtyards, mature trees, and wide walkways between buildings. Many families have lived in the same apartment for decades, so their apartments are impregnated with memories and history, relationships with their neighbours, and affection for the neighbourhood.[40]

Vazha-Pshavela Block No. VI is an entity in itself: quiet, but at the same time separated from the adjacent areas and closed off from its neighbours, which means that it is in danger of becoming a ghetto. So far, Vazha-Pshavela does not seem to be of interest to developers looking for projects in which to invest. On the one hand, this is a problem since very little or no money is invested in the neighbourhood, in renovating its buildings or in improving the open spaces. On the other han, it offers opportunities since Vazha-Pshavela Block No. VI still has affordable housing, an increasingly rare commodity in Tbilisi. The areas surrounding Vazha-Pshavela, such as the newly built neighbourhood to the west of it, consist of modern apartment buildings and co-working spaces, so are markedly different from the social strata – and housing prices – of the area under discussion. This large neighbourhood is accordingly shouldering increasingly needed social benefits for the city as a whole, thus relieving pressure placed on other districts by tensions on the housing market.

Vazha-Pshavela is undergoing dynamic spatial transformation shaped by individual engagement within the neighbourhood due to deficits

[39] Guthrie, Samantha, 'Tbilisi City Hall Moves to Initiate "Khrushchovka" Replacement Project', *Georgia Today*, 11 February 2019, <http://gtarchive.georgiatoday.ge/news/14427/Tbilisi-City-Hall-Moves-to-Initiate-%E2%80%98Khrushchovka%E2%80%99-Replacement-Project, accessed 3 January 2024.

[40] Ibid.

in housing supply and open spaces. At present, the outcomes of do-it yourself urbanism are fulfilling private needs but are also creating frictions with neighbourhood interests, violating safety regulations, and leading to functional problems. Moreover, transformation and reorganisation of buildings and open spaces are carried out without respect for the spatial configuration of the modernist layout. The result is degradation and destruction of the modernist heritage.[41]

At the same time, such transformation shows the neighbourhood's ability to adapt and modify itself to meet changing needs and new demands, demonstrating a high level of resilience. The bottom-up activities and household-level interventions illustrate civic engagement, responsibility, and stewardship of the neighbourhood and the living environment, which is a valuable resource and a prerequisite for a neighbourhood that people would want to identify with.[42]

The ongoing and future transformation of Vazha-Pshavela requires monitoring and guidance. A comprehensive form of planning is needed that will take into account the needs of citizens and new functional requirements, such as sustainable mobility concepts and climate adaptation and mitigation strategies – as well as respecting the spatial configuration of post-war modernism. It should also consider and balance the diversity of interests and give residents the opportunity to become involved in designing their living environment – and by doing so, sustaining and enriching Vazha-Pshavela's modernist heritage.

41 Salukvadze, Joseph and Van Assche, Kristof, 'Multiple Transformations, Coordination and Public Goods. Tbilisi and the Search for Planning as Collective Strategy', *European Planning Studies*, vol. 31, No. 3, May 2022, pp. 1–19, here: p. 4.

42 Bouzarovski, Stefan, Salukvadze, Joseph, and Gentile, Michael, 'A Socially Resilient Urban Transition? The Contested Landscapes of Apartment Building Extensions in Two Postcommunist Cities', *Urban Studies*, vol. 48, No. 13, 2011, pp. 2689–2714, here: p. 2711.

References

Asatiani, Nino, 'City Building Problems in 1960s–1970s Georgia (Based on the Example of Tbilisi)'. <https://www.academia.edu/35893557/Problems_of_Tbilisi_city_Planing_in_1960ies>, accessed 3 January 2024.

Asabashwili, Levan, and Mirzikashvili, Rusudan: 'Housing the Masses: Soviet Housing in Tbilisi' in Wheeler, Angela (ed.), *Tbilisi: Architectural Guide*, (Berlin: DOM publishers, 2023), pp. 347–351.

Bouzarovski, Stefan, Salukvadze, Joseph, and Gentile, Michael, 'A Socially Resilient Urban Transition? The Contested Landscapes of Apartment Building Extensions in Two Post-communist Cities', *Urban Studies*, vol. 48, No. 13, 2011, pp. 2689–2714.

Gogishvili, David, 'Competing for Space in Tbilisi: Transforming Residential Courtyards to Parking in an Increasingly Car-Dependent City', *Eurasian Geography and Economics*, 18 October 2021, pp. 1–27, <https://doi.org/10.1080/15387216.2021.1993292>, accessed 4 January 2024.

Gogishvili, David, 'Gldani: From Ambitious Experimental Project to Half-realised Soviet Mass-housing District in Tbilisi, Georgia', in Mariotti, Jasna, and Leetma, Kadri (eds.) *Urban Planning During Socialism: Views from the Periphery* (London; Routledge, 2023), pp. 191–205.

Guthrie, Samantha, 'Tbilisi City Hall Moves to Initiate 'Khrushchovka' Replacement Project', *Georgia Today*, 11 February 2019, <http://gtarchive.georgiatoday.ge/news/14427/Tbilisi-City-Hall-Moves-to-Initiate-%E2%80%98Khrushchovka%E2%80%99-Replacement-Project>, accessed 3 January 2024.

Ibrahim, Thomas, 'The House Is Never Complete: A Cartography of Idiosyncrasy in Socio-political Maelstrom', 2022, <https://repository.tudelft.nl/islandora/object/uuid:24e07142-b100-4291-9298-efc3aa490a4a/datastream/OBJ5/download>, accessed 10 January 2024.

Kiselevich, Lev N., and Rabinovich, Izidor L., *Kompozitsiya massovyh zhilyh domov i ansamblya zastroyki* (Moscow, 1973).

Kotzias, Nikos-Pavlos, 'Urban Renewal and Disconnect Varying Perceptions on the Value of Urban Development in Tbilisi, Georgia' (master's thesis, Utrecht University, 2023), <https://studenttheses.uu.nl/handle/20.500.12932/45389>, accessed 4 January 2023.

Mumladze, Mayram, 'Finding Happiness in a Krushchevka', 28 March 2018, https://chaikhana.media/en/stories/651/finding-happiness-in-a-khrushchevka, accessed January 7th 2024.

Municipal Development Fund of Georgia (MDF), 'Consulting Services for Organization of a Transportation Household Survey in Tbilisi Metropolitan Area. Final Report', 5 August 2016, <https://tbilisi.gov.ge/img/original/2018/4/20/THS_Final_Report_Eng.pdf>, accessed 12 January 2024.

Salukvadze, Joseph, and Javakhishvili, Ivane, 'Market Versus Planning? Mechanisms of Spatial Change in Post-Soviet Tbilisi', in Van Assche, Kristof, Salukvadze, Joseph, and Shavishvili, Nick (eds.), *City Culture and City Planning in Tbilisi: Where Europe and Asia Meet* (Lewiston, NY: Edwin Mellen Press, 2009), pp. 158–187, <https://www.researchgate.net/publication/290008134_Market_versus_planning_Mechanisms_of_spatial_change_in_post-Soviet_Tbilisi/link/57f7ea9908ae91deaa60683d/download?_tp=eyJjb250ZXh0Ijp7ImZpcnN0UGFnZSI6InB1YmxpY2F0aW9uIiwicGFnZSI6InB1YmxpY2F0aW9uIn19>, accessed 3 January 2024.

Salukvadze, Joseph, and Van Assche, Kristof, 'Multiple Transformations, Coordination and Public Goods: Tbilisi and the Search for Planning as Collective Strategy', *European Planning Studies*, vol. 31, No. 3, May 2022, pp. 1–19.

Tsitsagi, Mariam, Kharebava, Nino, Nikolaishvili, Dali, Kupatadze, Ia, and Gadrani, Lela, 'Tbilisi Through Time', *Georgian Geographical Journal*, vol. 2, No. 1, 2022, pp. 62–72.

Van Assche, Kristof, and Salukvadze, Joseph, 'Urban Transformation and Role Transformation in the Post-Soviet Metropolis' in Lara, J. (ed.), *Remaking Metropolis: Global Challenges of the Urban Landscape* (London: Routledge, 2013, pp. 86–102, <https://www.researchgate.net/publication/289986549_Urban_transformation_and_role_transformation_in_the_post-Soviet_metropolis>, accessed 4 January 2024.

Wheeler, Angela, *Tbilisi: Architectural Guide* (Berlin: DOM publishers, 2023).

13

Vyhurivschyna-Troieshchyna in Kyiv, Ukraine. A housing estate with supergraphics and colour composition

Semen Shyrochyn

Introduction

The city of Kyiv grew actively after World War II. The first new housing estates were built on vacant land outside the historical centre. Nearby areas saw further development until the late 1960s, but with not much empty land available for new construction, new residential estates have also been built on the site of earlier settlements since the late 1960s.

The starting point for the construction of large estates on the lower bank of the river was Rusanivka, built in the early 1960s. This experiment in hydraulic land reclamation offered a new opportunity for building new housing on land that had previously not been used due to spring flooding or had rural settlements that suffered from such floods. Since then, a number of new residential estates have been built on reclaimed land on both banks of the River Dnipro; they include Bereznyaky, Obolon, and parts of Livoberezhnyi.

From the late 1960s forwards, mass housing construction has given Kyiv new districts that have broken records in terms of population, each comparable to a medium-sized city. They have usually had much more developed infrastructure: not only schools, kindergartens, shops, and post offices but also hospitals, stadiums, sports halls, cinemas, and malls. In the 1960s the Mykilska Borshchahivka estate was built for 100,000 residents. In the 1970s construction began on the Obolon estate, designed for 200,000–250,000 people. Each of these estates was provided with rapid transport: Mykilska Borshchahivka had the world's first high-speed tram, and Obolon soon acquired a metro link. In the 1970s, however, the population grew faster, and even more estates were needed.

By 1980 planning of the largest housing estate had been completed. To be built on the site of two old villages – Vyhurivschyna and Troieshchyna[1] – in the northeast of Kyiv, the estate was initially planned for a population of 350,000 inhabitants (other sources give an even higher estimate of 400,000),[2] which would have made Troieshchyna the largest residential estate in Kyiv and the second most populous in Ukraine after Kharkiv's Saltivka (which had 410,000 residents by 2018).

---

[1] Blinova, G. N., 'Arhitekturno-prostranstvennaya kompoziciya novyh zhilyh rajonov Kieva', *Stroitel'stvo i arkhitektura*, no. 8, 1981, pp. 8–11.

[2] Shyrochyn, Semen, and Myhaylyk, Oleksandr, *Nevidomi Periferii Kyieva: Pivnichne Livoberezhzhya* (Kyiv: Sky Horse, 2022).

Figure 1:
Aerial view of Vyhurivschyna-Troieshchyna, 2014.
Photo: Semen Shyrochyn

13 Vyhurivschyna-Troieshchyna in Kyiv, Ukraine

Grand plans of/for the estate

The general plan of Troieshchyna housing estate was developed in the late 1970s and early 1980s by the Kyiv architects Yuriy Paskevich, Hryhoriy Slutskyi, Yevgeny Frolov, Mykola Dyomin, Valentin Yezhov, Vadym Hopkalo, and others. Architects who participated in developing individual micro-districts and residential groups included Georgy Gurenkov, Vadym Grechyna, Volodymyr Kolomiets, and Vsevolod Suvorov.

The estate was planned with two residential formations – in its east (on the site of the village of Vyhurivschyna) and its west (on the site of the village of Troieshchyna). The boundary between the two formations is Honoré de Balzac Street and the cascade of artificial lakes along it. The eastern formation was to be arc-shaped; the western, egg-shaped with a network of radial streets converging at its centre, conceived as a compositional accent for the entire estate.[3,4] A large industrial zone was planned to the east of the estate. New industrial businesses as well as expansions of existing factories were planned. It was expected that a large proportion of the residents would work there.

The original plan was to build the estate on the site of the villages of Vyhurivschyna and Troieshchyna. The main part of the village of Vyhurivshchyna was demolished in 1981–1984, and its eastern outskirts in the second half of the 1980s, leaving only the northern part of the oldest corner of Kuchanskyi. The village of Troieshchyna remained in place and avoided demolition.[5]

[3] Odnopozov, Igor, *Zvichajna nezvichna Troieshchyna* (Kyiv, 2021).

[4] Shyrochyn, Semen and Myhaylyk, Oleksandr, *Nevidomi Periferii Kyieva: Pivnichne Livoberezhzhya* (Kyiv: Sky Horse, 2022).

[5] Ibid.

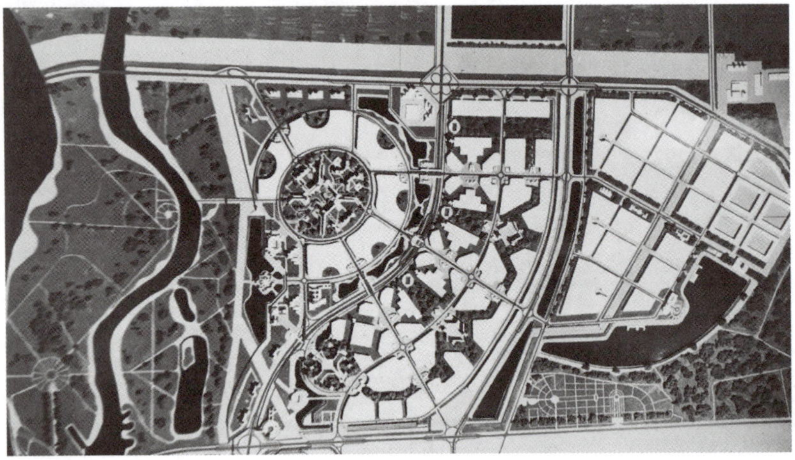

Figure 2:
Planned development of the Troieshchyna district, 1980. At the upper left is the unbuilt part of the estate.
Source: album of planned development in Kyiv

Figure 3:
The unbuilt part of the Troieshchyna district, 1980.
The village of Troieshchyna still exists in its original location.
Source: album of planned development in Kyiv

History of construction of the estate

Construction of the estate took place at the highest pace of construction ever seen in the history of Kyiv.[6] In the press in the late 1980s it was claimed that during the 11th five-year plan (1981–1985), more new residential areas were built in Kyiv than in the city's entire history from its foundation to World War II. In February 1981 engineering preparations for the new construction began with hydraulic reclamation, which had a significant impact not only on surrounding settlements, but also on the surrounding nature. In 1982–1990 multistage alluvial land reclamation led to the emergence of Lake Almazne, which is now the largest lake on the left bank of Kyiv. In 1988 a canal was built near Micro-district No. 1. In 1989 Lower Vygurivske Lake formed, and in 1990 the Upper and Middle Vygurivske lakes made their appearance. The five lakes along Balzac Street remained on the drawing board.

Construction of the estate was divided into three phases. During the first phase, from 1982 to 1986, micro-districts 1, 3, 5, 6, 7, and 8 – almost the entire southern part of the estate – were built Micro-districts 1, 5, and 6 were designed by the architect Georgy Gurenkov, and micro-districts 3, 7, and 8 by Vadym Grechyna.[7] In 1987 construction of the second phase of the estate began. Micro-districts 9, 11, 13, and 14 and the micro-districts in the north-eastern part of the estate, as well as micro-district 2 in the south-western part were built from 1987 to 1991. Micro-districts 9, 11, 13, and 14 were designed by Georgy Gurenkov, micro-district 2 by Vadym Grechyna. In 1991 construction of the third phase of the estate began based on a project by Vadym Grechyna. Located on the western side of Balzac Street, the third phase included micro-districts 21, 22, 23, 24, and 26. Development of these micro-districts was mainly carried out from 1991 to 1996, although some houses were built in the mid-2000s and even later. In addition to residential micro-districts, four non-residential districts (Nos. 4, 10, 12, and 27) were planned. These were to contain only parks and public buildings. In the end, only micro-districts 4 and 12 became green zones: these contain Desnyansky and Molodizhny parks. At the same time, it was decided to build two more neighbourhoods – Nos. 20 and 25 – on the site of medical facilities north of Myloslavska Street.

Despite the fact that the estate received additional residential neighbourhoods that were not originally planned, part of what had initially been planned was never built. This is evident both in the

6   'Konveyer bol'shikh novoseliy', *Stroitel'stvo i arkhitektura*, No. 4, 1984, pp. 16–17.

7   Shyrochyn, Semen, and Myhaylyk, Oleksandr, *Nevidomi Periferii Kyieva: Pivnichne Livoberezhzhya* (Kyiv: Sky Horse, 2022).

absence of micro-districts 15 to 19 and in the fact that Balzac Street, with its high-speed tram, has buildings on only one side for almost half its length. The reason for this is the five missing micro-districts which were supposed to replace the village of Troieshchyna, which became part of Kyiv on 26 August 1988. The village was supposed to be demolished during the fourth phase of construction, planned for the mid-1990s.

However, the collapse of the Soviet Union and the subsequent economic crisis, which made mass housing construction difficult, saved the village. The initial target population of 350,000 was no longer possible due to cancellation of construction on the site of the village of Troieshchyna. Under the original plans, the first two stages of construction were supposed to provide housing for 240,000 residents in 1990. The exact number of residents as of 2021 is unknown but is estimated at 280,000.[8]

8   Ibid.

Monumental art and infrastructure

The total standardisation that Soviet architecture underwent after the beginning of the campaign 'against architectural excesses', initiated by Nikita Khrushchev in 1955, left architects almost no scope for artistic expression. Their designs were now limited by sanitary and building regulations, the available range of existing structural elements, and urban planning, while their duties consisted in optimal placement of standardised buildings, which was also limited by

Figure 4:
A model of the first micro-district, 1985.
Source: *Stroitel'stvo i arkhitektura*

Figure 5:
Aerial view of the first micro-district, 2021.
Photo: Semen Shyrochyn

9 Pravnichenko, I. A., 'Obraztsovo-pokazatel'niy mikrorayon zhilogo massiva na Troeshchine', *Stroitel'stvo i arkhitektura*, No. 11, 1985, pp. 13–15.

10 Vlasova, T. Y., 'Troeshchina. Standart i raznoobrazie', *Stroitel'stvo i arkhitektura*, No. 8, 1986, pp. 11–12.

11 Kostenko, A. Y., 'Programmirovanie eksperimenta', *Stroitel'stvo i arkhitektura*, No. 8, 1986, pp. 13–14.

12 Inozemceva, A. S., 'Aktual'nye problemy arkhitektury massovogo zhilishcha v Kieve', *Stroitel'stvo i arkhitektura*, No. 8, 1984, pp. 10–12.

13 Pravnichenko, I. A., 'Obraztsovo-pokazatel'nyj mikrorajon zhilogo massiva na Troeshchine', *Stroitel'stvo i arkhitektura*, No. 11, 1985, pp. 13–15.

14 Vlasova, T. Y., 'Troeshchina: Standart i raznoobrazie', *Stroitel'stvo i arkhitektura*, No. 8, 1986, pp. 11–12.

15 Tovstenko, T., 'Zhiloy rayon Troeshchina v Kieve', *Arkhitektura SSSR*, No. 5, 1987, pp. 52–57.

16 Vlasova, T. Y., 'Troeshchina: Standart i raznoobrazie', *Stroitel'stvo i arkhitektura*, No. 8, 1986, pp. 11–12.

17 Pravnichenko, I. A., 'Tsvetnoy mikrorayon: Nuzhno li krasit' novuyu zhiluyu zastroyku?', *Stroitel'stvo i arkhitektura*, No. 4, 1987, pp. 2–3.

18 Vlasova, T. Y., 'Troeshchina: Standart i raznoobrazie', *Stroitel'stvo i arkhitektura*, No. 8, 1986, pp. 11–12.

various urban planning regulations. Under such conditions, there were two ways to artistically design a space: artistic arrangement of standardised houses and modification of the assortment of standard structural elements, which would make it possible to introduce something new into the typical monotony.[9,10,11] Troieshchyna's micro-districts 5 and 6 follow the common Stalin-era principle of symmetrical ensembles of residential areas, but the large micro-district built symmetrically on the side of Mayakovsky Avenue reproduces this principle on a much larger scale.

Micro-district No. 1 is rightfully considered one of the estate's most successful micro-districts from the point of view of urban planning and architectural and spatial composition. Designed by the architect Georgiy Gurenkov, the plan has a distinctive image composed of standard mass house designs.[12,13,14,15] The main feature of this micro-district is its chromatic and graphic composition, which was included in the integrated programme of architectural and artistic decoration of Kyiv, approved in 1984.[16] The design of the buildings uses super-graphics – large-scale geometric motifs. Introduced by the American architect Charles Moore, this technique operates through active engagement with form; the graphic elements are independent in relation to the structural basis of the architectural form. Supergraphics dynamically change the nature of the form and organise the surrounding space differently, giving it new meaning. In contrast to the murals that have gained popularity in recent years, supergraphics do not assert themselves by denying the real geometry of the underlying architectural forms but by creating a new compositional integrity based on them. The functions of colour here are diverse: the colours emphasise the idea of the volumetric-spatial composition, give individual features to individual groups of houses, and create independent colourful structures that shape the housing environment. Supergraphics can be used to focus attention on a group of buildings, an individual building, a part of a building's façade, or a detail, and so on. The first micro-district at Troieshchyna is the most vivid example of this technique in Kyiv.[17] The active colour tone gives this neighbourhood greater urban significance. Vertical and horizontal lines are accentuated with supergraphics, and compositions have been created from different building sections and separate buildings. The colours used are terracotta, brown, white, yellow, and blue; these are colours considered traditional for Kyiv.[18]

The implementation of this idea became possible thanks to the collaboration of architects, engineers, and artists as well as house-building

Figure 6:
A supergraphic in micro-district 1, 2020.
The 12- to 16-storey block has a painted façade instead of panels coloured with ceramic tiles.
Photo: Semen Shyrochyn

Figure 7:
A supergraphic on a nine-storey building in Micro-district 1, with high-quality ceramic tiles on the walls, 2020.
Source: Semen Shyrochyn

13 Vyhurivschyna-Troieshchyna in Kyiv, Ukraine

factories. Houses in Series 96 are clad with coloured ceramic tiles that were laid before the panels themselves were poured. As integral parts of the panels, these tiles have held firmly in place, unlike tiles affixed to the façades of brick houses from the outside, which could fall off over time. It was also planned to decorate panels for high-rise buildings in the T-4 series, but this proved not to be possible due to the technological conditions for production at the time. Instead of using ceramic tiles, the supergraphics were applied by painting the panels. However, the paint used was not water-repellent; the low quality of the pigments and the short-term durability of the dyes led to rapid fading of the colours and surface peeling.

Despite the undeniable novelty and boldness of this design approach, the result was received with ambivalence by critics, who drew attention to problems with the quality of the execution.[19,20] It was proposed to switch to the use of more durable decorative concrete panels in the future.[21] In addition, criticisms were made of the colour schemes of the glazed tiles, the supergraphics, etc. According to critics, the compositions on neighbouring buildings are not always related to each other, just as the end façades of nine-storey buildings in the form of geometric panels are not always related to the theme of the main façade and have too many yellow and brown tiles. Yellow was considered a bad colour from the point of view of chromatic stereoscopy, because it 'pushes forward' the elements.[22]

Local toponyms

An interesting feature of the estate is the policy by which its streets have been named. New streets were mostly named after writers, poets, architects, and historians. During construction of the first phase, in 1983, streets were named after Volodymyr Mayakovsky, Honoré de Balzac, Vikentii Beretti, Mykola Zakrevsky, the architect Nikolaev, and Theodor Dreiser.[23] Only two names were exceptions to this 'series of figures from the arts' – the street named after the soldier Oleksandr Saburov (now Serzh Lyfar) and the neutral Kashtanova Street. In 2022 Mayakovsky Avenue was renamed 'Chervona Kalyna', and in 2023 Theodore Dreiser Street became Ronald Reagan Street. During construction of the second phase this tradition was continued. In 1987 streets were named after Leonid Bykov, Volodymyr Vysotsky, Kostyantyn Dankevich, and Maryna Tsvetaeva. It is worth noting the commemoration of Volodymyr Vysotskyi and

Figure 8 (previous spread):
A mosaic on the wall of a polyclinic, 2021, with the same colour scheme as the supergraphics on the walls of most nearby buildings.
Source: Semen Shyrochyn

19 Pravnichenko, I. A., 'Obraztsovo-pokazatel'niy mikrorayon zhilogo massiva na Troeshchine', *Stroitel'stvo i arkhitektura*, no. 11, 1985, pp. 13–15.

20 Vasilenko, L. G., 'Tsvet v arkhitekture Troeshchiny', *Stroitel'stvo i arkhitektura*, No. 4, 1987, p. 3.

21 Pravnichenko, I. A., 'Tsvetnoy mikrorayon. Nuzhno li krasit· novuyu zhiluyu zastroyku?', *Stroitel'stvo i arkhitektura*, No. 4, 1987, pp. 2–3.

22 Vasilenko, L. G., 'Tsvet v arkhitekture Troeshchiny', *Stroitel'stvo i arkhitektura*, No. 4, 1987, p. 3.

23 Ibid.

Figure 9:
Supergraphics with a design in blue in Micro-district 3, 2021.
Source: Semen Shyrochyn

Maryna Tsvetayeva: Kyiv became one of the first cities in the world to have streets named in their honour. This trend was subsequently replaced by the preservation of ancient toponyms. On 17 February 1987 the estate was renamed 'Vyhurivschyna-Troieshchyna' to preserve the historical name of the lost village of Vyhurivschyna, but in everyday life people still call it 'Troieshchyna'. At the same time, this village was memorialised in the name 'Vygurivskyi Boulevard'.[24]

The tendency to preserve ancient toponyms was retained during construction of the third phase of the estate, which began in 1991. As early as 1989, Myoslavska Street was named after the ancient village of Myloslavychy (Myloslavshchyna). In 1991 the streets named 'Budyshchanska', 'Gradynska', 'Liskivska', and 'Radunska' were given historical toponyms.[25]

[24] Shyrochyn, Semen, and Myhaylyk, Oleksandr, *Nevidomi Periferii Kyieva: Pivnichne Livoberezhzhya* (Kyiv: Sky Horse, 2022).

[25] Ibid.

Current problems

Degradation of mass construction

Despite the collapse of the USSR, mass construction continued to a certain extent in the 1990s and 2000s, but the state was no longer able to provide sufficient funding. This led to a degradation of mass housing, a decline which is conspicuous in certain features that can be found in all mass housing districts built at this time. Here we look at how these changes are manifested in Vyhurivschyna-Troieshchyna.

- Absence of monumental art
  One of the first visible changes was the absence of monumental art. No mosaics, no monuments, no supergraphics. The new microdistricts became even more faceless and grey and looked much poorer than those built in the 1980s.

- Lack of infrastructure
  The second trait of degradation is a lack of infrastructure. Hospitals, retail and sports centres, a palace of youth, and a wedding hall all remained unbuilt. This was partly compensated by construction of new commercial malls in the 2000s and 2010s, but the lack of social infrastructure remains. The main hospital, which was designed as the central clinical hospital for the whole of Ukraine, with helipads on the roofs of the operating theatres, remains unfinished after more than 30 years.

Degradation is especially evident in the infrastructure for children. Construction of schools and kindergartens was often left for the future. For example, Micro-district 24 saw completion of its first residential houses in 1998, but the first kindergarten did not appear until 2011, followed by a second one in 2020 – 22 years later, when the first children from these houses were already adults.[26] This micro-district likewise has not a single school, even though it is required to do so by the urban development regulations.

In Micro-district 26, built between 1993 and 1997, one of two planned schools remained unfinished until 2016, when it was demolished to make room for new commercial housing, a project that was later declared illegal and never completed.[27]

· Lack of greenery

Another sign of degradation is the lack of greenery. It is common for hydraulic reclamation to remove not only previous buildings but also all trees. New housing is then built on a sandy soil without grass or trees. In the 1980s trees were planted at the time when the new buildings were built, but this practice ceased in the 1990s due to the economic crisis. So the most recent micro-districts have been built without proper greenery; some self-seeded trees and bushes have since appeared.

As mentioned above, the estate was to have four micro-districts reserved for parks. Two of these indeed became green zones, but the other two, micro-districts 10 and 27, remained vacant until the 2000s. Micro-district 10 was to accommodate the wedding hall in the centre of a green zone. Micro-district 27 was planned as another green zone. Despite the plans, these micro-districts were filled with dense high-rise construction without even a single school in either district. This is another visible sign of degradation: the housing was not only faceless and grey but also taller and denser. The most recent micro-districts have been built up mainly with 24-storey houses; this is the maximum height allowed by fire-safety regulations for standard buildings.

· Unfinished construction

A further sign of degradation is unfinished construction. Vyhurivschyna-Troieshchyna was the first residential area in Kyiv in which residential skyscrapers were planned. In 1999 it was decided to build six 35-storey buildings, each 108 metres high, at Balzaka Street 2 to a project by the architect Oleksandr

Moskovchuk. Intended to house employees serving in the internal forces of the Ministry of Internal Affairs of Ukraine, these buildings were supposed to be the tallest in Kyiv and to form a strong architectural accent at the entrance to Troieshchyna. They were designed with helipads on their roofs, high-speed lifts, an autonomous power supply, and multi-stage water pumps.[28]

28   Ibid.

For the first two years three floors were built every month. In 2003 construction was suspended with the buildings at various stages of completion. One was only 16 storeys high, while the rest had reached their full planned height. One remained frozen in the form of a completely finished skeletal frame; another had started to be faced with bricks; a third was partially clad with façade panels; and yet another even had a significant number of glazed windows already in place. Only one tower was almost completely clad, with windows installed and a decorative metal structure on the roof. After seven years in an unfinished state, two of the buildings were found to have tilted by ten centimetres. There was talk of completing the towers by 2012, but nothing was done. As of 2023, they have stood unfinished for 20 years, and it is doubtful that they will ever be completed.

The crisis of the 1990s led not only to degradation of mass housing, but also to cancellation of the plans for building a large industrial zone. Only the power plant, a money-printing factory, and several small businesses were built in the 1980s. As a result, the inhabitants of Troieshchyna have to work far from home. This is, in fact, the key disadvantage of this estate.

Transportation problems

From the very start, it was clear that the new estate required transport links. So, on 10 July 1984, a trolleybus route was opened running along Mayakovskiy Avenue to Lyfarya Street, connecting Troieshchyna with Petrivka (now Pochayna) metro station. On 6 November 1986 a tramline dedicated to a single route was opened from Zakrevskogo Street to Lyfarya Street. The trolleybus line was extended along Mayakovsky Avenue, with a further extension to Myloslavska Street in 1990. The estate also had a bus service: four routes in 1985, six in 1987, and seven in 1989.

But the transportation needs of such a populous area could not be covered without high-speed rail transport. After the city's blue metro line reached the Obolon estate in the early 1980s, it was

Figure 10:
Unfinished 35-storey buildings, 2013.
Source: Semen Shyrochyn

reasonable to expect the next line to be built on the left bank. This line first appears on perspective images in 1974 (even before the commissioning of the blue metro line), where it is called 'Prydniprovska'. The same planning scheme is repeated on maps from 1976 and 1981. A diagram produced in 1984 depicts the line in schematic form, without reference to terrain. Thus, in the 1970s and 1980s, the left bank line existed only as an intention depicted in perspective images; no technical drawings were ever executed or implemented.

When the Troieshchyna estate was being planned, it was decided to provide it with two types of high-speed rail transport – metro and high-speed tram. The metro was supposed to pass under Mayakovsky Avenue, which was accordingly made 130 metres wide. The odd side of the avenue up to the intersection with Tsvetaeva Street has an undeveloped pedestrian mall 50 to 70 metres wide. The future metro line was supposed to run under this alley, then turn right near Tsvetaeva Street to reach a depot located on the section between Upper and Middle Vygurivsky lakes.[29]

The high-speed tram was placed on Honoré de Balzac Street, which at 180 metres wide is the widest street in Kyiv. It was decided to place the tram line in low-lying areas, creating intersections with expressways at different levels. On each side of the tramline there are two-way vehicular carriageways. The plan for the left-bank high-speed tram was finally approved in 1990. The idea was to connect the Troieshchyna estate in the north of Kyiv with Poznyaki, another large modern housing estate, in the south of the city. In fact, the high-speed tram was supposed to replace the Prydniprovska metro line. Construction of the tramline began in 1993 and progressed very slowly. The section between Myloslavska and General Vatutin Avenue stations was not completed until 2000 but only connected different micro-districts on the same estate without solving the problem of providing access to the rest of the city.

In 2003 when a start was made on constructing Podilsko-Voskresensky Bridge, construction of a new metro line was announced to connect the left and right banks of the Dnipro. In order to link Troieshchyna with the newly approved line, in 2005 it was proposed to convert the high-speed tram line into a metro line and extend it to the southern part of Kyiv's left bank, mostly following the proposed high-speed tram route. Due to a lack of space, some of the route along the railway line was to be built as two tunnels placed one on top of the other.[30]

29 Ibid.

30 Kurinnij, V., 'Probudzhennya spal'nogo rajonu: mistobudivna rada skhvalila skhemu livoberezhnoi linii metro "Troieshchyna-Osokorky"', *Hreshchatyk*, No. 72, 2007, p. 4.

Because construction of the bridge was taking much longer than expected (in fact, it has not yet been finished, as of 2023), another attempt to solve the problem was made in 2009. This time, the city authorities decided to use the railway bridge to accommodate part of the daily passenger traffic. An urban rail service was launched, together with a new station, Troieshchyna-2. As the railway was quite a distance from the estate, the tramline was extended to reach this new railway station. On 25 October 2012 a tram service finally began running to the new station. But the tram was often late, and the urban rail service only ran twice an hour. This, combined with the frequent mismatch of timetables, different payment methods (tram tickets and city rail tokens), and low passenger throughput, meant that this turned out to be a poor solution. Since then, the idea of a metro line has resurfaced. As in the original proposal, the idea was that the line would run under Mayakovsky Avenue; this makes good logistical sense. However, the crisis that began in 2014 with the war in eastern Ukraine has shifted the prospect for this construction project to far into the future. As of 2023, it has been 40 years since the first residential building was completed on the estate, but Troieshchyna has never had proper transport links to other parts of the city.

Reputation as depressive and a place with a high crime rate

From the very beginning this distant and poorly accessible housing estate was considered to be disadvantaged. In urban folklore there is a phrase: 'Жизнь дала трещину – переехал на Троещину', meaning 'My life is broken, so I moved to Troieshchyna'. This reflects popular stereotypes and people's reluctance to live in the district. Although all housing was state-owned in the USSR, people would try to take advantage of their personal contacts to obtain apartments in better houses and locations. But those who could not were happy to inhabit new houses here. For many it was their first private home after years of living in dormitories and communal apartments.
The economic crisis of the 1990s confronted Troieshchyna with numerous social problems. The industrial companies that employed the workers here went bankrupt; many people lost their jobs. Unemployment led to poverty and a sharp rise in crime. The situation was aggravated by the social structure and the estate's poor reputation. People who could afford housing in safer and more easily reachable parts of the city moved away. At the same time, others

who could not afford to continue living in the city centre sold their apartments and moved here. So there was a process of migration within the city that exacerbated the situation and made the estate more and more depressive.

Troieshchyna was considered dangerous in the 1990s because of criminal gangs, who controlled trade and other commerce and established control – as a state within a state – over the neighbourhood. Since the 2000s the gangs have dissolved: some of their members have been killed; others have been imprisoned or have died due to drug abuse, while still others have moved away or found a legal occupation. The estate has become much safer as generations have changed. But the stereotype of Troieshchyna as a dangerous place remains.

Since the 2000s, another population change has occurred here. Because Kyiv is the capital and has higher salaries, many people have moved here from other regions, attracted by better job prospects and a better quality of life. Numerous shops, cafes, and restaurants have appeared. All this has made Troieshchyna less depressive, less blighted by crime, safer, and more socially diverse.

Changing perceptions; proposals for improvement

Despite the above-mentioned problems, Vyhurivschyna-Troieshchyna is a well-thought-out and well-organised urban district and a good place in which to live. Consideration of the above overview of its history, problems, and advantages leads to a number of recommendations for future improvement. The following urban proposals require long-term funding and can improve the comfort of the environment. Their aim is to give the estate new advantages and change the quality of life on it. The more symbolic proposals, which are generally easier to implement, are more about changing perceptions, popularisation, and value recognition.

Transport

Since the key problem that makes Vyhurivschyna-Troieshchyna a disadvantaged estate is its lack of rapid transport, the most important thing is to solve the transportation problem. The best solution would be a metro line; this has been planned for many years, and locations for station have already been chosen. But construction of the metro cannot start until Podilsky Bridge is finished. The bridge has been under construction for 20 years already and because of the war is not expected to be completed soon. The metro is an expensive and long-term project in any case, so the first step in developing rapid transit could be to extend the high-speed tram to create a single line across the left bank with several stops where passengers can change to urban rail, metro, and other forms of public transport.

Another approach is to increase the use of public transport, especially at rush hours. Many people use private cars instead of public transport because crowded buses and trams are hard to board and uncomfortable to travel on. But if the city puts enough buses and trams on the routes and creates dedicated public transport lanes, this will make public transport easier and faster. Public transport will only be attractive when it is fast and convenient.

Infrastructure

Although new malls and numerous supermarkets provide commercial activity to compensate for the previous absence of retail and entertainment, there is still a lack of social infrastructure. The city authorities should finance construction of medical and educational institutions. The state clinical hospital should finally be completed, as should the frozen skyscrapers.

Greenery

As two of the micro-districts that were planned as green zones have been built up with housing, new green zones should be created on areas near the estate, for instance on the unused part of the industrial zone to the east of Troieshchyna. New recreational zones can also be created around the lakes that border the industrial zone. Currently, most of these lakes are surrounded by metal garages. The latter could be replaced with multilevel car parks to free up space. Although recommendations concerning infrastructure and transport are difficult to implement and require the will of the city authorities, substantial funding, and a long implementation time, they are crucial for residents' comfort. Another group of recommendations will not directly change the quality of life itself but can affect attitudes and values, which is also important.

Protection

One of the hardest tasks is to preserve the estate's artistic heritage and to promote the district as a site of urban design heritage. A special focus must be placed on the estate's planning structure and supergraphics as valuable local features. Supergraphics are not destroyed intentionally but gradually lost when wall insulation is installed, a measure which has become popular since the late 2000s as a means to reduce heat loss, especially in panel housing. As installation is carried out haphazardly, each resident only insulates his or her part of the wall and the façade begins to look like a patchwork quilt. Adding to this, chaotically glazed balconies, satellite dish antennas, air conditioning units, and other parasitic structures completely change buildings' appearance, making it seem that they are not part of the same coherent design.

Currently there is no legal way to protect supergraphics because they are not well-defined objects, and no building can be considered valuable enough to be listed as a monument simply because of its supergraphic façade. So the legislative approach to protection would be the most difficult. This does not, however, mean that recourse should not be had to legislative measures to preserve this estate's unique, colourful design. Supergraphics should be given the status of protected heritage, and parasitic structures should be removed.

Popularisation

Besides protection, popularising the heritage on the estate is also important. Since the late 2010s perceptions of Vyhurivschyna-Troieshchyna have been slowly changing among citizens. More and more people, especially generations that never experienced the USSR, are becoming interested in the urban context and its features. Vyhurivschyna-Troieshchyna has been presented in several books that have explored its history and features of its urban design. The Ukrainian modernism community conducts guided tours of this estate, pointing out valuable examples of supergraphics, monumental art, and urban design. Although infrequent, these tours are making a difference: they help make this context valuable and historic for future generations.

Apart from these occasional tours, however, there is nothing being done to promote the heritage on site. There are no signs, posters, or routes pointing out things of value. Vyhurivschyna-Troieshchyna should be covered in in guidebooks; valuable objects should be identified on public transport routes; and special signs and information stands should be erected to make it easier for tourists to find everything that is of value. People should know that Vyhurivschyna-Troieshchyna is a beautiful place with a precious heritage.

References

Blinova, G. N., 'Arhitekturno-prostranstvennaya kompozitsiya novykh zhilykh rayonov Kieva', *Stroitel'stvo i arkhitektura*, No. 8, 1981, pp. 8–11.

Inozemtseva, A. S., 'Aktual'nye problemy arkhitektury massovogo zhilishcha v Kieve', *Stroitel'stvo i arkhitektura*, No. 8, 1984, pp. 10–12.

'Konvejer Bol'shih Novoselij', *Stroitel'stvo i arkhitektura*, No. 4, 1984, pp. 16–17.

Kostenko, A. Y., 'Programmirovanie Eksperimenta', *Stroitel'stvo i arkhitektura*, No. 8, 1986, pp. 13–14.

Kurinnij, V., 'Probudzhennya Spal'nogo Rajonu: Mistobudivna Rada Skhvalila Skhemu Livoberezhnoï Liniï Metro "Troieshchyna-Osokorky"', *Hreshchatyk*, No. 72, 2007, p. 4.

Odnopozov, Igor, *Zvichajna nezvichna Troieshchyna* (Kyïv, 2021).

Pravnichenko, I. A., 'Obraztsovo-pokazatel'niy mikrorayon zhilogo massiva na Troeshchine', *Stroitel'stvo i arkhitektura*, No. 11, 1985, pp. 13–15.

Pravnichenko, I. A., 'Tsvetnoy mikrorayon. Nuzhno li krasit' novuyu zhiluyu zastroyku?', *Stroitel'stvo i arkhitektura*, No. 4, 1987, pp. 2–3.

Shyrochyn, Semen, and Myhaylyk, Oleksandr, *Nevidomi Periferii Kyieva: Pivnichne Livoberezhzhya* (Kyiv: Sky Horse, 2022).

Tovstenko, T., 'Zhiloy rayon Troeshchina v Kieve', *Arkhitektura SSSR*, No. 5, 1987, pp. 52–57.

Vasilenko, L. G., 'Tsvet v arkhitekture Troeshchiny', *Stroitel'stvo i arkhitektura*, No. 4, 1987, p. 3.

Vlasova, T. Y., 'Troeshchina: standart i raznoobrazie', *Stroitel'stvo i arkhitektura*, No. 8, 1986, pp. 11–12

Index

Architects, developers, house-building factories

Bakradze, A. 193
Bartashevich, Konstantin 77
Brėdikis, Vytautas 93
Bulatov, M. 35
Čekanauskas, Vytautas 93
DSK-1 and DSK-2, house-building factories 143
Dyomin, Mykola 212
Egohouse 151
Egorev, S. 77
Fil, Oleksandr 152
Frolov, Yevgeny 212
Grdzelidze, D. 193
Grechyna, Vadym 214
Gurenkov, Georgy 214, 217
Hopkalo, Vadym 212
Kalinina, Nataliya 152
Kavlashvili, I. 193
Kavlashvili, Sh. 193
Khajakyan, M. N. 77
Kolomiets, Volodymyr 212
Kornfeld, Yakov 77
Krūminis, B. 99
Kubasov, V. S. 77
Lamze, Arnolds 127
Latgiprogorstroi 132
Mazūras, Česlovas 101
Moore, Charles 217
Moskovchuk, Oleksandr 225
Novikov, Feliks 77, 78
Ose, L. 131
Paskevich, Yury 212
Pilsētprojekts 133
Plakane, L. 131
Pokrovsky, I.A. 77
Reinfelds, A. 131
Rostov Regional Design
 Institute Rostoblproekt 54
Rusteika, Jonas 101
Semyakin, Hleb 152
Slutskyi, Hryhoriy 212
Standard-Design Department, Vilnius Urban Construction
 Planning Institute 99
Suvorov, Vsevolod 212
Sverdlovskgrazhdanproekt 81
Tyulpa, Leonid 143
Vilnius House-Construction Combine 99
Yezhov, Valentin 212
WZMH Architects 151

Individual buildings

Bolshevik Kyiv Machine-Building Plant 78
Palace of Culture, Khimmash 74–91
Palace of Pioneers, Moscow 77, 78
Ural Chemical Machinery Plant (Uralkhimmash) 78

Mass housing, series

Series 1-451P 20
Series 1A-450 20
Series 90-K 161
Series 96 222
Series 103 ..... 114, 133
Series 104 114
Series 105 114
Series 114 114
Series 169–129 81
Series 310 35
Series 464 133
Series 467 ..... 114, 133
Series 602 ..... 114, 133
Series I-310 36
Series I-464 ..... 99, 193
Series LT 99
Series-M3 130
Series T-4 222

Residential areas, microrayons, housing estates

Ajapnyak, Yerevan, Armenia ..... 12 ff
Chilanzar, Tashkent, Uzbekistan ..... 34 ff
Chulkovo, Tula 125
Dubki, Taganrog, Russia ..... 46 ff
Farsta, Sweden 95
Fennpfuhl, Berlin, Germany 184
Gorbitz, Dresden, Germany 184

Khimmash, Sverdlovsk-Yekaterinburg, Russia .... 74 ff
Lazdynai, Vilnius, Lithuania .... 92 ff
Microrayon No. 41, Kamensk-Uralsky, Russia .... 60 ff
North Saltivka, Kharkiv, Ukraine .... 140 ff
Novye Cheryomushki, Moscow 125
Olaine, Latvia .... 108 ff
Purvciems, Riga, Latvia .... 124 ff
Solnechny, Samara, Russia .... 156 ff
Toulouse-Le-Mirail, France 95
Universitetsky, Irkutsk, Russia .... 172 ff
Vazha-Pshavela, Tbilisi, Georgia .... 190 ff
Vällinbgy, Sweden 95
Vyhurivschyna-Troieshchyna, Kyiv, Ukraine .... 208 ff

Microrayons: characteristics, features, problems, challenges

Apartment building extensions (ABEs), unauthorised
    minor building alterations, carried out by residents 197–199
Churches, construction of on land assigned to schools and
    kindergartens in microrayons in Russia, (post-1991) 160
Common space, regarded as 'unclaimed' as opposed to
    'collectively managed' 135
Compact City approach, implementation of 160
Courtyards, informal privatisation of 204
Fundamental planning principle of micro-districts 173
'Focusing' method, general principle of spatial development 143
Garages
    private garages, problem of 20, 149
    residents' reluctance to consent to removal of 169, 170
    unorthodox uses of 164, 203
'Group development', late-Soviet principle for arranging
    buildings in a microrayon 162
Homeowners' associations (HOA) 157
Inefficient utilisation of space 160
Lack of borders between land around houses
    in a microdistrict 164
Panel buildings
    construction quality, contributory factor in impact of 1988
    earthquake 20
    resilience in war 154
Parking, unregulated, especially in
    courtyards 164, 179, 197, 201
Privatisation of housing, effect on housing maintenance 195

Resident participation,
    desirability of 69, 154, 170, 187, 206
    Exit-Voice-Loyalty-Neglect model 72
    passivity among residents 71
Resilience through capacity for transformation 206
Russo-Ukrainian war, impact of 145, 149–151
Speedstac, modular building block construction system 151

Laws, regulations, state programmes affecting development of micro-districts

Campaign 'against architectural excesses',
    initiated by Nikita Khrushchev in 1955 .... 35, 76, 215
'Comfortable Urban Environment', Russian national
    programme, 2018–2024 .... 66, 181
EU Cohesion Fund 117, 121
Free privatisation of housing in Russia, effect on building
    maintenance 157
First five-year plan (1928–1932) 78
'Housing', Russia state programme (initiated 2011), impact of .. 157
Kharkiv, new master plan for, led by architect Norman Foster .. 150
Law on Decentralisation and Privatisation, Uzbekistan, 1990 38
Law on Property, Uzbekistan 38
Perm, master plan for, example of a new
    urban planning approach in post-Soviet Russia 160
Purvciems district, detailed planning project for 131
Regulations governing permanent registration in Uzbekistan 42
Regulations on Use and Development of Territories
    in Tbilisi Municipality, 2016 204
Restitution of land to former owners in Latvia 136–137
Rules for the Use and Development of Territories in
    the City of Tbilisi, March 2009 204
Solnechny microrayon, new master plan for .... 166 ff
Stadtumbau Ost (Urban Redevelopment East),
    redevelopment programme for East Germany 185
Sverdlovsk Region, Strategy for the Development of
    Housing and Communal Services until 2035 69
Urban Planning Code of the Republic of Uzbekistan 41

Other initiatives

Art space *podyezd* 'Podyezd' 72–73

Authors

Hlib **Antypenko** is a PhD candidate at the Faculty of Architecture, Department of Urban Planning and Design, at Budapest University of Technology and Economics. In 2018 he graduated from Kharkiv National University of Civil Engineering and Architecture with a master's degree in architecture and city planning. He has been the recipient of several academic awards and scholarships, such as the INFINITY Erasmus Mundus (2015–2016) and Stipendium Hungaricum (2019–2023). He is the author of seven academic papers published in international journals, four of which are listed in Scopus. He has also participated in several international conferences and workshops on urban design and architecture and is a practising architect. His doctoral dissertation is titled 'Functional Diversification of Large Housing Estates: Perspectives from Budapest and Kharkiv'.

Elena **Batunova** is an urban and regional planner and a senior researcher at RWTH Aachen University in Germany. She holds a PhD in urban planning, design, and policy from Politecnico di Milano in Italy; her PhD course included periods studying and researching abroad at Leibniz Institute for Regional Geography in Leipzig, Germany and at KU Leuven in Belgium. Elena's research interests and project activities include urban shrinkage, post-socialist cities, small and medium-sized cities, urban governance, urban planning, and institutional practices of built heritage preservation and use. She had a leading role in several national and international research projects in urban shrinkage, heritage protection, innovations in urban planning, and the impact of mega-events on local development.

Ivan **Bushlanov** holds a bachelor's degree in public policy and social sciences and a master's degree in social and cultural activities from Ural Federal University. He is researching problems of heritage preservation in Russia, in particular in monotowns. Bushlanov actively promotes the heritage conservation agenda in Kamensk-Uralsky, where he is developing a local history media project, 'Slonolen', about the city's architecture and landscaping as seen through a critical lens. Also in the field of civic activity, he has organised the volunteer project 'City of Our Moment' together with other activists, runs the art project podyezd *'Podyezd'*, and has completed the restoration of several sculptural compositions.

Māris **Bērziņš** is an associate professor at the University of Latvia. He has chaired the Department of Human Geography. His research interests involve population geography and urban studies – in particular, various forms of human geographical mobility and patterns of socio-spatial differentiation in urban areas. Dr. M. Bērziņš has been involved as a researcher in several national and international research projects.

Elena **Chernysheva** is an independent researcher, urban activist. She graduated from the Department of Clinical Psychology at Southern Federal University in Rostov on Don.

Albina **Davletshina** holds a master's degree in architecture from Ufa State Petroleum Technical University and a master of science in urban planning and policy design from Politecnico di Milano. The main scope of her research interests covers urban heritage, social cohesion, and sustainable policy design. She has professional experience in the fields of architecture and urban planning from Russia, USA, and Italy, and has taught at Politecnico di Milano. She has been conducting independent research on heritage practices in Sweden and has volunteered on several projects in Germany and Russia with European Heritage Volunteers. Currently she is a member of the 'Cities Building Culture' research team.

Barbara **Engel** (Prof. Dr.) is a German architect and urban planner. She was awarded her PhD in 2004 and worked as a visiting professor at Kent State University in the US in 2007/2008. In 2008–2013 she was head of the department for the inner city at the City Planning Office in Dresden. Since 2013 she has been a professor of international urban planning and design at Karlsruhe Institute of Technology. Barbara Engel is head of design committees in Halle and Nuremberg and vice president of the Deutsche Akademie für Städtebau und Landesplanung (DASL). Her research interests focus on urban development in post-Soviet countries, metropolitan areas, public spaces, and science communication.

Ekaterina **Gladkova** is a PhD candidate and a researcher at Karlsruhe Institute of Technology (KIT) in Germany. She holds a bachelor's degree in architecture and a master's in urban planning from Irkutsk National Research Technical University (IRNITU); her studies included periods of study and research abroad at Karlsruhe Institute of Technology (KIT). Ekaterina is a practising urban planner and organizer of international urban planning workshops. She is working on planning strategies for the sustainable urban development of large settlements built in the 1960s and 1970s. Her research interests and project activities include methods, concepts, and approaches to the renovation of residential neighbourhoods built in the 1960s–1970s.

Polina **Gundarina** studied history, ethnography, and journalism in Russia, Norway, and Germany. Since 2020 she has been publishing cultural essays, and journalistic pieces in Russian-, English-, and German-speaking media and from 2021 has been working at the Leibniz Institute for History and Culture of Eastern Europe (GWZO) as a research associate. Polina Gundarina is currently finishing her doctoral manuscript on the history of late-Soviet leisure and culture in houses of culture at the University of Leipzig.

Ludmila **Kozlova** received her diploma in architecture at Irkutsk National Research Technical University (IRNITU). Her research interests are development of public spaces in the structure of Irkutsk city, the features and qualitative characteristics of such spaces, and principles for their improvement. She has presented the main results of her research at international conferences and integrated them in international research projects focused on understanding mass housing heritage and its transformations – 'Unloved Heritage Socialist City?' (2016–2019) and 'Living Laboratory' (2021–2023). She is author of publications in the field of urban environment and architecture.

Dona **Kulmatova** is an expert in conservation and restoration of architectural heritage and an interior designer. A member of ICOMOS since 2018, she obtained an MSc degree in conservation and preservation of monuments from the University of Applied Sciences in Potsdam in 2015, following her BA in architecture and design at Tashkent Architecture and Construction Institute. Since 2022 Kulmatova has been teaching architecture at Bucheon University in Tashkent and running *The Art Station* art gallery in Samarkand. Kulmatova's work as an exhibition designer and curator reflects her passion for Uzbekistan's cultural heritage. She has also participated in various research projects related to architectural heritage preservation.

Kārlis **Lakševics** is a researcher at the Department of Anthropology at the University of Latvia. His research covers social, political, and environmental inequalities in post-socialist development projects. Additionally, he is involved in activism initiatives for social housing, environmental justice, and the eradication of homelessness.

Dr. Anastasia **Malko** is an architect, an urban planner, and a senior researcher at Karlsruhe Institute of Technology (KIT) in Germany. She is a specialist in protection of architectural, historical, and cultural heritage. She holds a PhD in engineering from Technical University of Dresden (Germany). Her work experience includes research in urban planning workshops at Les Ateliers Internationaux de Maîtrise d'Oeuvre Urbaine (Cergy-Pontoise, France) and Ecole de Chaillot (Paris, France). Her research interests and design activities focus on preservation and development of the historical architectural and urban environment, including from the era of Soviet modernism.

Heghine **Pilosyan** is an architect and urbanist with a focus on affordable-housing studies and sustainable transitions. Her academic qualification include degrees in sustainable architecture and multidisciplinary studies from the polytechnics of Turin and Milan and a postgraduate diploma in developing social housing projects from the IHS, Erasmus University Rotterdam. From 2018 to late 2019 she worked as an architectural manager in China for a Beijing-based German company designing projects to passive-house standards and for an American-Chinese company in Tianjin. Since 2015 she has been teaching at a faculty of architecture and has developed and delivered courses called 'Introduction to Sustainable Architecture' and 'Urban Economics'. In 2019 she co-founded the re.de architectural studio.

Marina **Sapunova** is a research assistant and a PhD candidate at Karlsruhe Institute of Technology and a co-founder of MÊTRE –a project that makes investigative documentaries about housing and urban regeneration. She has a background in urban planning, teaching, and research in cross-disciplinary teams and self-initiated projects. Her research interests include urban governance, urban planning, zoning legislation, housing and property policy, and its (post)-socialist transformation.

Guido **Sechi** is a researcher at the Department of Human Geography at the University of Latvia. His main research interests are in the domain of urban and regional studies, with a focus on socio-spatial (in)justice and neoliberal policies in the context of post-socialist transition. He has investigated spatial segregation, availability of green and public spaces, and regional peripheralisation in FSU countries. He also works on cultural projects focused on Soviet/socialist urban planning heritage and its afterlives.

Dr. Semen **Shyrochyn** was born in 1988 in Kyiv. He received his PhD in engineering science in 2015. Semen is a researcher into socialist architecture in Ukraine. His research focuses primarily on interwar and post-war modernism and Stalinist Neoclassical architecture. His research subject is the architecture of Kyiv and Ukrainian industrial cities. In 2016 he began campaigning publicly to protect the heritage of the socialist period, which has been endangered following the start of the decommunisation campaign in Ukraine. In 2017–2023 he published 20 books and numerous articles on architectural heritage and its preservation. Shyrochin has taken part in conferences on interwar and post-war socialist architecture and participated in multiple outreach and exhibition projects in Ukraine and the EU. In 2018–2019 he was the curator of the exhibition *Reconstruction of Khreshchatyk: Competition and Design* in Sofia Kyivska. He has also participated in round tables on the protection of cultural heritage and helped prepare substantiation for several buildings to receive state protection.

My thanks go to all the authors for their expertise and efforts, to my colleagues in the research project who created the content framework for this publication, and to the Federal Ministry of Education and Reserch for its financial support.
For his careful copy editing with valuable critical questions, I am grateful to David Koralek.
I would also like to thank the team at DOM publishers for their constructive and engaged assistance.

Barbara Engel

The Deutsche Bibliothek lists this publication
in the Deutsche Nationalbibliografie; detailed
bibliographic data is available on the Internet
at http://dnb.d-nb.de

ISBN 978-3-86922-892-1

© 2024 by DOM publishers, Berlin
www.dom-publishers.com

This work is subject to copyright. All rights are
reserved, whether the whole or part of the material
is concerned, specifically the rights of translation,
reprinting, recitation, broadcasting, reproduction on
microfilms or in other ways, and storage or processing
in data bases. Sources and owners of rights are given
to the best of our knowledge.

Proof reading	John Nicolson
Copy editing	David Koralek
Graphics editing	Nora Staab Maurice App Ksenia Gulyaeva Aurélie Pha Mariia Tumureeva
Layout	Masako Tomokiyo
Printing	Tiger Printing (Hong Kong) Co., Ltd. www.tigerprinting.hk

SPONSORED BY THE